DIRECTORS'

D0316880

the cinema of
MIKE LEIGH

a sense of the real

garry watson

 **WALLFLOWER PRESS** LONDON & NEW YORK

First published in Great Britain in 2004 by
Wallflower Press
4th Floor, 26 Shacklewell Lane, London E8 2EZ
www.wallflowerpress.co.uk

A catalogue for this book is available from the British Library

ISBN 1-904764-10-X (paperback)
ISBN 1-903364-90-6 (hardback)

Book design by Rob Bowden Design

Printed in Great Britain by Antony Rowe, Chippenham, Wiltshire

CONTENTS

This book grew out of an earlier version of the chapter on *Naked* and I want to thank Robin Wood, who published it in *Cineaction*, for his generous response to it. My brother suggested I contact Wallflower Press and I am grateful for that since working with Yoram Allon there has been a real pleasure.

Mike Leigh has helped by spotting errors of fact, by loaning me some hard-to-find videos, and by graciously answering e-mail enquiries throughout the time while I was working on this project. Thanks too to his assistant Claire Broughton at Thin Man Films for all her help, especially in providing the still used on the cover image. My colleagues Susan Hamilton and Josh Nodelman helped track down film reviews, and Thomas Elsaesser of the University of Amsterdam read and made invaluable comments on an early version of the chapter on *Naked*.

Working on Leigh's films is bound to make one think of family, and mine have contributed to this project in various ways over the past few years. My mother shared her love of books, theatre and film with me; and the lively interest of the next generation – Sophie and Martin, Molly and Hannah, Michael and Aengus – has helped keep me on my toes.

My wife Betsy read the entire manuscript as it came hot off the computer and, whatever its shortcomings, she has certainly helped make this into a better book than it would have been without her. Her enthusiasm is at least as clear-eyed as my scepticism and I may have grown to depend on it. Her bullshit detector, her eye for detail and her sensitivity make her an ideal movie-going companion.

The works of writers of genius ... give us, in the guise of fiction, something equivalent to the actual density of the real, that density which life offers us everyday but which we are unable to grasp...

          – Simone Weil (1977b: 292)

Each day a few more lies eat into the seed with which we are born, little institutionalised lies from the print of newspapers, the shock waves of television and the sentimental cheats of the movie screen. Little lies, but they pipe us toward insanity as they starve our sense of the real.

          – Norman Mailer (1966: 21)

In just over a thirty-year period, from 1971 to 2002, Mike Leigh has made the following sixteen full-length films (eight of them – from *Hard Labour* in 1973 to *Four Days in July* in 1985 – for television): *Bleak Moments* (1971); *Hard Labour* (1973); *Nuts in May* (1976); *The Kiss of Death* (1977); *Who's Who* (1979); *Grown-Ups* (1980); *Home Sweet Home* (1982); *Meantime* (1983); *Four Days in July* (1985); *High Hopes* (1988); *Life is Sweet* (1990); *Naked* (1993); *Secrets and Lies* (1996); *Career Girls* (1997); *Topsy-Turvy* (1999); *All or Nothing* (2002).

During this time Leigh has also made three shorts – *The Five-Minute Films* (1975),[1] *The Short and Curlies* (1987) and *A Sense of History* (1992); and three Television Studio Recordings – *The Permissive Society* (1975), *Knock for Knock* (1976)[2] and *Abigail's Party* (1977). In addition to all this, between 1965 and 1993 he wrote and produced over twenty plays for the theatre. Except for a section on the televised recording of *Abigail's Party*, this book will have nothing to say about Leigh's work in the theatre. It will focus exclusively on Leigh the film-maker, which is to say on those films he has both directed and (with the sole exception of *A Sense of History*) written. Not surprisingly, then, I will be drawing on, and engaging with, an assortment of writers on film. In addition to his biographer (Michael Coveney) and the author of the first critical study on his work (Ray Carney), these will include many of the reviewers and critics of his work and three film theorists – Andrew Klevan, Stanley Cavell and Slavoj Zizek – whose work I have found particularly useful.

What might surprise some, however, is my decision to open a book on film with citations from Norman Mailer and Simone Weil. I have done this for two reasons: the first is that I agree with Colin MacCabe's claim that discussion of film needs to be placed 'in the widest possible intellectual and cultural context' (2001: vii). Hence the references throughout this book, not just to Weil and Mailer, but also to such writers as George Eliot, Dickens, Conrad, Flaubert, Thoreau and D. H. Lawrence, in addition to an assortment of film critics and critical theorists. The second reason is that, like Weil in the 1930s and Mailer in the 1950s, I too think that 'our sense of the real' is under various kinds of threat and that it needs special attention to prevent it from dying. This is why Leigh's work matters: because it can strengthen our sense of the real, providing it with some of the nourishment it so desperately needs.

This book is divided into three parts. Part One identifies and begins to question some of the expectations that have played their part in determining the reception of Leigh's work so far. The opening three chapters attempt to establish a new set of expectations and thus a new context for thinking about Leigh's work; they also offer some fresh perspectives that I hope will be more appropriate, in the sense of being more productive, in generating deeper insight into his films: chapter one introduces the concept of traumatic realism (to revitalise thinking about Leigh's realism); chapter two draws on two recent books on 'the everyday' (to help us reflect on what might be involved in Leigh's commitment to 'ordinary' life); and chapter three suggests something of what might be at stake in the unusually long period of preparatory work Leigh and his actors go through for each film in their pursuit of the real.

Parts Two and Three are devoted to discussions of the individual films and some of the questions they raise. Part Two takes four chapters to look at all the films (two shorts, *Abigail's Party* and eleven full-length films) from *Bleak Moments* to *Life is Sweet*, while Part Three devotes a separate chapter to each of the last five films, from *Naked* to *All or Nothing*.

As Ray Carney has noted, in his earlier work, Leigh's style is 'unrhetorical in the extreme – no editorial razzle-dazzle, visual sublimities or acoustic stylisation' (2000: 241). The fact that Carney thinks this changes in *Naked* makes it, for him, 'a "problem" film in Leigh's oeuvre', one that marks 'a serious change of direction … [that] is quite troubling in its implications' (2000: 278). I think Carney is right to observe that *Naked* marks a break in Leigh's work, a break that is immediately apparent in the film's style (both visual and acoustical) but also in its content. I think

Leigh himself is acknowledging as much in his response during the 2002 session at the National Film Theatre in London to a questioner who had said that his upper-middle-class characters 'seem to be rather stereotyped in films like *High Hopes*':

> I think *High Hopes* has a satirical element to it. That's not what I normally do. Satire is not my natural tendency. I think *High Hopes* contained that in a very specific way. That results in the portrayal of the upper-middle-class characters. I think all of my films up to and including *Life is Sweet* had broader comic elements. From *Naked* onwards, I moved on to a different kind of feel and relationship to the characters. (Malcolm 2002: n.p.)

In a similar vein, in another interview given in the same year, Leigh states:

> It was in *Naked* that I went beyond making films that merely depicted an interesting collection of relationships between people. *Life is Sweet* is the last of those films. With *Naked* I broke into my own and constructed the epic out of the domestic. The other films followed from it. (Quart 2002a: 39)

For my part, I agree that *Naked* marks a significant turning point in Leigh's oeuvre and my decision to devote separate chapters to each of the films from *Naked* onwards is meant to highlight his recent work.

But at the same time, I do not want this division to be at the expense of the earlier films to which Leigh himself is grossly unfair when he says that they merely depict interesting collections of relationship between people. Even though the books by Coveney and Carney were necessarily focused on the earlier work, I hope to show that there are still new things to be said about it. Moreover, the astonishing achievement of the later films is only likely to be fully recognised by those familiar with such earlier ones as *Bleak Moments, Nuts in May, Grown-Ups, Home Sweet Home, Meantime* and *Four Days in July,* all of which seem to me important films by any standard. Though none of them get individual chapters to themselves, they have been grouped in such a way as to try to bring out aspects of Leigh – his feminism, for example, or what some of his films have in common with certain classic Hollywood comedies – that seem to have gone unnoticed. Finally, in the last chapter, I will try to bring out some of the deeper issues raised by my choice of title: *A Sense of the Real.*

The primary goal of this study is to try to win wider recognition for Leigh's achievement so far and, rightly or wrongly, I have thought that my best chance of doing this was by means of a two-pronged approach: (i) offering the sort of detailed descriptions of many of the films that will encourage readers to seek them out or to see them again; and (ii) creating the kind of cultural and intellectual contexts that will place the films in the richest possible light. In general, I try to allow the text I am discussing to suggest the most relevant approach. Sometimes it does so immediately, other times only after a number of viewings (or readings). In the case of *Naked,* for example, it was in the first instance Johnny's reference to Sophie's 'proclivity for negation' ('I suppose she thinks it's progressive') that made me think of the letter in which Georges Bataille once spoke of 'unemployed negativity'. With *All or Nothing* it was Leigh's use of the term 'redemption' (in a discussion at the NFT that marked the film's release) that made me think of a passage in Adorno's *Minima Moralia* that seemed to me to be almost crying out to be used.

In addition to the names already mentioned, I also make use in the following pages of such thinkers as (among contemporaries) Jonathan Lear and Adam Phillips and (among earlier figures) Freud, Winnicott, Benjamin and Marcuse. If this seems like a long list of names, I can only say that these sixteen films are all quite different from each other and that many of them call for the different approaches that these authors can help to provide. At the same time, there are certainly important continuities in Leigh's oeuvre that need to be brought out and I should note two of the things a number of these figures have in common. The first is an interest in psychoanalysis, which seems appropriate as the kind of 'real' Leigh pursues and explores in his films is – in one way or another – frequently *traumatic*; the second is that a number of them work as well within the orbit of leftist critical theory, which also seems pertinent considering that Leigh identifies himself as a socialist.

It will be clear from the above that I like to make connections, especially between the ways in which certain questions and topics get raised and explored on different levels of culture, as in academic/philosophical/psychoanalytical/political thought on the one hand and in film on the other. And of course the connections made inevitably reveal a great deal about my own interests and point of view. Indeed, one of the ways in which I know that these interests *are* my own is the kind of configuration that is formed by the names I have made a point of mentioning. While many readers will be interested in some of them, I doubt if anyone will be interested in them all – everyone's configuration will be different. If there is to be the basis for a fruitful conversation then there probably has to be some significant overlap but, in the last analysis, everyone who has a point of view will have his or her (slightly or very) different (and evolving) list of favourites/companions/guides/fellow-explorers/reference points.

While I do hope that I bring something to Leigh's work, I do not expect my readings to produce complete agreement (either in Leigh himself or in anyone else). Given, over and above our shared interests, the inevitable differences that remain, I do not see how that could be either possible or desirable. What seems to me desirable is a form of give and take: both between the critic and the films and between the critic and the reader. So that though I am trying to illuminate the films, I recognise that in some cases the sharpest illumination might come from someone I have provoked or stimulated into disagreement.

PART ONE

Establishing a New Context

What is important, it seems to me, is that you share questions with the audience, and they have to go away with things to work on.

You do not walk out of my films with a clear feeling about what is right and wrong. They're ambivalent. You walk away with work to do. My films are a sort of investigation. They ask questions...

And I do believe it's necessary for you to walk away from these kinds of films with questions unanswered, and work to do, and matters to be faced.

I want my films, in a Talmudic way, to raise questions and posit possibilities.

– Mike Leigh (Movshovitz 2000: 63, 103–4, 121, 134)

CHAPTER ONE

The Reception of Leigh's Work: Revising Our Expectations

> Whatever film you watch, assuming you've seen a film before, you immediately go into one programme or another, or plug into an expectation system. If the film is any good, these expectations are constantly confounded.
> – Mike Leigh (Movshovitz 2000: 65–6)

Of the sixteen full-length films Leigh has made so far, it is probably true to say that *Naked* (1993) and *Secrets and Lies* (1996) are the two for which he is best-known, at least internationally. While many of his other films have their admirers, these two were particularly well-received, especially at Cannes, where *Naked* won both the Best Director and (with David Thewlis) the Best Actor awards in 1993 and *Secrets and Lies* both the Palme d'Or (Best Picture) and (with Brenda Blethyn) the Best Actress awards in 1996. *Secrets and Lies* went on to become Leigh's biggest commercial success and *Naked* the film for which he is most admired by the critics. Thus, with reference to the latter, in a recently published poll in which the Canadian journal *Cinemascope* had asked 155 film programmers and critics from 15 different countries to list the films and the directors they considered to be the 'Best of the Nineties', *Naked* was ranked the ninth-best film and Leigh the eighth-best director. Furthermore, among the 67 Canadian participants in the poll, *Naked* was ranked as the second-best film of the 1990s and Leigh as the second-best director.

In the face of this particular poll, then, it might seem that Kenneth Turan was not greatly exaggerating when he told his readers in *The Los Angeles Times* in 1996 that Leigh is 'considered by many critics the preeminent film-maker in the English-speaking world' (Movshovitz 2000: 84). One can, moreover, find support for this view in Michael Coveney's (1996) lively and extremely helpful biography, in Ray Carney and Leonard Quart's (2000) pioneering study of the films up to *Naked*, and from many of the interviewers found in Howie Movshovitz's (2000) very useful collection of Leigh's interviews. And considering all of this, some will no doubt think that Leigh has already received his fair share of praise. Enough is enough; it is now time for a more negative assessment of his work. Or so it might seem. This is not, however, my own view.

For one thing, other polls tell a very different story. Take, for example, the September 2002 *Sight and Sound* poll on 'The Ten Greatest Films Of All Time' which, as Ian Christie notes, makes it perfectly obvious that 'the stakes are now clearly loaded in favour of Hollywood, with little or no chance of a British film reaching anywhere near the top 20 (if we ignore Kubrick, *The Third Man* and *Lawrence of Arabia* come highest this time, at number 35 and number 45 respectively)'. Or (perhaps even more revealingly) consider the results of a 'mini-poll of UK critics' on 'the best films of the last 25 years' that – because it was disappointed with the first poll's failure to include anything more recent than 1974 – *Sight and Sound* published in December of the same year. This time one fine English film (Terence Davies' *Distant Voices, Still Lives*) did get into the list of the top ten films but there is nothing at all by Leigh and the bias in favour of US cinema is striking. It is not just that, as Nick James happily reports, Martin Scorsese was 'by a long way the top-ranking director' – no fewer than six of the top ten films are American (Francis Ford Coppola's *Apocalypse Now*, Martin Scorsese's *Raging Bull* and *GoodFellas*, David Lynch's *Blue Velvet*, Spike Lee's *Do the Right Thing* and Ridley Scott's *Blade Runner*) and a seventh (Sergio Leone's *Once Upon a Time in America*) is set in the US. In addition, one of the top ten directors is (in fifth position, no less) Michael Mann, whose votes, James tells us, were 'cast largely for his epic heist movie *Heat* and psychological thriller *Manhunter*'. Despite James's claim that 'the US cinema chosen by our pollsters is hardly from the mainstream', Lee's *Do the Right Thing* seems to me the only example of what might loosely be called America's alternative cinema to be listed. In this kind of critical climate, how could Mike Leigh receive his due?

While agreeing, then, with those critics who think that it is Leigh, not Scorsese, who has become 'the preeminent film-maker in the English-speaking world', I would go further and raise the stakes even higher. It seems to me that Leigh's achievement in film has been that of a major artist, who is as potentially important to our time as, say, Beckett and Godard were in earlier periods. In short, I feel that Leigh's work has not yet been sufficiently – by which I mean, widely enough – appreciated and understood. But why does this seem to be especially the case in his own country?

Though it is true that *Bleak Moments*, Leigh's first film, was hailed by the US movie critic Roger Ebert as 'a masterpiece' when it was released in 1971, the fact remains that most North American filmgoers did not become aware of Leigh until the appearance of *High Hopes* in 1988. This means that many had not seen either the numerous works that Leigh had written and directed for the theatre or any of his work for television. In fact, the view of the UK that North American audiences had been used to getting from television and the movies over the previous two decades had been largely restricted – not exclusively but predominantly – to what was shown on Public Television's *Masterpiece Theatre* and the so-called Heritage Films. As two of Leigh's American interviewers explain, 'the Public Broadcasting System, an outlet that was eager to ply Americans with the genteel pleasures of *The Forsyte Saga* and *Upstairs, Downstairs*, was never tempted to broadcast the less soothing but infinitely more challenging Leigh films of the 1970s and 1980s' (Movshovitz 2000: 60). As a result, when North Americans did finally get a chance to see Leigh's earlier work, they could at the very least appreciate how different it was to the kind of thing they had come to expect from the UK.

Indeed, in my local Canadian video store (in Edmonton, Alberta) Leigh's films (almost all sixteen of them) can be found *not* in the fairly substantial British section but – under the heading 'Outlaw Film-makers: Independent Alternative Cinema' – alongside the films of Hal Hartley, Pedro Almodovar, Spike Lee, Wim Wenders, John Waters, Andrei Tarkovsky, Werner Herzog, Rainer Werner Fassbinder and Satyajit Ray.[1] I have personally noticed, furthermore, while visiting family members (rather than carrying out any kind of scientific survey) over the last two or three years, that all or almost all of Leigh's films are also readily available in at least three other North American video stores, one in Washington D.C., one in New York and the third in Portland, Oregon. And in each of these cases one gets the impression that the owners also think of Leigh as belonging in the kind of international and decidedly heterogeneous company just identified.

In contrast, most British viewers were aware of Leigh long before the arrival of *High Hopes* in 1988. Not because they remembered *Bleak Moments* in 1971 – very few of them would have seen that in the first place. But because many would have seen some of the films Leigh had made for television. In an interview given in 1997, Leigh made the following observation:

> The fact is that if you made *A Play for Today* as they were called on the BBC, you could be pretty sure you could get eight or nine million viewers in one evening. Now eight or nine million people seeing the film you've just made is not bad. I mean, I don't know how long it will take for eight or nine million people to see *Secrets and Lies* for all its success. It'll take quite a while. (Movshovitz 2000: 118)

That eight or nine million viewers saw the first showings of films like *Hard Labour*, *The Kiss of Death*, *Home Sweet Home* and *Meantime* seems to me an astonishing comment on the cultural richness of a certain (one-and-a-half decades long) moment in the history of British television. And if, when he reflected on this moment in 1996, Leigh understandably felt deep frustration mixed with gratitude – 'They'd be shown once and that was it. I went mad for 17 years' (Movshovitz 2000: 91) – the good news is that the situation in which we now find ourselves has, in one respect at least, changed for the better. Thanks to the arrival of video, it is now possible to see these films again.

But what I wish to do here is to note the significance of the fact that more people have seen one work in particular – *Abigail's Party* – than any other of Leigh's works. As Coveney explains, 'on its third showing, there was an ITV strike, an unattractively highbrow programme on BBC 2 (Channel 4 had not yet been invented) and a raging storm throughout the British Isles. This was how, apart from its intrinsic merits, *Abigail's Party* attracted no less than sixteen million viewers and a permanent place in the nation's affection' (1997: 114). But as Coveney also notes, it is 'a cruel irony that the piece of work for which Mike Leigh and Alison Steadman together remain best known [in the UK] is a flatly photographed, crude studio recording' (1997: 112). What makes this popular success all the more ironic is that it was *Abigail's Party* that provoked what is probably the most vitriolic attack ever made on Leigh's work, in which Dennis Potter claimed – in *The Sunday Times*, in 1977 – that the play was 'based on nothing more edifying than rancid disdain, for it was a prolonged jeer, twitching with genuine hatred, about the dreadful suburban tastes of the dreadful lower-middle-classes' and sinking 'under its own immense condescension'. It was, according to Coveney, after Potter's review that 'words like "condescension" and "patronising" started to appear regularly in reviews [of Leigh's work]' (1997: 119).

My point is that when British reviewers first saw *High Hopes* (1988), *Life is Sweet* (1990) and *Naked* (1993), they often reacted as if they already knew what to expect. What they expected to see was something that would confirm the impression of Leigh that they had formed mostly in response to *Abigail's Party*. Let us quickly look at two examples taken from two of the reviews of *Naked* in 1993. In *The Sunday Times*, we find Julie Birchill suggesting that this 'Mike Leigh film … would have been far better on TV in the first place … In his way Leigh has developed as instantly recognisable a collection of stereotypes as the *Carry On* team in their heyday' (1993: 9). She maintains that at its best the dialogue 'is good sitcom, *not* great cinema' (ibid.) In the *New Statesman*, on the other hand, after noting how everything in the film is 'the deathly grey of urban sludge', Jonathan Romney claims that it is 'this monochrome – meticulously art-directed in street scenes, interiors, clothes, even the characters' lard-pallid faces – that make *Naked* the one Mike Leigh film that really looks like a film through and through. *Naked*, for once, is its own universe, not simply a filmed amplification of sitcom conventions' (1993: 34). It looks to me as if both Romney and Burchill expected more or less the same thing but Romney did not find it and Burchill did. Or to put it another way, Romney was partially surprised out of his prejudices, while Burchill found hers confirmed. On one thing they continue to agree: for Romney almost all and for Burchill all of Leigh's films are not really films.

In order to see the wider significance of this, we need to look at two more reactions – the first from a great admirer, the second from someone who would seem to share Burchill's strong dislike of Leigh. The first is Andy Medhurst's overview of Leigh's career that appeared in *Sight and Sound* when *Naked* was first released. Here Medhurst claims that no one excels Leigh in 'making moving (in both senses of the word) pictures that evoke the horrors and humours of being English over the past 20 years ... only Alan Bennett and Victoria Wood come close to matching Leigh's successes, and they too have had to look to audiences, rather than critics, for their primary recognition' (1993: 7). What concerns Medhurst, however, is that with *Naked* 'Leigh is likely to be applauded for ... moving on up into the rarefied arena of European art cinema' (ibid.). As Medhurst sees it, 'British social comedy is far more important [than] the European art cinema club that *Naked* might give him an open passport to' (1993: 10). In other words, like Romney and Burchill with their references to 'sitcom', Medhurst also sees Leigh as belonging to 'British social comedy' rather than to 'European art cinema'. The difference is that Medhurst *values* British social comedy more than the other two, and that – as he tells us in a later review of *Topsy-Turvy* – he would 'insist' that Leigh is 'Britain's greatest living film-maker' (2000: 36). But it seems to me unfortunate that such praise rests on the insistence that Leigh's films must be seen as belonging to only one side of that overly rigid dichotomy, that they must not be seen as having any connection with 'European art cinema'.

After all, John Caughie, who provides us with our next reaction, would be happy to agree both that Leigh's films do not belong to the latter and also that they do belong to 'British social comedy'. It is just that, as he sees it, this justifies his refusal to take Leigh's work in film seriously. And I have to admit that this is one of two points on which I agree with Caughie: if it were true, then he would be justified. Here, then, is the entry devoted to Leigh and written by Caughie in *The Companion to British and Irish Cinema* published by the influential and – in film terms – establishmentarian British Film Institute in 1996:

> *British director*, most of whose work has been in theatre and television drama since the 1970s, with only four feature films to his credit, and a seventeen-year gap between his first feature film, *Bleak Moments* (1971), and his next, *High Hopes* (1988), which won the Critics' Award at Cannes. Since 1988, his films have attracted increasing international attention. His extensive work in theatre and television established a highly individual working method in which scripts were developed out of improvisation, the director/writer's role being to 'sculpt' characters and situations out of the material which the actors threw up. The detailed observation is often astonishing, but his aesthetic owes more to the *Carry On* tradition than to the critical realist tradition, a comedy of character which ruthlessly exposes vulnerability and social pretension but ends up assuring the audience of its own superiority. In his third feature film, *Life is Sweet* (1990), the revelation that people without taste are not necessarily people without feeling seems patronising and predictable, while in *Naked* (1993), which brings a new level of intensity to its performances, the lingering question of whether Leigh's misogyny is a

thing in itself or just an aspect of misanthropy seems to be resolved on the side of misogyny. (1996: 100–1)

This seems to me to gets things so seriously wrong that the temptation is strong simply to dismiss it, by pointing either to *Life is Sweet* (anyone who thinks its characters can be accurately summed up as 'people without taste' is unintentionally revealing more about himself than about the film) or to the ending of the review of *Naked* in *The New York Review of Books* where Ian Buruma placed Leigh in the company of some of the greatest film-makers: 'Like other wholly original artists, he has staked out his own territory. Leigh's London is as distinctive as Fellini's Rome or Ozu's Tokyo' (1994: 10). But though I agree with Buruma that this is indeed part of the company to which Leigh belongs, and though he and I are far from being alone, there remains nevertheless considerable resistance to this view. I want to avoid if possible talking only to the already persuaded. I have quoted Caughie's dismissal in its entirety because I think it usefully summarises the position held by many of Leigh's detractors. For the same reason, I will respond to it in some detail.

The distinction Caughie insists on making between British television and British film is finicky at best and basically untenable. As Leigh says, a 'film is a film, whether made for the cinema or television' (Movshovitz 2000: 63). Judging by the following excerpt from his entry on Stephen Frears, Caughie himself would agree with this:

He made his first feature film, *Gumshoe*, in 1971, but between 1971 and 1984, when he made *The Hit*, he worked in television drama. *My Beautiful Laundrette* (1985) was also made for television, but its surprise success earned it a cinema release in the United States and an Oscar nomination. This film and *Sammy and Rosie Get Laid* (1987), both made collaboratively with Hanif Kureishi, are key films of the 1980s, unpicking the social fabric of Thatcherism into its multicultural and multisexual threads. (1996: 69)

The idea that 'Thatcherism' had 'multicultural and multisexual threads' makes no sense to me. This aside, however, it would seem that if, for Caughie, Frears' *My Beautiful Laundrette* is a film and Leigh's *Meantime*, say, is a 'television drama', this can only be because the former secured 'a cinema release' and the latter did not. And since most of Leigh's 'television drama[s]' have in fact been shown in cinemas, in various retrospectives of his work as a film-maker, Caughie's final criterion turns out to be whether or not a film has been *commercially* released. This, I submit, is unacceptable.

Basically, Caughie makes three charges: (i) that Leigh's work cannot be taken too seriously because it essentially belongs to 'the *Carry On* tradition'; (ii) that his films typically encourage their audiences to feel 'superior' to – or to 'patronise' – the films' characters; and (iii) that Leigh and his films are 'misogynistic'.

What about 'the *Carry On* tradition'? It is true, and important to notice, that there are certainly elements of farce in many of Leigh's films and, as he himself has pointed out, 'to some degree, [his] roots are in Ealing comedy':

There's a broader British comic tradition. I grew up in the age of radio comedy, and then television comedy, as well as the movies. Certain of the Ealing films – *Kind Hearts and Coronets*, *The Man in the White Suit*, *The Lavender Hill Mob*, *Passport to Pimlico* and Alexander Mackendrick's *The Lady Killers* – had a great impact on me. (Leigh quoted in Movshovitz 2000: 74)

But the *Carry On* films are not in the same league as these. Since I would guess that most younger readers are not likely to have seen any of the movies in question (and most older readers not likely to have seen any of them for a good many years), here is an excerpt from the entry Caughie provides in *The Companion to British and Irish Cinema*:

The films belong in the music-hall tradition of George Formby and Max Miller, and their humour is in the tradition of the seaside postcard ('pinched bums, big tits, screaming queens and henpecked husbands are the conditions of their existence … their most celebrated feature, their great comic glory, is the reliance on innunendo' – Andy Medhurst). (1996: 43)

Based on the sample that I have recently made a point of seeing – *Carry On Camping* (on the offchance that *Nuts in May* might be in any way indebted) and a few excerpts from other *Carry On* movies – I would say that at least the last part of this (concerning the seaside postcard, if not the music-hall tradition) gives us an accurate description of what they have to offer. The idea that Leigh's aesthetic owes anything to the *Carry On* movies seems to me insulting.

Part of the problem would seem to be that when Caughie wrote his entry on Leigh he was not familiar with the whole of the latter's oeuvre up to that point. On the other hand, I think it is clear that he had seen at least some of the work Leigh had done for television. In fact, the idea that Leigh belongs to 'the *Carry On* tradition' is only likely to appear at all plausible to someone who has not seen any of the *Carry On* films for a long time and is thinking, where Leigh's work is concerned, primarily of *Abigail's Party* (and to a lesser degree, perhaps, of *Nuts in May* and one memorable sequence near the end of *Grown-Ups*). It is, to put it mildly, ludicrously wide of the mark as a summary of what even these works have to offer; but my immediate concern here is to draw attention to the way in which while, on one level, Caughie excludes a significant part of Leigh's work as a film-maker, on another, his sense of one of Leigh's television films – ironically, the one that least deserves to be thought of *as* a film (as Coveney says, '*Abigail's Party* is not a television film but a hastily compiled television studio play which merely replicates the Hampstead Theatre production' [1997: 112]) – appears to have consciously or unconsciously determined his view of the films made directly for the cinema.

Of course, I cannot prove that Caughie's judgement of Leigh's work is disproportionately influenced by *Abigail's Party,* but this is the best explanation I can offer for what is definitely a serious misrepresentation. In any case, if, as I will argue later, Dennis Potter's view of *Abigail's Party* is a mistake, it is at least an understandable mistake. What is *not* so understandable or excusable is the larger mistake, which still continues to be made today, according to which Leigh's work as a film-maker is supposed to be *typically* condescending and patronising. Think of such films as, say, *Bleak Moments, Hard Labour, The Kiss of Death, Meantime, Four Days in July* and *Life is Sweet* (astonishingly, the middle four of them not counting for Caughie as a contribution to British cinema). And it is worth noting, incidentally, that the first two of these films *could* be seen – indeed, as I hope to show, *should* be seen – as deeply feminist works. Not that this in itself disproves the third of Caughie's accusations, the allegations of misogyny that he levels against both Leigh in person and his film *Naked*. But it should at least give pause to those inclined to agree with Caughie on this. Here too, however, if only in the case of *Naked* (and perhaps *Abigail's Party*), we are dealing with an at least partially understandable mistake, one that deserves to be taken seriously, and the courtesy of a careful rebuttal, which it will receive.

Now I assume that we all have expectations of one kind or another and I certainly did not mean to suggest that North American viewers came to *High Hopes* and *Life is Sweet* without any at all. Leigh claims, as we have seen, that a good film can confound our expectations, but unfortunately this only holds true if the viewer is sufficiently open to the experience to allow his or her expectations to be confounded. Sometimes our expectations are so strong that they prevent this from happening, which is why part of the task of the critic is to try to help us become at least more aware of the preconceptions, expectations and prejudices that we bring with us – in the hope that awareness can be a first step in a process of change and opening up.

I will now admit that the first Leigh films I saw were *High Hopes* and *Life is Sweet*. I saw them when they came out and was not particularly impressed. They certainly did not strike me then as being the work of a major film-maker. In my mind, the most important film-maker was still Godard, even though I was dissatisfied with most of the work he had produced since 1968. And it would be difficult to think of anything much further removed from Godard's highly self-conscious and essentially Brechtian approach to the cinema than – to use the labels that I no longer find satisfactory but which irresistibly came to mind at the time – the naturalism or neo- (or social-)realism of *High Hopes* and *Life is Sweet*. The last thing I was expecting at the time was the emergence of a major artist who would be found working that particular vein, the possibilities of which were surely exhausted ages ago.

It must have also been the last thing certain others were expecting too. I am thinking, on the one hand, of Christine Gledhill's reminder of how, in the early 1970s, 'structuralist neo-Marxism, in critiquing the notion of "popular art", identified "realism" as the anti-value, in which could be exposed at once literary critical tradition, bourgeois ideology and the manipulations of the capitalist culture industries' (2002: 8).[2] I am also thinking, on the other hand, of the subsequent growth of a sensibility and a climate that has come to be known as postmodern. From the point of view of the latter, Leigh's account of the formative experience he had while studying in a life-drawing class at Camberwell School of Art is bound to seem hopelessly old-fashioned. Here is Mirra Bank's summary of it:

He'd go out with a sketchpad to work from something real – an approach he'd never encountered in his acting training. His 'clairvoyant flash' – that working from the source was the key to making a work of art – gave Leigh his method as a director. (Movshovitz 2000: 117)

Working from 'the source'! What, from the point of view of those formed by the assumptions of the postmodern, could seem more naive? But perhaps it is easier now than it may have been ten or twenty years ago to see this as an example of the pot calling the kettle black?[3]

In any case, what changed my own attitude was seeing *Naked*, a film that I found highly disturbing but that also immediately struck me as being, quite unmistakably, an extremely powerful work of art. And when *Secrets and Lies* was released, I was won over. What amazed – and still amazes – me is the fact that the same man made both of these films. As a result, I at first wanted to write a monograph on *Naked*, which would have contained a large section on *Secrets and Lies*. When I finally got around to watching the films that preceded *High Hopes*, my initial overall impression was decidedly mixed. This seems to me crucially important because, going by my own experience, I would say that (more than most other films) many of Leigh's films absolutely require that we give them at least a second viewing (and ideally more than that) before most of us are likely to be able to take what they have to offer.

Why is this? Why, if I am right, are most of us likely to find some of Leigh's films – *Naked* and *All or Nothing*, for example, in their entirety, and parts of a number of others – so difficult to take on a first viewing? For the same reason, I suggest, that, as D. H. Lawrence once explained, we generally find it 'hard to hear a new voice', which is that a new voice offers a new experience and the 'world fears a new experience more than it fears anything'. But again, if this is so, why, according to Lawrence, do we fear new experiences?

Because a new experience displaces so many old experiences. And it is like trying to use muscles that have perhaps never been used, or that have been going stiff for ages. It hurts horribly.

The world doesn't fear a new idea. It can pigeon-hole any idea. But it can't pigeon-hole a real new experience. It can only dodge. (1933: 7)

I am not so sure myself that the world does not fear new ideas too but, leaving this aside, I would say that (often despite their air of surface familiarity) Leigh's films offer us new experiences and, while frequently being funny – sometimes hilariously so – and in other ways entertaining and pleasurable, they are also often painful, so painful that it is difficult at first to resist the temptation to dodge them.

In itself, this will not seem in any way controversial. No doubt Andy Medhurst was expressing a common sentiment when he maintained that the humour of Leigh's films is the only thing that keeps them 'from being too wounding to bear' (1993: 8). But to be more specific, let us look a bit more closely at a moment in Dennis Potter's

1997 review of the televised version of *Abigail's Party*: 'As so often in the minefields of English class-consciousness, more was revealed of the snobbery of the observers rather than the observed.' By 'the observers' Potter obviously meant Leigh and his actors observing lower-middle-class life ('the observed'). But of course Potter was one of the observers too, inescapably. And a good deal is revealed by *his* reaction, in particular by his response to the performance, which he finds 'memorably nasty', 'of Alison Steadman as the dreadful, blue-lidded Beverley':

> Her cretinously nasal accents made the hairs prickle on the back of my neck, and every moment, every gesture was honed into such lethal caricature that it would not have been too surprising if she had suddenly changed shape in the manner of the fat, thin or elongated reflections in a fairground mirror.

However improbable it may at first appear, I submit that on reflection it can be seen from Potter's highly visceral reaction – the mixture of revulsion and accusation, the hairs prickling on the back of his neck – that he experienced *Abigail's Party* as the kind of site that for Henry Krips marks the intrusion of the Lacanian Real: 'a site of anxiety where the symbolic order breaks down' (1999: 37); 'a site where the subject experiences an excessive or "unrealistic" anxiety' (1999: 102).

What, I would therefore suggest (without intending any personal criticism whatsoever), made Potter so deeply uncomfortable was the fact that he was finding himself in such close and distressing proximity to the real, the real in the form of an encounter with class, an encounter that for him at least was traumatic. If, as Lawrence maintains, a new experience 'hurts horribly' just because it is new, there is another reason why the experiences many of Leigh's films offer us hurt; they are experiences of the real, often of the traumatic real.

I realise that this is bound at first to sound a little odd but I am thinking, among other things, of what the American art critic Hal Foster has to say in a recent book entitled *The Return of the Real: The Avant-Garde at the End of the Century*. Here, Foster asks why in so much avant-garde work today there is 'this fascination with trauma, this envy of abjection?' (1996: 166). He suggests that part of the explanation is that 'there is dissatisfaction with the textualist model of culture as well as the conventionalist view of reality – as if the real, repressed in poststructuralist postmodernism, had returned as traumatic' (1996: 166). Or to put it slightly differently: 'Repressed by various poststructuralisms, the real has returned, but as the traumatic real' (1996: 239).

It is obvious that Leigh started his explorations of the traumatic real before 'poststructuralist postmodernism' arrived on the scene and the scene in question was mainly academic anyway. So I am definitely not suggesting that this explains why Leigh was drawn to explore this form of the real. When I say that the experiences Leigh's films offer us are of the 'real', I want to make it plain that my usage of this term differs from Foster's in that I do not intend mine – as he intends his – to *exclusively* conform to any of the definitions provided by the French psychoanalyst Jacques Lacan. On the other hand, since some of these often seem to me highly suggestive and helpful when one is trying to think about the encounters with the real staged by Leigh, I will later (as I have already started to do in my references to Krips and Foster) be drawing on some of the Freudian/Lacanian-derived usages. As we shall see, the effects of trauma are evident in most of Leigh's films and the term itself is explicitly invoked in both *Career Girls* (in a flashback to the lecture-room where the concept actually gets explained) and *Secrets and Lies* (in the course of the social worker's interview with Hortense – 'it's a very traumatic journey we're embarkin' on').

Here is Foster's explanation as to why we need to experience the kind of art-works he is discussing twice:

> For Freud, especially as read through Lacan, subjectivity is not set once and for all; it is structured as a relay of anticipations and reconstructions of traumatic events ... One event is only registered through another that recodes it; we come to be who we are only in deferred action ... On this analogy the avant-garde work is never historically effective or fully significant in its initial moments. It cannot be because it is traumatic – a hole in the symbolic order of its time that is not prepared for it, that cannot receive it, at least not immmediately, at least not without structural change ... the avant-garde project in general develops in deferred action. (1996: 29)

But surely I am not implying that Leigh belongs to the avant-garde? Not exactly, no. But let us consider, for a moment, some of the resemblances, under four headings:

(i) *Leigh's uncompromising attitude.*

Coveney and other commentators often claim a kind of outsider status for Leigh and he obviously (and rightly) takes pride in the fact that his art is both confrontational and uncompromising. He tells us that his credo is that 'if you don't give in, you don't sell out and compromise, you've got half a chance' (Movshovitz 2000: 33). When asked about the 'abrasive qualities' of *Naked*, Leigh responds as follows:

> Life is abrasive for a lot of people ... and there is no getting around it. I think a function of art – and the cinema not least – is to confront these things ... I'm absolutely committed as a film-maker to be entertaining and to amuse; but I am also concerned to confront, as I did in *Life is Sweet* and other films. (Movshovitz 2000: 43)

In keeping with this, Leigh is critical of Hollywood and of the unfortunate influence he sees it having had on some British films, films that have earned considerable praise from the critics:

> A large proportion of Channel Four films throughout most of the 1980s – although they were independent films and they were successful – continued,

and some still continue, to genuflect towards Hollywood. *The Long Good Friday*, or even for example, *Mona Lisa* – are basically Hollywood genre films. British, and other European film-making, has a desire to be what is basically pastiche Hollywood fare. (Leigh quoted in Movshovitz 2000: 119)

In a similar vein, he tells another interviewer (with reference to the innocent-seeming request of a potential Hollywood producer to see only 'half a page' about a projected film), that you 'cannot compromise on anything so basic and fundamental' (Movshovitz 2000: 57).

(ii) *Leigh's method*

As Amy Taubin put it in her *Village Voice* piece on *Naked*, 'Leigh has developed lengthy, improvisory rehearsal methods, which are as legendary as Cassavetes' or Scorsese's, and even more radical' (1993: 70). As even Caughie is willing – or obliged – to recognise (this is the second point on which I agree with him), the 'detailed observation' that this produces, 'is often astonishing'. Astonishing, yes, but also, therefore, well worth pondering. I shall have more to say about this in chapter three but will simply note for now that nothing in Leigh's practice seems more avant-garde than his deep commitment to a method of radical experimentation.

(iii) *Leigh's rejection of glamour*

It seems relevant here to note David Thomson's statement concerning the central importance of melodrama in our experience of the cinema, in the sketch on Douglas Sirk in *The New Biographical Dictionary of Film*:

> Cinema – as an entertainment, an art form, an academic topic, or an institution – is addicted to melodrama. What greater contrast of chiaroscuro is there than that between burning screen and darkened audience? ... What medium is so dependent on sensation, with the screen so much larger than life and the constant threat that in a fraction of a second the image we are watching can change unimaginably? And what are the abiding themes of cinema but glamour, sexuality, fear, horror, danger, violence, suspense, averted disaster, true love, self-sacrifice, happy endings, and the wholesale realisation of those hopes and anxieties that we are too shy to talk about in the daylight? Why is it dark in cinemas? So that the compulsive force of our involvement may be hidden. (2002: 815)

As this eloquent passage can forcibly remind us, Leigh does not only consistently reject the glamour that is a staple of the vast majority of films; many of his films – in fact, almost all of them up to *Naked* and *Secrets and Lies* – also largely reject the various modes of melodrama itself. And whatever else is to be said about this, it would be difficult to deny that, in its way, it too is a measure of his radicalism.

(iv) *Naked*

'A hole in the symbolic order'. This brings us to the one film by Leigh that most closely resembles an avant-garde work. When *Naked* was first released, its effect on the reviewers (especially the British ones) does seem to have been almost traumatic. To use Foster's words, which seem entirely appropriate here, 'the symbolic order of its time' was obviously 'not prepared for it'; the reviewers could not 'receive it'. Let us look at some examples, starting with Jonathan Romney, the title of whose review ('Scumbag Saviour') was preceded by the claim (or boast?) that 'Jonathan Romney is exposed to Mike Leigh's blast of hatred'. As it happens, Romney explicitly refers to trauma, claiming that *Naked* is 'immersed to the hilt in a traumatised conception of the real – the real London of homelessness, violence, sexual exploitation and despair'. For Romney, the experience of watching *Naked* was 'like being trapped for two hours in a railway carriage with a charismatic preacher who might possibly have an axe under his coat'. I take it that, even if Romney's fear of the non-existent axe testifies to a misunderstanding of the film's central character, Johnny, it was nevertheless a real fear. More realistically, Romney also thought that Johnny was 'cruising compulsively for the inevitable bruising'. In a similar vein, Burchill likened the experience of watching the film to 'a mugging'; in the US, Georgia Brown, who judged it to be 'a brilliant, radical' and 'brave' work, said that it 'could be called a laceration' ('It's painted in bruise colors, especially black and blue'); and (back in the UK) Claire Monk found it 'gruelling viewing for the wrong reasons'.

These reactions go some way toward registering just how shocking an experience these reviewers found the film to be. And if we recall Hal Foster's description of a traumatic experience – as one that cannot be digested at the time it is undergone, that can only be digested in a later reconstruction, in an action that is deferred – then the larger-than-usual number of mistakes they made might suggest that they came close at least to having such an experience. I will explain why I think they are mistakes but first let us look at three instances:

(a) Monk seems to be doing her best to be fair, which makes the following two examples from her review all the more striking: 'Johnny asks the melancholy waitress if he can stay the night; she panics and tells him to go, which he does after pushing her around … The truly homeless characters, Archie and Maggie, are treated as heartlessly as Leigh's past bourgeois targets.'

Johnny does not push the waitress around, Archie and Maggie are not treated heartlessly. (I discuss the latter scene in the chapter on *Naked*.)

(b) Under the title of the second review ('Crass struggle') we read: 'Julie Burchill says *Naked*, Mike Leigh's new film, is British class prejudice at its worst'. Unbelievably, the prejudice Burchill detects is against the working class. What she finds throughout Leigh's films (as well as in this one) is 'an impotent, slightly preening rage at the rather sweet pretensions and foibles of the English working-class, over and over.' (Talk about condescension!) 'Doesn't Leigh', she therefore asks, 'ever feel the need to tilt at the ruling class, just for a change?' Presumably

Burchill simply has not seen *Who's Who* or *A Sense of History*, but these comments make one wonder which of Leigh's films she thinks she *has* seen.

I'll let Georgia Brown make the most important point about Burchill's review:

> Released in Britain last month, the movie elicited a scandalous personal attack in the *Sunday Times* by Julie Burchill. In the midst of an incoherent diatribe, Burchill accused Leigh of disguising his middle-class, and Jewish origins: 'His father is a doctor – and his family's original name was Lieberman … his films look a great deal more cruel and patronising if not made by One of Us.' Astonishing. (1993: 70)

(c) An even greater mistake than these, however, is one made by most of *Naked's* reviewers. Almost all of them think that it begins with a rape. Even Brown makes this mistake, though she at least immediately corrects herself:

> *Naked* opens with a rape. At least it looks like one. Given what we later see of Johnny's modus operandi, probably consensual sex turned nasty. (Ibid.)

But this is a matter of some importance. Whether he is or is not a rapist makes – or should make – all the difference in the world, in the way we relate to him.

How do I know – or why do I think I know? – that the mistakes identified above really are mistakes? The kind of evidence I am *not* relying on can be found in something David Thewlis (the actor who plays Johnny) tells Amy Taubin about *Naked's* opening scene:

> He's not a rapist. At the beginning, that's not a rape. It's sex that gets out of hand. That's not to condone it. Obviously he's out of order. And with Sophie, it's not a rape. And the woman in the window – he pulls away from her. She says 'hurt me' and he pulls away and hurts her verbally. He says some very nasty things, but it's not rape.

It is true that usually we would of course expect the actor involved to know such things. But what counts is the evidence on the screen. The first viewing of *Naked* is bound to be a distressing experience and it is more than usually difficult, when one is deeply distressed, to see things clearly. I am arguing, after all, that *Naked* (along with, but even more than, Leigh's other films) positively *needs* to be seen at least twice.

So much, then, for some of the ways in which Leigh's work resembles the practice of – and produces some of the effects we expect to be produced by – the avant-garde. Yet, however much his work has in common with typical avant-garde practice, there are of course certain obvious and important differences. Thus, after telling us about 'Leigh's anger whenever "media studies" people and TV comedy buffs draw simple analogies between his work and sitcoms and soaps', Coveney quotes Leigh's reaction to this as follows:

I get angry because there is nothing, no situation, in my films that is inorganic. But if the commentators simply mean that there are populist elements in my work, I'm happy with that. I have no wish to be seen only by a few people in art houses. I want my work to be popular, mainstream, and enjoyed by the greatest possible audience. I try for that all the time. (1997: 110)

As a statement of intent, this deserves to be taken seriously. Yet, at the same time, I do not mind admitting that I am not happy to think of Leigh as a populist, if only because I associate populism with the philistinism he elsewhere rightly complains about ('there is [in the UK] a great tradition of acting – extraordinary in such a philistine country that there should be a great tradition of anything creative but there is' [Movshovitz 2000: 21]). The point is that, while Leigh genuinely does want to reach the largest audience possible, he wants to reach it *only on his own terms*.

Changing our expectations

No doubt the principal expectation of a Leigh film is that it will be in some way a work of realism. So it is worth noting that, under the title 'Nul Britannia', while commenting in September 2002 on the miserable showing of British films in the *Sight and Sound* ('Ten Greatest...') poll, Nick James wondered 'whether realism [had not] ruined their chances'. After all, it has, as he says, 'been widely assumed that realism is what the British do best' and the poll in question does seem to reflect a 'general shift in cinema tastes toward spectacle and away from the reflection of ordinary life'. Unless it might be more accurate to say that the larger film-going public has always tended to prefer spectacle to the reflection of ordinary life; and that it may now be even less willing to sit through reflections of the latter than it used to be. But if this is the case, then the author of a new book on Leigh – whose most successful film in the poll (indeed, the only one mentioned) is, as James points out, 'his paean to High Victorian fantasists Gilbert and Sullivan' – would be well-advised to take it into account.

I may as well admit, then, that I am as bored as anyone could be by some of the categories that frequently get applied to Leigh's work; some of them ('social realism', 'kitchen-sink realism', 'council-estate realism') ought to be immediately consigned to the scrapheap and others ('naturalism', even 'realism' itself) ought be used much more selectively.[4] At the same time, there is clearly no point in denying either that most of Leigh's films offer precious little in the way of spectacle or that they are mostly distinguished by precisely their focus on ordinary life. And of course his films do undoubtedly offer at least a kind of realism. But what kind? As I have begun to explain, my own answer is traumatic realism, part of the point of which is that it shifts the discussion from 'realism' as such to the 'real'. More on this later.

In the next chapter I shall consider Leigh's interest in ordinary life. And here again I will be trying to slightly (but I trust significantly) shift the emphasis of the discussion – this time with the help of two recent books on 'the everyday' – from the related concepts of the 'ordinary' to the concept of 'the midst of life'.

CHAPTER TWO

The Extraordinary Element of Too-Muchness at the Heart of the Ordinary

Directly, objectively, yet compassionately, it [Olmi's *The Tree of the Wooden Clogs*] puts on the screen the great, hard, real adventure of living and surviving from day to day, and from year to year, the experience of ordinary people everywhere.

I do not share Ermanno Olmi's religious views, although I empathise with his spirituality ... Behind the wholesome simplicity of the characters' lives is their faith, and for all one's own late-century urban atheist scepticism, one cannot but be moved by the total harmony of their lives.

– Mike Leigh (1995a: 114, 117)

'My films', Leigh maintains, 'are actually about things like work, surviving, having an aged parent or whether it's a good idea to have kids, the problems that everybody cares about' (Fuller 1995: xxi–xxii). In other words, his films are primarily interested in investigating 'day-to-day ordinariness' (Fuller 1995: xi). What Leigh is basically trying to do is what he has praised Ermanno Olmi for doing in his 1978 film *The Tree of the Wooden Clogs*: he wants to give us the 'experience of ordinary people everywhere'.

I see two potential difficulties here, the first of which is the kind of scepticism that wonders whether there are indeed 'problems that *every*body cares about', or whether the same experience is shared by 'ordinary people *every*where'. What could such experience – or such experiences – be? The second has to do with the word 'ordinary'. It is so familiar that it is difficult not to take it for granted, not to use it mechanically. Considering, therefore, how unavoidable it is in any discussion of Leigh's work, I think that we need to pause here and draw on two recent attempts to rethink the topic that this and the related term 'everyday' mark out.[1]

Andrew Klevan on the Uneventful, the Festive and the Everyday

> For most people in the world … life is hard work; it's tough … It's about coping. Most movies are about extraordinary or charmed lifestyles. For me what's exciting is finding heightened drama, the extraordinary in the ordinary – what happens to ordinary people…
>
> – Mike Leigh (quoted in Carney 2000: 14)

Approximately two-thirds of Andrew Klevan's *Disclosure of the Everyday: Undramatic Achievement in Narrative Film* are given over to close readings of four films – Robert Bresson's *Diary of a Country Priest* (1950), Milos Forman's *Loves of a Blonde* (1965), Yasujiro Ozu's *Late Spring* (1949) and Eric Rohmer's *A Tale of Springtime* (1990). We are invited to see them as being 'exceptional' in that, unlike the great majority of films that either 'avoid … or transform' the 'everyday', these four simply '*acknowledge*' and '*disclose*' it (Klevan 2000: 30). Whereas 'most narrative films are in an overtly dramatic, melodramatic or comic idiom', the narratives of the four films Klevan singles out are organised 'around a range of life experiences unavailable to the melodramatic mode as it has developed in world cinema – life experiences based around the routine or repetitive, the apparently banal or mundane, and the uneventful' (2000: 1–2).

At first glance it might well appear that this perfectly describes a number of Leigh's films too – such films as *Bleak Moments*, *Hard Labour*, *The Kiss of Death* and *Life is Sweet*, among others. Nor should this be too surprising since Ozu is the director Leigh is most often compared to. And, in fact, in film after film, there can be no doubt about the depth of Leigh's commitment to the ordinary and the everyday. It is especially clear, for example, in *Four Days in July* (1985), the film set in Northern Ireland. If ever there was an obvious opportunity to exploit the dramatic, this was it. But instead, Leigh decided to tell the story of two couples, one Catholic and one Protestant, both of whom are expecting babies, which arrive more or less together as the two mothers occupy adjacent hospital beds. Here, in the case of childbirth (and all that surrounds it), we have an example of the kind of 'experience' that can indeed be said to be that 'of ordinary people everywhere', even if not everyone experiences it directly.

Another such example can be found in Leigh's short television play *The Permissive Society* (1975). The point here is that, even in a society that is widely thought of as being 'permissive', there will always be someone like Les, a youngster who is still virginal but interested in sex and struggling with the problem of how best to approach, or court, another youngster, Carol, who just happens to be more experienced in these matters than he is. Again, a clear case of one of 'the problems' that, at one point or another in their lives, virtually '*every*body cares about'.

So far, then, it would appear that some, at least, of Leigh's films belong in the category of those works that acknowledge and disclose the everyday. But, as Klevan reasonably points out, '"coming to terms with the everyday" will depend on not mistaking it for something else' (2000: 2), and it is easy to make this mistake, if only because it is easy to confuse 'aspects of realism(s) with the everyday' (2000: 36). Klevan argues that it is important to recognise, therefore, not only that the 'quest for the ordinary cannot be expressed simply as the search for the "more real"' but also that the pursuit of the 'more real' does not necessarily result in a greater 'sensitivity towards the everyday – the everyday as uneventful'. And with this in mind, Klevan examines films – including Satyajit Ray's *Pather Panchali* (1955), Ken Loach's *Kes* (1969) and Roberto Rossellini's *Paisan* (1946) – 'conventionally described as providing pictures of everyday or ordinary life, but which are all, in fact, organised around events or crises' (ibid.).

Let us take just one example, a scene in *Paisan* in which an Italian boy and a drunken American soldier 'sit together on the rubble of a bombed-out site'. Klevan suggests that here it is the 'cacophony of street noise and irregular spontaneity of movement that we might mistakenly characterise as the ordinary'. Whereas 'its down-to-earth(i)ness (its in-the-earthness), its roughness and crudity are precisely the opposite' of what *he* means by 'the everyday and the ordinary, which is not turbulent or unruly but repetitively rigid' (2000: 44). Of course, in many parts of the world there are people who are forced to live everyday in conditions that are highly 'turbulent' and 'unruly'. It is not as if Klevan is insensitive to their plight: his point, I take it, would be that they are forced to live the extraordinary every day, that the horror of their situation is that they are *denied* the ordinary.

Here things begin to become more complex. After all, the life Leigh's films explore is often 'organised around events or crises' (even if they are invariably low-keyed) and – as a result, no doubt, of his 'pursuit of the real' (2000: 45), or 'the "more real"' (2000: 36) – they are not infrequently rough, crude, turbulent and unruly. But it would seem that, from Klevan's point of view, this would make them the very opposite of 'the everyday and the ordinary'. What are we to make of this?

We can start by noting that Klevan is influenced here by the thought of the American philosopher and film critic/theorist, Stanley Cavell. In particular, it would seem that he is committed to the idea of (what Cavell calls, in the title of one of his essays) 'The Ordinary as the Uneventful'. In this essay – with the example of the French '*Annales* Historians' in mind – Cavell tries to envisage 'a history of the human being to which we are blinded by the traditional histories of flashing, dramatic events' (1984: 190). As Cavell understands it, 'the turning away from events as made by exceptional individuals proposes that history turn to an interest in a different set or class of people, call them the unexceptional. Beyond this, it suggests that history, that the human being thinking historically, is *to interest itself differently* in human existence, whatever individual or class it turns its attention to' (1984: 191).

It is tempting to say what seems at least partially and importantly true, that Leigh's films offer us versions of precisely such a history. Yet, as already noted, it is also true that his films are often 'organised around events or crises'. But if this is a contradiction, it is Cavell's, as well as Leigh's. Because, as Klevan knows very well, Cavell himself tries in his other writings to remain faithful both to the 'ordinary' *and* to the idea that it might be in some sense eventful.

We have seen that, while celebrating those films that *disclose* the ordinary and everyday, Klevan divides all other films into two categories: those that *avoid* the ordinary and everyday, and those that *transform* it. Most films presumably fall into the avoidance category and we need not concern ourselves with them here. What we do need to briefly consider, though, are some of the films that Klevan thinks *transform* everyday life, in particular the ones Cavell has grouped together as a genre under the heading of *The Hollywood Comedy of Remarriage*, the subtitle of his book *Pursuits of Happiness*. Cavell has chapters on each of the following: Preston Sturges' *The Lady Eve* (1941), Frank Capra's *It Happened One Night* (1934), Howard Hawks' *Bringing Up Baby* (1938), George Cukor's *The Philadelphia Story* (1940), Howard Hawks' *His Girl Friday* (1940), George Cukor's *Adam's Rib* (1949) and Leo McCarey's *The Awful Truth* (1937).

As Klevan notes, these are all films 'where the couples have to learn to live with the repetitions of the everyday', marriage, as he sees it, being 'crucially connected to any discussion of the everyday because it entails the decision to live with one person every day of one's life' (2000: 23). But for us here, the key point is that, whereas (in Cavell's words) 'classical comedy may be expected to conclude [with a] festival ... say a wedding ... [the] courage, the powers required for happiness are not something a festival can reward, or perhaps so much as recognise, any longer' (1981: 239). So that, as Klevan explains, in these Hollywood comedies 'true ratification of the marriage is provided from within the continuous festivity of the union itself' (2000: 25). And here is Cavell's summary of what this means in practice:

> When [in *The Awful Truth*] Lucy acknowledges to Aunt Patsy her love for Jerry after all, what she says is, 'We had some grand laughs.' Not one laugh at life – that would be a laugh of cynicism. But a run of laughs, within life; finding occasions in the way we are together. He is the one with whom that is possible for me, crazy as he is; that is the awful truth. 'Some grand laughs' – is this comedy's lingo for marriage as festive existence. (1981: 239)

Klevan is certainly not unappreciative of this but what he wants to emphasise is that if the 'conception of the everyday' that Cavell celebrates in these comedies eradicates 'the necessity of a notion of once-and-for-all events', it does not dispose 'of events *per se*'. The fact is that *The Awful Truth* 'does have a series of little events' (2000: 26) and, while they 'may not quite be events in the sense of crescendo happenings to which are attached a fairly definite importance (such as a wedding ceremony) … they are not felt to be only routine happenings' (2000: 27). Yet, while he is by no means indifferent to the achievement of these films, Klevan wants to draw our attention to the films that do *not* transform the everyday, but only disclose it, in all its *un*eventfulness.

How can this help us to situate Leigh? How can it sharpen our sense of where *his* films belong? Consider again *Four Days in July*. Not mentioned previously is the fact that the births occur in the midst of the annual Protestant festivities, questioning whether this film automatically belongs alongside the four Klevan celebrates. Because if, in one sense, giving birth is an activity that clearly belongs to ordinary life, it obviously does not occur everyday – not, at least, in the life of the same family. On the contrary, it marks a very special occasion. So it is highly significant not just that (on Wednesday 11th) Eugene, the Catholic husband, should express the hope that his and his wife Collette's baby should be born on the following day – 'We need something to celebrate on the 12th … bands an' all laid on for it' – but that this wish should be granted. This suggests that perhaps *Four Days in July* has more in common with the films that transform everyday life than with those that concentrate on disclosing it.

It certainly *looks* more like the films by Bresson, Forman, Ozu and Rohmer, having, like them, none of the surface glitter of the Hollywood comedies, nor of course their investment in the star system. But, on the other hand, it is important to note that *Four Days in July* attaches just as much – and a similar kind of – importance to humour as does *The Awful Truth*. It can be clearly seen in, for example, Collette's comment on the departure of the wise-cracking Dixie (Stephen Rea): 'He's a tonic, that Dixie fella.' And then, to her husband: 'If you didn't have a laugh, you'd go mad.' Maybe, says Klevan (thinking of the humour in the Hollywood comedies), 'this is what we mean when we say that the comic helps us "get *through* life"; the comic moments prevent us from needing to avoid it' (2000: 25). But Dixie is far from being the only one of Leigh's characters who have what Klevan (thinking specifically of 'Lucy's giggles' in *The Awful Truth*) calls 'a continuing commitment to laughter' (ibid.) – think, for example, among others, of the giggling Wendy (Alison Steadman) in *Life is Sweet*, of Johnny (much of the time) in *Naked*, and of many of the actors in *Topsy-Turvy*. Just as Eugene and Collette are not by a long stretch the only characters of his who exhibit (as they so splendidly do) the courage that Cavell maintains is 'required for happiness'.

It is tempting, then, in the light of this, to say of Leigh – at least the Leigh of *Four Days in July* – what Klevan says of Cavell, that his 'interest in the ordinary … is one of turning it … into [or of showing it to potentially be] a site of festivity' (2000: 31). Even though we immediately have to add that by no means all of Leigh's films feel as good-natured and as festive as do *Four Days in July* and (for much of the time) *Life is Sweet*. As noted in chapter one, many of them feel like sites more of anxiety than of festivity. What is striking, however, as soon as one starts to reflect upon it, is the extent to which they are organised – in the absence in almost all of these films up to *Secrets and Lies* of any real plot – around (or with important reference to) special, ritualistic and potentially (at least) festive occasions. These are the kind of events that are so undramatic, so small-scale, that they usually do not get recognised *as* events. Leaving aside the countless tea-drinking sessions and ordinary meal-times, here – for all its obvious inadequacies – is a provisional list of only some of these special occasions: (i) *Bleak Moments* – courtship; (ii) *Hard Labour* – Sunday family visit, confession; (iii) *Nuts in May* – holiday in the countryside; (iv) *The Kiss of Death* – courtship, death, a funeral, and marriage; (v) *Who's Who* – dinner party; (vi) *Grown-Ups* – a sort of extended housewarming, deciding to have a child; (vii) *Home Sweet Home* – Sunday dinner; (viii) *Meantime* – family visiting; (ix) *Four Days in July* – childbirth, Protestant celebrations; (x) *High Hopes* – mother's birthday; (xi) *Life is Sweet* – teaching dance, restaurant opening; (xii) *Naked* – opportunities for Socratic dialogue; (xiii) *Secrets and Lies* – Roxanne's 21st birthday, dating one's daughter, housewarming; (xiv) *Career Girls* – friends' weekend reunion; (xv) *Topsy-Turvy* – art, acting, theatre; (xvi) *All or Nothing* – karaoke, promise of a holiday; (xvii) *The Short and Curlies* (short film) – courtship; (xviii) *Abigail's Party* – welcoming evening for new neighbours.

It is of course true that if, as suggested, there is potential festivity on these special occasions, usually this potential is far from being realised. On balance, the mood is probably more often negative than positive, and sometimes – as in the case of *Abigail's Party* – it is nightmarish. But then, as Leigh says, his 'films are, at the same time, a lamentation and a celebration of the human experience as I feel it' (Fuller 1995: xxxiii). And if, as Georgia Brown recalled, at the beginning of her review of *Naked*, lamentation is 'a good biblical word', it is also worth noting that the first *OED* definition of 'celebration' is the 'performance of a solemn ceremony; *spec*, the action of celebrating the eucharist' (the first *OED* definition of 'celebrate' being to 'perform publicly and in due form any religious ceremony, a marriage, a funeral, etc.'). Briefly, then, we should consider something Leigh said in 1988: 'A great deal can be conveyed to an audience about the way the world *might* be, by showing the way the world *is*" (Movshovitz 2000: 12, my italics).

We may now be in a position to see that what Leigh's films may be typically doing is *both* acknowledging and disclosing the ordinary *and* transforming it. Or to be more precise: while acknowledging and disclosing the ordinary, Leigh's films simultaneously reveal the transformative potential that is continually being generated within it. So that if there is a key to Leigh's elusiveness, it may lie in his paradoxical determination to find 'the extraordinary in the ordinary'. Up to a point, we can understand 'the extraordinary' here as the transformative potential to which I have just referred. But we need to dig more deeply than this and to help us do so we can now turn to the second of our two books on the everyday.

Eric Santner on Too-Muchness: The Psychotheology of Everyday Life

My canvas is quite wide, actually, and my self-imposed creed is to be quite open as to what the world is and whom I am depicting.
– Mike Leigh (Fuller 1995: xxiii–xxiv)

The subject matter of my films is not English, but universal…
— Mike Leigh (Movshovitz 2000: 33)

Like Klevan's, the title of Santner's book – *On the Psychotheology of Everyday Life: Reflections on Freud and Rosenzweig* (2001) – also promises to shed some light on the *everyday*. But Santner's title introduces a new element, that of *Psychotheology*, and the book itself redirects our attention not so much *away* from the ordinary and everyday as towards an enriched, more ethically-charged, conception of them, which Santner sums up in the words 'the midst of life'.

In a nutshell, Santner's argument is that reading Freud and the much less well-known Franz Rosenzweig (regarded as 'one of the crucial figures in the renaissance of German-Jewish culture in the first third of the twentieth century' [2001: 4]) in conjunction with one another can enable us 'to rethink what it means to be genuinely open to another human being or culture' (2001: 5). As Santner sees it, we typically operate out of a 'global consciousness' on the mistaken assumption that 'every stranger is ultimately just like [us], ultimately familiar; his or her strangeness … a function of a different vocabulary, a different set of names that can always be translated' (2001: 5–6). Whereas the truth is that 'what makes the Other *other* is not his or her spatial exteriority with respect to my being but the fact that he or she is *strange*, and not only to me but also to him- or herself, is the bearer of an internal alterity, an enigmatic density of desire calling for response beyond any rule-governed reciprocity; against this background', Santner maintains, 'the very opposition between "neighbour" and "stranger" begins to lose its force' (2001: 9). This gives us the gist of the biblically-derived 'ethical conception of ordinary or "everyday" life' – of the universal rather than global consciousness – that Santner finds implicit in Freud and Rosenzweig. And, according to Santner, it is when 'we shift from the register of the global to that of the … universal-in-becoming [that] we truly enter *the midst of life*, that … we truly inhabit the proximity to our neighbour, assume responsibility for the claims his or her singular and uncanny presence makes on us not only in extreme circumstances but *every day*' (2001: 7).

With regard to Leigh, then, an initial suggestion is that having these reflections in mind can help us appreciate a number of the things that we might otherwise miss: such things, for example, as the full significance of the way Cyril and Shirley take in Wayne at the beginning of *High Hopes*, and then carefully see that this neighbour/stranger catches the right bus to take him home. I would also suggest that when we ponder both Cyril and Shirley's decision to have Cyril's mother (Mrs Bender) living with them in *High Hopes* and Dick and Mandy's acceptance of Mandy's difficult, needy sister Gloria at the end of *Grown-Ups*, it can be useful to recall the Rosenzweigian conception of communities that are, as Santner explains, 'constituted … in relation to the remnant'. Especially in the light of Emmanuel Levinas' reminder that the 'Torah demands … concern for the stranger, the widow and orphan' (quoted in Santner 2001: 117).

But by giving Rosenzweig (and the Torah) such prominence, does this not risk making Leigh's sensibility seem more Jewish than it actually is? Judging by some of the comments he has made, Leigh himself would seem to be ambivalent on the subject. On the one hand, Coveney tells us that Leigh 'has always regarded himself as Jewish, rather than a Jew'. And that Leigh 'claims that religion has played no part in his life: "I walked away from that as early as I can remember and certainly, by the time of my bar-mitzvah, I did not believe in God. And I still don't"' (1997: 54). On the other hand, in a 1996 interview, Leigh says that he 'feel[s] sometimes that [he carries] on a great Jewish tradition of a *rebbe* surrounded by Talmudic students, talking things out' (Movshovitz 2000: 89).

In 1994 Leigh admitted to having 'slightly mixed feelings' on the subject of whether or not his Jewish background has any relevance when it comes to understanding his work. He thought 'it could be distracting and distorting':

> Very much in passing, however, it's possible to see a certain kind of Jewish influence. But I think it would be wrong to label these films 'Jewish', or for a whole new kind of interpretation to grow out of this. I think it would be nonsense, I really do. On the other hand, given that there's a consistent tragicomic thing going on, it's possible that's a perspective you could put on it ... There is a thesis on Pinter which says the same thing – his background is also Jewish – but it would be eccentric to say that Pinter is like Isaac Bashevis Singer. (Movshovitz 2000: 76)

Fair enough. But of course the purpose of my remarks is definitely *not* to make the absurd claim that Leigh is 'like Isaac Bashevic Singer'. It is simply to suggest that 'the ethical conception of ordinary or "everyday' life" that Santner finds in Freud as well as in Rosenzweig may shed some light on the conception we find at work in Leigh's films.

It's true, however, that Santner does insist on bringing God into the discussion and for those of us who share Leigh's (and Freud's) atheism, this is troubling. What ought we to make of it? We can start off by noting that, if a common assumption about the Judeo-Christian God is that He is supposed to inhabit – and to be inviting us to share – 'a life beyond this one' (2001: 10), this is definitely not the kind of God Santner is talking about. Santner claims that Freud and Rosenzweig are 'emphatically post-Nietzschean thinkers in the sense that' for them the 'death of God' is precisely 'the death of such an Elsewhere, such a "beyond" ... What', he maintains, 'both Freud and Rosenzweig help us to grasp is that with the "death of God" the entire problematic of transcendence actually exerts its force in a far more powerful way in the very fabric of everyday life.' It is, therefore, this 'immanent transcendence' (2001: 10) that Santner has in mind when he refers to 'the Psycho*theology* of Everyday Life'. In short, he tells us that, in the view he is 'distilling from Freud and Rosenzweig, God is above all the name for the pressure to be alive to the world, to open to the too much of pressure generated in large measure by the uncanny presence of my neighbour' (2001: 9).

Whether or not we want to call it 'God', I would argue that nothing is more characteristic of Leigh's work than the ways in which it exerts on us precisely this kind of 'pressure'. And it seems that the minimalist understanding of a '"spiritual" dimension' that Santner provides – one located in 'the constitutive "too-muchness" that characterises the psyche' (2001: 8) – can help us to better understand something Coveney tells us Leigh once said on the subject: 'that he is "a deeply spiritual person", which is obvious, he reckons, from his work' (1997: 54). After all, if one thing about his work seems undeniable, it is that the psyches of so many of his characters are so obviously constituted by various forms of 'too-muchness'. Hence, too, the suggestiveness – where Leigh's highly idiosyncratic characters are concerned – of Santner's emphasis on singularity: on 'his or her singular and uncanny presence', 'the singularity of our own out-of-jointness' (2001: 7), the 'singular something that ... resists generic identification' (2001: 73).

As Santner understands it, for both Judaism and Christianity human life is characterised by a 'constitutive "too-muchness"' that 'bears witness to a spiritual and moral calling, a pressure toward self-transformation, toward "goodness"' (2001: 8). Prompted by this, I want to make three points: about the presence in Leigh's work of the spirit, goodness and love. In this connection it is worth pondering, among other things, (i) Carney's claim that 'Leigh's subject is the possibility of self-transformation' and that, 'in this respect, his work is essentially as spiritual as that of Dreyer and Tarkovsky' (2000: 17); (ii) Leigh's drawing our attention to something that he claims viewers sometimes overlook, the fact that 'Secrets and Lies is also about goodness' (Movshovitz 2000: 107); (iii) the significance of the extraordinary moment in *Hard Labour* when Mrs Thornley confesses that she does not '*love* people enough' and the agonising plea for love at the end of *All or Nothing*.

Finally, there remains, as Santner says, a paradox, which is 'that in our everyday life we are for the most part *not* open to [the] presence [of our neighbour], to our being "in the midst of life"':

> Everyday life includes possibilities of withdrawing from, defending against, its own aliveness to the world, possibilities of, as it were, not really being there, of dying to the Other's presence.

This, Santner notes, is why 'both Freud and Rosenzweig, not unlike a number of other modern thinkers, orient their thought around the various ways in which we remove ourselves from this midst, the ways in which we *defend* against this very sort of aliveness' (2001: 9–10).

Leigh's films are also concerned to make us aware of our defensive tendency to remove and defend ourselves from the midst of life, but they are animated as well by a pursuit of the real and this is what we need to turn our attention to in the next chapter.

CHAPTER THREE

In Pursuit of the Real

My point is that no work of art is truly naturalistic. Art is not real life, and has to be organised, designed and distilled because it's dramatic. There is nothing accidental, it's all contrivance. What is real is a very complicated, epistemological question.

– Mike Leigh (in Movshovitz 2000: 132)

Whatever else is to be said about Leigh's work, it is obviously driven by a pursuit of the real. There cannot be many artists who have taken such pains to capture 'the texture of real life' (Movshovitz 2000: 83).

Leigh's pursuit of the real invites discussion on a number of different levels, two of which – the importance he attaches to what it seems appropriate to call (in the words of the Russian literary critic Mikhail Bahktin) 'the material bodily principle' and the role played in his films by class – will be explored in the last chapter. This chapter will be restricted to a few remarks on his method, by which is mainly meant his distinctive way of relating to his actors, which Timothy Spall calls 'this science he's invented to achieve what he does' (quoted in Howe 2002).

The Method

As a film-maker with pretensions to making films about real life, I am often asked whether I have used actors or 'real' people. My answer is of course always appropriately shocked and outraged: how could I possibly achieve this reality with people 'off the street'? Only highly sophisticated, professional actors could possibly achieve such performances, never amateurs!

– Mike Leigh (1995a: 115)

At one point in *The World According to Mike Leigh*, Michael Coveney paints a vivid picture of a minor character in *Home Sweet Home* (1982), 'a strange, limping, waiflike creature' whom Stan, the postman, first picks up in a laundrette, then takes 'to the pub, then back to his bed':

> Sheila Kelley [the actress who plays the woman] … is only on screen for a few minutes – in the pub, then dressing after sex with Stan and leaving, never expecting or wanting to see him again – but in this desolate, polio-stricken creature she paints a whole life of someone who haunts laundrettes, not to wash clothes, but to make human contact. When the veteran film-maker Michael Powell attended a showing in San Franscisco in 1986, he asked Leigh, 'She's not an actress, is she?', so disturbingly real did Kelley's performance seem to him. (Coveney 1997: 161–2)

Like Powell, I too had the uneasy feeling when I first saw *Home Sweet Home* that Janice, the young woman in question, was genuinely polio-stricken and somehow played, as it were, by herself. In truth, this left me not just uneasy, but feeling sick to my stomach. It felt as if I had witnessed something in some way shameful. I was greatly relieved when I discovered that Janice was indeed played by a proper actress, Sheila Kelley, who plays Honky, a very different character, in Leigh's earlier *Nuts in May* (1976).

I mention this for two reasons: (i) because I have never had this experience with the films of any other director, and (ii) because it would seem – judging by what Leigh says in his piece on Olmi – to be a fairly common reaction to his characters. For me too, in other words, a Leigh film is often, among other things, 'a site of anxiety'.

How does Leigh manage to get his actors to do this? Why does he go to such trouble? And what precisely is he trying to achieve? I shall address the 'How?' question first. He has explained his method of working to interviewers on numerous occasions, at least in its broad outlines, and what follows is distilled from these accounts.

When he assembles his actors together for the first time, he has no script, not even, apparently, a one-page outline of one. Here is the account of what then happens that Leigh gave to John Lahr in 1996, after the release of *Secrets and Lies*:

> The first thing I say, and it's terribly important that I say it, is 'In five months' time – or three months, or whatever – we are going to go out on location with a film crew and make up a film. What we are going to do between now and then is merely to assemble the raw materials to arrive at the premise for that investigation. We are not going to create a piece of work in that time.

We are not going to create the artifact itself.' The inquiry takes the actors' minds off immediate, appealing results – frees them, as Leigh says, from 'the idea of having to be interesting, funny or sad,' from everything 'but *having to be real*' (Lahr 1996: 54, my italics)

Five or even three months of preparation is of course quite a long period of time and it has not always taken that long. In 1982, when *Home Sweet Home* was being shown on television, Leigh had this to say to Nicholas Wapshott: 'First the whole cast does a lot of research. For *Home Sweet Home*, which is about three postmen in Hitchin, we all spent six weeks in Hitchin.' A number of things seem to have remained constant, however, not the least important of which is the fact that, as Ian Buruma explained in 1994,

> Leigh's actors literally have to find their characters, through improvisation and research into the ways people in specific communities speak and behave. The setting for Leigh's stories can be in Northern Ireland (*Four Days in July*), or in a modern South London slum (*Meantime*), but wherever it is, Leigh and his cast immerse themselves in the local life before creating the story. (1994: 7)

At each stage of the process of making his films, it would seem that the main criterion for Leigh is that it has to be real. Here, for example, is David Thewlis talking to Amy Taubin:

> When you work with Mike, you take a source character, who is someone you know and you build the character on top of a real person. It's not an impersonation but it's inspired by a real person. Of course, for any character, you draw on all sorts of people. In Johnny's behavior there's bits of my friends, my brother, my wife, an old girl-friend. At the same time, Mike is tweaking the character, pushing me in certain directions and pulling me back, influenced, presumably, by people he knows. And that's how Mike directs in terms of creating a character who is neither me nor the original person but someone entirely new. (Taubin 1993)

Another constant feature of the process is that Leigh works individually with each of the actors in turn so that, up until the very end, there is a sense in which – at least as far as the overall, complete picture is concerned – each actor is kept in the dark. So it is not so surprising if, in these circumstances, the emotional involvement of the actors becomes exceptionally intense. And an example of just *how* intense the actor's involvement in this process can be is provided by Thewlis, who 'describes Leigh spending a day after *Naked* had finished shooting doing improvs with Lesley Sharp (the remarkable actress who plays Johnny's ex-girlfriend), allowing her character an opportunity to resolve her feelings about being abandoned once again' (quoted in Taubin 1993).

What makes this sort of thing necessary is the fact that the emotions Leigh and his actors are working with are real ones. 'As you know', Leigh told an interviewer in 1994, 'I go to considerable lengths to be sure that when we film, we're filming some kind of actual emotion. The tension's really there' (Movshovitz 2000: 52). Take, for example, the tea-shop scene in *Secrets and Lies*, in which Cynthia suddenly remembers what up until then she has deeply repressed, the fact that she did, when very young, have sex with a black man after all, so Hortense is not mistaken, she *is* Cynthia's daughter. As Kenneth Turan notes, 'we see the memory literally flood Cynthia's face as she breaks down into convulsive sobs': 'That moment is devastating,' agrees *Secrets and Lies* cinematographer Dick Pope. 'You can't believe it's acting, the emotion is so true' (Movshovitz 2000: 88). Even with the qualification Leigh provides – 'some *kind* of actual emotion' – the claim being made here is a strong one. And it suggests a radically different attitude to the one Slavoj Zizek highlights in the title – *The Fright of Real Tears* – of his recent book on Krzysztof Kieslowski. Here is Zizek's explanation, followed by only part of the passage he goes on to quote from Kieslowski:

> Towards the end of the documentary *First Love* (1974), in which the camera follows a young unmarried couple during the girls's pregnancy, through their wedding and the delivery of the baby, the father is shown holding the newly born baby in his hands and crying. Kieslowski reacted to the obscenity of such unwarranted probing into the other's intimacy by referring to the 'fright of real tears'. His decision to pass from documentaries to fiction films was thus, at its most radical, an ethical one: 'That's probably why I changed to features. There's no problem there … I can even buy some glycerine, put some drops in her eyes and the actress will cry. I managed to photograph some real tears several times. It's something completely different. But now I've got glycerine. I'm frightened of real tears. In fact, I don't even know whether I've got the right to photograph them…' (Zizek 2001: 72)

It is easy to see why Leigh's attitude might strike some as being simply naive, a kind of throwback, perhaps, to the 1960s, when, as Buruma reminds us, 'spontaneity was the rage' and 'happenings' the latest theatrical fashion. But, as Buruma points out, on the one hand, 'happenings didn't interest [Leigh]' and, on the other, 'some remarkable things emerged from the dross' (1994: 7), one of them being the theatrical experimentation of Peter Brook, that Leigh has been happy to acknowledge as one of the formative influences on his work (see Movshovitz 2000: 102, 116). My point, then, is that, like Peter Brook, Leigh is actually a highly sophisticated artist and that what his films force us to admit is that certain forms of art – which are not only not 'truly naturalistic' but which are in a certain sense 'all contrivance' (Movshovitz 2000: 132) – *can* and *do* bring us into contact with more than one face of the real.

This, then, is what Leigh's method is designed to bring about, often during moments of great intensity. Again, as Leigh told Buruma:

To get everything right for that one moment on film, that's what interests me. You want the spontaneity of the theatre to happen at that white-hot moment when the camera is rolling. (1994: 7)

In fact this point (concerning the importance of certain key moments) seems to me crucial and it is worth quoting Terrence Rafferty developing it at some length in his review of *Life is Sweet*:

He prepares us to accept the moments of piercing, almost miraculous clarity that arise, as if by happy accident, at the end of his best films. These moments are modest, unspectacular … long after we've given up trying to figure out what the whole thing is supposed to mean, Leigh comes up with a stunning scene in which Wendy and Nicola discuss Nicola's dissatisfaction with life … as it progresses we sense how this moment of mutual unguarded honesty has emerged from the apparent chaos of the women's recent experiences. And we realise, too, that Mike Leigh's unusual film-making process is designed to generate scenes like this, to bring forth acting that is as pure and direct as Alison Steadman's and Jane Horrocks' … What he's searching for in his movies is the possibility of seeing the world through someone else's eyes – someone specific, whose life can be shared only through patient observation of its random and stubbornly idiosyncratic details. His art consists of making such moments of sudden, profound understanding seem worth any amount of pain, muddle and slapstick catastrophe. (Rafferty 1991: 104)

One could say that such moments are by no means confined to the end of Leigh's films. But this aside, Rafferty's commentary is sensitive, subtle and penetrating. In addition, it may be helpful to think of these moments – which are of course the product of collaborative creation – as constituting (what in a different context Eric Santner calls a kind of '*surplus of the real within reality*' (2001: 74). They are, after all, extraordinary moments and what *is* the 'extra' in 'extraordinary' if not, precisely, a kind of 'surplus'?

In a word, this, then, is what Leigh may well be after. And as noted in the last chapter, it is precisely here – in this 'surplus' (or 'too-muchness') – that we might find evidence of a '"spiritual" dimension', one that belongs to this world and that makes possible the kind of 'immanent transcendence' that exerts its force 'in the very fabric of everyday life' (Santner 2001: 10).

PART TWO

The Films (I)
From *Bleak Moments* (1971) to *Life is Sweet* (1990)

CHAPTER FOUR

The Feminist Leigh: Two Women 'on the other side of silence'

Nor can I suppose that when Mrs Casaubon is discovered in a fit of weeping six weeks after her wedding, the situation will be regarded as tragic. Some discouragement, some faintness of heart at the new real future which replaces the imaginary, is not unusual, and we do not expect people to be deeply moved by what is not unusual. That element of tragedy which lies in the very fact of frequency, has not yet wrought itself into the coarse emotion of mankind; and perhaps our frames could hardly bear much of it. *If we had a keen vision and feeling of all ordinary human life*, it would be like hearing the grass grow and the squirrel's heart beat, and *we should die of that roar which lies on the other side of silence*. As it is, the quickest of us walk about well wadded with stupidity.

– George Eliot, *Middlemarch* (1961: 207, my italics)

By the twentieth chapter of George Eliot's *Middlemarch*, the young heroine, Dorothea (now Mrs Casaubon), is on her honeymoon in Rome. She is deeply unhappy and has just been crying. She is beginning to realise that her new husband is not what she had imagined him to be, that up until this point she had been relating not so much to him as to a fantasy figure of her own construction. The above passage reflects on and in effect universalises her plight. Here, Eliot gives us a glimmer of understanding as to what the real is often like. Only a glimmer, however, because 'our frames could hardly bear much of it' – if we were to somehow truly see and experience 'that roar which lies on the other side of silence', we should die of it.

In his first two films – *Bleak Moments* and *Hard Labour* – Leigh begins his exploration of that other side of silence. Except for the fact that their central characters are female, their joint motto might well be Thoreau's famous line: 'The mass of men lead lives of quiet desperation' (1966: 5). One of the differences, however, is that *Hard Labour*'s Mrs Thornley seems much closer to being resigned to a life of quiet desperation than *Bleak Moment*'s Sylvia. Another is in terms of the works' quality. Though the ending of *Hard Labour* is quite devastating, and though it is impressive in other ways, the film is technically much rougher, seeming more primitive, than *Bleak Moments*. Yet my first priority is to demonstrate why it is worth taking seriously. My contention, then, is that each of these two films gains when seen in the company of the other and that the two together form an extraordinarily powerful feminist statement.

Bleak Moments

What does woman want? If Freud asked this question near the beginning of the twentieth century, it has been raised again by some feminist thinkers in recent years and even, in one instance, chosen (by Shoshana Felman) as the title of a book. In Sylvia's case, the answer seems fairly clear. 'There you are dear', says the cashier as, very early on, he hands her the bottle of sherry she has just bought. 'Enjoy yourself.' The phrase is of course utterly commonplace yet, on one level, that is exactly what she does want: to be able to enjoy herself. But if this gives us a short and provisional answer to the question as to what this one woman, Sylvia, wants, it leads, in turn, to another question. What can a woman *do* to *get* what she wants?

Sylvia (Anne Raitt) is living with and looking after her mentally impaired, 29-year-old (probably slightly younger) sister, Hilda (Sarah Stephenson). Sylvia works as a secretary in the office of a Chartered Accountant, alongside another secretary, Pat (Joolia Cappleman), who is living with and looking after her bed-ridden mother.

Bleak Moments opens with some shots of empty streets in a residential part of London. The first person we see – from a distance, in long shot – is a woman (Sylvia) making haste to meet a man (Peter [Eric Allan]) who has evidently been waiting for her. She apologises for being late and they then walk together. When the path they are on reaches a road, they go in different directions, agreeing that they will see one another the next day. It is morning and they are on their way to work.

The following morning we see Sylvia again meeting Peter in the street; but this time, when it is time for them to part, he wonders, hesitantly, shyly, if her sister might not like to go for a walk with them the following Sunday. It would seem that he and Sylvia have only met quite recently and that this is his indirect way of proposing that they might start the process of getting to know one another better.

Shortly after this, Peter pays his first visit to Sylvia's home. We learn that he is a teacher and we see that he is tied up in knots. On his arrival, he first has difficulty closing the garden gate and then stands, as if paralysed, outside the door of the house while Sylvia is on the inside, waiting for him to knock. He does not knock and, after a few seconds, Sylvia opens the door and lets him in. Apart from the fact that Hilda clearly does not like him, we see very little of this first visit but, judging from Sylvia's smile at the office the next day, she seems to think that it has not gone off too badly.

As it happens, Peter only makes one more visit to Sylvia's; but before he does so, some young men turn up on her doorstep in response to an advertisement in which she had offered to rent out her garage. They form some sort of musical group and live in a commune. Their idea is that one of them, Norman, will use the garage to produce copies of their magazine (which is called *Open Family*) on a duplicating machine.

This is one of those Leigh films in which, if not exactly nothing, then certainly – in terms of significant, outward *action* – very little actually occurs. Like *Hard Labour* in this respect, it could reasonably be called uneventful. Yet, at the same time, it can also be said that whereas, only a short while before, Sylvia had apparently had *no* men in her life, she now has two of them, Peter and Norman, if not precisely *in* her life, at least on her horizon.

The next evening Sylvia is giving Hilda a bath when the sounds of Norman (Mike Bradwell) singing to his own guitar – 'Pretty baby won't you stay all night. Cocaine, it's all around my brain' – waft in from the garage and Sylvia decides to invite him in for a cup of tea. If it soon becomes obvious that Norman is even more awkward socially than Peter, at least Sylvia finds it easier to put him at his ease. She does this very simply. It is as if she has a natural gift for it. After he has declined her offer of something to eat, she first explains that she has five nuts and then begins to eat them, slowly, counting down, one at a time, until he smilingly accepts the last one, a biscuit to go with his tea and a cigarette. A sweet exchange then follows in which, after explaining that his last job was in a toy factory in Doncaster, he asks her what she does. 'I'm President of Venezuela', she tells him. Yes, we realise, this is indeed how a playful conversation might begin, and in his own, quiet way, Norman starts to enter into the spirit of it. When he learns that she is not married, he admits that he is not really from Doncaster (he is from Scunthorpe, which he thinks sounds less impressive), and this prompts her to jokingly confess in turn that she is 'not actually the President of Venezuela', that she 'gave it up to be a secretary, for [her] sins'.

What this exchange reveals is that, if Sylvia is to truly enjoy herself, she needs to find someone with whom she can have 'a meet and happy conversation'. Stanley Cavell places at the heart of his reflections on the 'Hollywood Comedy of Remarriage' a passage in John Milton's *Doctrine and Discipline of Divorce*. In this context, as Cavell makes clear, 'conversation' signifies 'a mode of association, a form of life', and, besides meaning 'talk', it 'also carries the sexual significance, as well as the social', that we perhaps more usually associate today with the word 'intercourse' (1981: 87–8). So to say that what Sylvia wants is conversation is by no means to deny what later becomes dramatically obvious, that she also wants sex. The point is that – ideally, at least – she wants the latter *within* conversation, with this understood as a shared form of life.

To put it another way, Sylvia wants happiness. Like the central characters in the Hollywood comedies of remarriage, Sylvia is engaged in her own pursuit of happiness, the kind that can only be found in 'a meet and happy conversation'. How frustrating, then (as we can see from her dour expression), when she is *told* by the cashier – in that automatic way – to enjoy herself! He might as well have said, 'Be happy!' It would have been no less fatuous.

Apart from the fact that Sylvia appears to love her sister and Pat clearly hates having to look after her mother, the main difference between these two women is that, while Sylvia is looking for a mate, Pat is searching for forms of other-worldly consolation. Thus, for example, when they are back in the office after the Sunday when Peter made his first visit to Sylvia, Pat reveals that the highlight of *her* weekend was the meeting she attended during which a 'medium' from Belfast managed to bring certain members of her audience into contact with the spirit world. And when they are in the office the day after Peter's second visit, which ends disastrously, Pat tries to interest Sylvia in another of her meetings, this one about faith healing. This time, moreover, Pat is sounding desperate and is insisting that Sylvia allow her to take Hilda with her to such a meeting. Under considerable pressure from Pat to give in, Sylvia calmly refuses. So that, in effect, the film is framed by these two appeals that Pat makes to the supernatural, which helps us to see that, by contrast, whatever transcendence Sylvia may be seeking, it is in this world here.

We can now examine the longest sequence in the film, the one that we might think of as potentially marking Sylvia's big moment or opportunity since it is organised around Peter's second visit. It lasts just over fifty minutes and, for the sake of convenience, we can break it down into seven sections.

Now, it would seem, Peter and Sylvia have the chance – especially since Sylvia has arranged for Pat to come and take Hilda out for the evening – to seriously begin getting to know one another. But before either Pat or Peter arrive, Sylvia – seemingly on the spur of the moment – invites Norman over to sing and play his guitar for Hilda. This then forms the beginning of the sequence.

(i) *The opening*

Though Sylvia looks slightly depressed at first, she soon relaxes and, very quickly, she, Norman and Hilda are spontaneously laughing and giggling together. Sylvia and Hilda are sitting on each side of the rather child-like Norman, who is playing 'Candy Man', and all three are unselfconsciously having a merry time.

(ii) *Pat's arrival*

'What a shame', Sylvia then declares when the doorbell rings. It seems as if she has got so caught up in the fun that she has forgotten Pat was coming. From this point on, the mood starts to deteriorate. Pat is either unable or unwilling to throw herself into things and her clumsy interruptions – first noisily throwing Hilda a present (some sweets), then asking Norman why he cannot sing something they can all join in, something happy – soon bring the proceedings grinding to a halt.

(iii) *Peter's arrival*

Peter arrives next and by now the atmosphere has definitely soured. It is not made any better by the more formal introductions that everyone seems to feel his entrance demands. Sylvia tries to lighten things up a little by suggesting that they have 'a brew up'. But this falls flat. Even her gift for putting people at their ease is not, it seems, going to work here. Within a matter of seconds, the company is reduced to silence, a silence that Leigh intensifies and prolongs by isolating, one after the other, each of the five characters in close-up. Ian Buruma nicely summarises the effect as follows:

> Like an English Bergman or Dreyer (there is something Scandinavian about the English affinity for unhappiness) Leigh trains his camera on their faces, one by one: Peter, anxious, disapproving, jaws working, lips pursed; Sylvia, unsure, unhappy, eyes darting about the room; Pat, embarrassed, sucking a chocolate; Norman, catatonic, fidgeting; Hilda, close to tears. (1994: 10)

It is agonising, Peter, Pat, Norman and Sylvia all squirming, the first three deeply self-conscious, none of them able to think of anything – either to say or to do – that might improve the situation, all of them failing miserably to rise to the occasion.

(iv) *Peter and Norman*

Somehow, Pat then manages to leave with Hilda, whom she promises to return by 10pm, and for a few minutes, while Sylvia sees to their departure, Peter and Norman find themselves alone in the living room. At this point Peter asserts himself. As if unconsciously wishing to emphasise his pedagogical authority, he tightly holds onto three or four of Sylvia's paperbacks (with the cover of *Wuthering Heights* showing at the top of the pile) and proceeds to grill Norman, asking him if he reads much, where he went to school, and so on. In the midst of this interrogation the camera cuts to Sylvia's bedroom where we see her having a drink on her own and saying 'cheers' to no-one. Finally, after she has shown the frightened-looking Norman out, she and Peter, both visibly uncomfortable, are left alone and the latter proposes that they go out for dinner.

(v) *Pat's mother's bedroom/Chinese restaurant*

The fifth section is actually made up of two scenes, in each of which things go from bad to worse. Pat has taken Hilda to her house for the evening and so, while we watch Peter and Sylvia in a Chinese restaurant, we get glimpses of Pat interacting with her mother and Hilda in Pat's mother's bedroom. At one point the mother (Liz Smith) tells Hilda that Pat 'don't half get on [her] wick' and it soon becomes obvious that Pat feels the same way about her. Pat is especially incensed by her mother's habit of leaving her false teeth in a glass by her bed – even when she has company. Pat thinks this gives a terrible impression and, ironically, given Pat's desire to create a good impression, she and her mother are soon screaming at one another.

In the Chinese restaurant, no-one is screaming but the mood is heavy. For one thing, it is almost empty; there is only one other customer there. For another, the waiter is bossy and Peter discovers that it is now his turn to be in a position similar to the one he had earlier put Norman in. Since they are in public, and since Peter evidently believes that it is important in public to create a good impression, he is defenceless. In effect, he can only behave in public in one way, 'politely'. As a result of which the gratuitously rude waiter can walk all over him. On the other hand, the other customer, a single man, has no such scruples. When *he* wants something, he gets the waiter's attention quickly with a crude 'Oi. Get us some peaches and cream, will you.' And now we discern a major new development. Even before this point, we have seen from the eye contact Sylvia has exchanged with the strange man that she is interested in him. Now she is visibly impressed. But she still has not given up on Peter, whom she encourages to talk by asking him if he has any friends. As stiff as ever, he mumbles something about one friend, whom he sums up as being 'materialistic'. Finding this 'a strange way to describe a friend', Sylvia, whom we now learn went to school in Scotland, treats him to another of her little comic fantasies, asking him if he knows that, by running about on the highlands and the plains, the haggis in Scotland have developed two little legs on the one side. Peter laughs a little at this; but Sylvia's joke also seems to have aroused the interest of the strange man. And a bit later, after Sylvia has visited the Ladies room, there is a moment when she pauses, seemingly uncertain as to which of the two tables she should return to. She chooses Peter who does not appear to have seen her hesitation but then, when they both start to leave soon afterwards, she again looks at the strange man, as if strongly tempted to go to him.

At this point, our sense of what Sylvia might be capable of begins to change. Or it ought to. Suddenly, very quietly, she has revealed herself to be tempted by a kind of transgression that might trump the kinds promised in some of Norman's songs ('Mama don't allow no marijuana here/We don't care what Mama don't allow'), the kind of wild abandon that would clearly terrify Peter if he had any inkling of it. Unknown to him, he is about to encounter this new and terrifying woman.

(vi) *Peter and Sylvia: 'take your trousers off'*

By the time Peter and Sylvia arrive back home, Pat has put Hilda to bed and so the next order of business is Pat's departure, which she manages with maximum awkwardness while trying, with a greatly exaggerated sense of diplomacy, to signal that she wants to go as swiftly and with as little fuss as possible. So finally Peter and Sylvia are alone in private, in her living room.

Declaring that it was not much fun in the restaurant, Peter now makes it clear that he blames the waiter. He admits that he gets angry with waiters who do not do their job. Sylvia seems distant, uncooperative, but then asks him if he would like some sherry and, when he declines (he is fine with his coffee), she refuses to take no for an answer. She tells him that she is 'going to have some so [he will] have to join [her]' and she instructs him as she herself was instructed earlier: 'Enjoy yourself.'

In an attempt to regain control of the situation, Peter next asks her which she finds easier: 'Watching the television or the radio?' To which Sylvia – still trying to open a space for play, to keep alive the possibility of a conversation – explains that she finds it 'easier watching the radio'. But instead of lightening up, Peter then starts to deliver a lecture on communication, with particular reference to the ideas of Marshal McLuhan.

Sylvia points out that he is not drinking his sherry but he ignores this and before long is explaining that he 'never know[s] quite what to say to [Hilda]'. Sylvia tells him he 'can say whatever [he] want[s] to say' but he maintains that the 'usual conversation gambits [do not] seem to be any use.' At this point, Sylvia starts to become more aggressive, telling him she does not think 'conversational gambits are ever of much *use*', that they seem to her 'an invasion of what's going on'. And when he stubbornly persists – 'It depends how you define conversational gambit' – she makes a decisive move by getting up and then, even though he refuses ('No, no, I'm fine'), pouring him some more sherry ('Too late'), up to the brim. 'What are you going to do?' she asks him. 'Hold it very steadily', he answers.

There is silence for a while but before long Peter is starting another speech, this one (on design) more rambling that the previous one, however, and after it has petered out Sylvia gets up, asks him if he wants more nuts, explains (when he says he does not) that there aren't any left anyway, and then bursts into laughter. When he asks her what's the matter, she then drops a bombshell. She explains that she was saying something to him in her head: 'I was saying to you, take your trousers off.' There is a pause here during which Sylvia laughs and Peter looks dismayed. She then tells him 'it was a sort of joke'. This produces another pause, during which she drinks some more sherry. 'Actually', she then tells him, 'it wasn't a joke. It wasn't a joke, believe me.' And then, haltingly and with great courage, she manages to say this: 'I mean ... since that ... you [she presumably means here: if we] could ... ever get around to touching one another, it wouldn't be a bad thing.' But this is precisely what Peter seems to be incapable of. It is true that he does now get up and he somehow manages to hold her, even to stroke her hair and lightly kiss her. But there is nothing spontaneous or remotely convincing about these movements, which he starts ('Sorry I ... er ... didn't know what to say') and ends ('I really didn't know what to say') with a panicked-sounding apology.

Here, then, in this 'brilliantly excruciating scene' we have the first of what Andy Medhurst has aptly called Leigh's 'case studies of strangulation' (1993: 8). As he says, the 'comic torture' can sometimes seem almost 'too wounding to bear' and, since this inevitably creates a pressure to look away, we need to make an extra effort to be sure that we have actually seen what is going on. As a small example of this, one could cite Medhurst's comment on this scene in which, according to him, 'Sylvia and Peter can't quite manage to seduce each other, their hormones buckled down by the niceties of protocol' (1993: 7–8). Yet what Medhurst may actually be responding to is something very different. In addition to her wonderful capacity for taking the initiative, Sylvia also demonstrates here and elsewhere, what – if we are thinking in terms of our chances of encountering the Other – may be equally important: namely, a willingess to wait, to give the Other a chance to respond.[1] But of course, if so, this only makes the failure of the encounter even sadder.

In Eric Santner's terminology, this is the moment when, 'in the singularity of [his] own out-of-jointness', Peter has the chance to open himself to 'the internal alienness' that Sylvia suddenly reveals, the chance to 'pass from one logic of being-together' (in which 'every stranger is just like me') to another (in which 'every stranger is just strange') (2001: 7, 5–6). But he cannot open himself in this way and it is left to Sylvia to get them both out of the situation by asking if he would like a coffee or something. He says that he would – but when she goes into the kitchen he grimaces, scrunching up his eyes, obviously in real anguish. At this point, I think that we, the viewers, encounter Peter in a way Sylvia herself never does.

When Sylvia is in the kitchen, Peter is emboldened by the slight margin of safety this gives him to ask her – as politely as ever – if she would mind if he 'changed [his] mind about the coffee. I think', he explains, 'I should be getting along.' 'Why?' Sylvia asks in a cold and angry voice. But she then shows real concern ('Are you all right?'), regains her composure, and lets him out.

(vii) *Norman*

As she is standing in the hall after Peter's departure, Sylvia hears the faint sound of Norman singing 'Mama don't allow...' coming from the garage and so, not yet ready to call it quits, she knocks on his door and asks if he would like to join her for 'a binge'. He declines, however, explaining that he is planning to leave shortly for a folk club in the West End. The idea that he might invite her to accompany him never seems to occur to him.

The following day, Sylvia bumps into Peter outside the post office and it is soon obvious that it is all over between them. When she and Hilda then arrive at their house, they discover that Norman's friends are driving him and their duplicating machine away. They explain that they are having to lay Norman off. Sylvia is disappointed that he had not let her know. So now it is all over between Sylvia and Norman too.

Since Hilda is also obviously saddened by Norman's departure, when the two sisters enter their house, Sylvia tries to comfort her by playfully singing the following ditty:

> Two old ladies locked in a lavatory
> They've been there from Monday to Saturday.

Considering Sylvia's very uncertain future, her humour sounds brave (as usual) but also dark and a bit chilling.

The film ends on a gesture of female solidarity. Pat turns up and makes a confession, explaining that she needs to get out of her house. She then starts sobbing hysterically. In her moment of breakdown she is able to ask for help: 'I don't suppose Hilda would like to come to the pictures would she?' Sylvia seems happy to let them go off together, but this means that, in the film's very last shot, she is alone in her house, her back to us, playing some jarring, dissonant notes on her piano.

The film's achievement

The moments when Sylvia seems drawn to the strange man in the restaurant, and also when she fills and refills Peter's glass with sherry, seem reminiscent of some moments in Harold Pinter's *The Homecoming*, which was first performed in 1965. Briefly taking note of this similarity may help to better appreciate Leigh's achievement in his first film.

In so far as Sylvia is a strongly sexual being (someone who is not willing to give up on her desire) and Peter is not, they resemble – however slightly – Teddy and his wife Ruth in Pinter's play. Like Peter, Teddy is a teacher, though he teaches in an American university. Unlike Sylvia, Ruth is a former prostitute, whom her husband has brought home to London with him to meet his father and brothers. Lenny, a pimp, is by far the most vocal of the brothers and, in one of his exchanges with Ruth, he tries to take away her glass of water:

Lenny: And now perhaps I'll relieve you of your glass.
Ruth: I haven't quite finished.
Lenny: You've consumed quite enough, in my opinion.
Ruth: No, I haven't
Lenny: Quite sufficient, in my own opinion.
Ruth: Not in mine, Leonard.
    (*Pause.*)
Lenny: Don't call me that, please.
Ruth: Why not?
Lenny: That's the name my mother gave me.
    (*Pause.*)
    Just give me the glass.
Ruth: No.
    (*Pause.*)
Lenny: I'll take it, then.
Ruth: If you take the glass ... I'll take you. (Pinter 1970: 33–4)

Though in many ways obviously quite different, I think this bears some resemblance to the moment in *Bleak Moments* in which Sylvia insists on filling Peter's glass with sherry. One of the differences, of course, is that Peter is more like the ineffectual

Teddy than he is like Lenny. Another is that, unlike Ruth, though Sylvia is also a strong woman, she does not get what she wants.

But then, if in *The Homecoming* Ruth does get what she wants, this is largely because the play is staging such a potent male fantasy – one in which woman voluntarily chooses to play the whore and derives her power over men from this choice. I would suggest, furthermore, that insofar as the play also stages the defeat of the middle-class, educated, but ineffectual Teddy (by the lower-class, uneducated but street-wise and relatively virile Lenny), it is – like a number of Pinter's other works, most notably perhaps his screenplay for *The Servant* – staging a displaced, fantasy-fulfillment of the class struggle.

In contrast, even if she is defeated, Sylvia remains a strong woman and it is an essential part of the strength of *Bleak Moments* that Leigh refuses to stage a fantasy resolution to her struggle. I would say that Leigh's treatment of class is also more believable, not at all dependent on the kind of displacement that we get in *The Homecoming*, which transforms the working class into a semi-criminal underclass. When we see Peter interrogating Norman – his interest in the fact that Norman went to a grammar school, his disapproval of Norman's failure to finish his A-levels – we begin to understand something of the oppressive nature of the system that has made both men so nervous. When we notice Pat's concern over appearances, over how things will *look* to others, we start to grasp the extent to which a poisonous, basically middle-class ideology of 'good manners' – which paradoxically only manages to guarantee that the manners will be bad (paralysing rather than liberating) – has her and the two men in its grip; and our understanding of this system – and the real effects it produces in the lives of real people – deepens. To a much greater degree than Sylvia, who is witty, inventive and challenging (there can be no question of our simply feeling sorry for her), all three of these characters are its victims.

Sylvia herself is made of tougher material, which is (in the glimpse of the paperback) briefly associated – as it was to be again, much later, in *Career Girls* – with the world of *Wuthering Heights*. Furthermore, Leigh was right to maintain, in a 1994 interview, that 'if Sylvia was more articulate, she would speak to Johnny [in *Naked*]. She'd get on with Johnny, for sure' (Movshovitz 2000: 71).

We noted, in chapter two, Santner's claim that, when we read them in conjunction with one another, Freud and Rosenzweig can help us 'to rethink what it means to be genuinely open to another human being'. But what happens when the problem is more like the reverse of the one Santner is addressing? What happens when, being herself genuinely open to – indeed, wanting nothing more than – the possibility of entering into relationship with another human being, a person is forced to realise that the *other* human being is not up to it, is unable to meet her? This is the situation in which Sylvia finds herself and, like the situation George Eliot describes, it is of course not at all unusual. What make Sylvia's situation even more usual – and thus, according to the narrator of *Middlemarch* (who thinks that we should not 'expect people to be deeply moved by what is not unusual') even less likely to win our sympathy – is the fact that the other human beings she wants to enter into relationship with are male. And for a few years, this in itself would have been enough to have earned Sylvia active disapproval, at least in some circles – Kate Millett's *Sexual Politics*, for example, having appeared just one year before *Bleak Moments*, in 1970. Indeed, from this disapproving point of view, the kind of woman who believes she needs a man in her life in order to feel fulfilled is simply deluding herself. What she really needs is not so much sympathy as to be emancipated from such nonsense.

Though Thoreau is not normally thought of as a feminist, he might have agreed with this. 'I went', Thoreau tells us, 'to the woods because I wished to live deliberately, to front only the essential facts of life, and see if I could not learn what it had to teach, and not, when I came to die, discover that I had not lived' (1966: 61). Like Thoreau, Sylvia gives the impression of being someone who passionately wishes to *live*, of someone who wants at all costs to avoid having to discover, when it is time for her to die, that she has *not* lived. As it is for Thoreau, 'life' for her means something *more*, it is a matter, by definition, of a *surplus*, of something *extra* (extra-vagant, as Thoreau liked to put it), over and above what is involved in merely existing, or coping. But *un*like Thoreau, Sylvia is not ready to believe that she can live life fully while on her own, in (or in some equivalent of) the woods, as it were. What she evidently believes is that we need one another. Of course, many of the women who were discovering feminism in the 1970s would have not have disagreed. They did not believe in going off to the woods as individuals: they believed in giving one another support. It is just that – for good historical reasons – they also believed that the time had come for women to demonstrate that they could, if necessary, do without *men*.

But it is one thing to see the importance of standing on one's own feet, and quite another to be certain of what other people want or need. Looking around, my own impression is that very few of us are best off when left to ourselves, like Thoreau. Almost all of us need one another and, for most but clearly (and importantly) not all of us, the one other in particular that we need to be our closest partner has to be of the other sex. There can be no serious doubt but that some of those who have for whatever reason done without such a union have lived incomparably fuller lives than many of those who have experienced very little of adult life outside of a partnership with someone. So that to say that we *need* one another is *not* to say that brave and admirable lives cannot be lived in relative isolation. Nor of course is it to deny the possibility of feeling isolated and miserable *within* a marriage, like George Eliot's Dorothea, for example. It is simply a matter of trying to acknowledge (what Eliot calls) that 'element of tragedy' in human lives that many of us overlook simply because of 'the very fact of [its] frequency' – even 'the quickest of us walk[ing] about well wadded with [the kind of] stupidity' that desensitises us to it.

Leigh's extraordinary achievement in his first film, then, is to be found in the sensitivity he shows to Sylvia's plight. I hope it may be a bit easier now than when the film was first released to recognise an impressive kind of feminist sensibility in Leigh's keen awareness of the tragic element in her situation. To put it very simply, it is a terrible thing when those who crave physical, human touch are denied it.

Hard Labour

If Sylvia's plight seems (and is) bad, she is much younger than Mrs Thornley (Liz Smith) and so can perhaps be seen as having time on her side. Mrs Thornley's plight seems far worse.

Unlike Sylvia, Mrs Thornley has a man, her husband, and her unhappiness is largely caused by the fact that her husband is a bully. As Milton memorably put it, 'no effect of tyranny can sit more heavy on the commonwealth than this household unhappiness on the family' (quoted in Cavell 1981: 180). Milton wrote these words in his great tract on divorce but Mrs Thornley is a faithful Catholic and so for her divorce is not an option. She is stuck in (what Milton calls) an 'ill marriage' (ibid.), with no way out.

Hard Labour is set in Salford, which is where Leigh grew up. Mrs Thornley lives in one of 'the old Salford back-to-backs' (Movshovitz 2000: 40), similar to the one the Albert Finney character inhabits in *Saturday Night and Sunday Morning*. She works as a cleaning lady for Mrs Stone, who lives in a middle-class, Jewish neighbourhood and, in fact, Leigh has explained that 'the house that Mrs Thornley cleans is actually next-door-but-one to the house where [he himself] lived'. He also tells us, incidentally, that Mrs Thornley is 'directly drawn from ... an Irish Catholic woman who cleaned for [his] mother' (Fuller 1995: xxii).

If anything, in terms of outward actions or events, even less happens in *Hard Labour* than in *Bleak Moments*. Mr Thornley (Clifford Kershaw) works as a night-watchman looking after a huge warehouse full of toys, novelties and travel goods and the film opens with his returning home to have the breakfast his wife has prepared for him and for their grown-up daughter Ann (Polly Hemingway). It is obviously no accident that the first shot of the house is from an extremely awkward camera angle at the top of the stairs looking down on Mrs Thornley, who is calling her daughter to come for breakfast. But if this immediately establishes the cramped conditions in which they live, the bad temper displayed by both father and daughter makes things worse. Their opening exchange sets the tone – Him: 'Up at last, are you?'/Her: 'Oh, shut up.' Basically, then, we see Mrs Thornley waiting on these two hand-and-foot, serving them meals, vacuuming after them, and all the while silently enduring their endless bickering. And when she is not working in her own house, she is working for Mrs Stone. In fact, we only really see her stop working on two occasions, once when she goes to mass, and once when she pays her Sunday visit to her son Edward (Bernard Hill), a car mechanic who lives with his wife Veronica (Alison Steadman) on a new housing estate (and even then, she tries to help clear the dishes after tea, only to be reprimanded for doing so by her daughter-in-law).

But if nothing much occurs in the way of external action, on another level, involving the inner life of the spirit, two major developments occur. First, Mrs Thornley goes to confession and confesses that she does not love people enough; more specifically, that she does not love her husband. In its context, this is dramatic and it reveals that, however undemonstrative she may be on the surface, she is actually experiencing a deep spiritual crisis in her life. This in turn helps us to see the significant change that has been occurring throughout the film to Ann, who has been falling *into* love (with Naseem [Ben Kingsley], the Pakistani cab driver), as her mother has been falling out of it.

When we first see Ann, near the beginning of the film, her mother is calling her down for breakfast and Ann is lying, fully clothed, on her bed, looking anxious. We gradually realise that this is probably due to her worrying about her friend Julie's unwanted pregnancy. But by the end of the film Ann is much happier. Not only has Naseem helped (at Ann's request) to arrange Julie's illicit abortion, he has behaved in such a kind, considerate and responsible manner that he has clearly earned Ann's trust and made her feel much more confident.

There is an important scene near the end of the film, a scene whose centrality is flagged by the film's title, *Hard Labour*. In it the daughter is alone with her mother and gets her to talk about what it was like when she was pregnant with, and gave birth to, Ann. A number of the details clearly surprise Ann, not least the mother's explanation as to why, despite the intense suffering involved, she would not have wanted to take any pain-relieving pills – because the pain helped her to know when she needed to bear down.

If the Ann we see in this exchange seems very different to the Ann we saw at the beginning (gentler, more vulnerable, more thoughtful and not at all closed-off), it is also true that her mother talks more openly in it than anywhere else in the film. The exchange is followed, however, by the arrival first of Veronica and then of Edward and his father back from the pub. Almost immediately they are all getting at one another, Veronica reprimanding Edward for putting his wet coat next to hers when he comes in, Mr Thornley complaining that his tea is too hot, and so on. And as all of this goes on, Leigh's camera slowly moves in to give us a close-up of Mrs Thornley's expressionless face.

This scene is immediately followed first by our seeing Mrs Thornley rub cream onto her husband's hairy back and then by her confessing to the priest that she does not love her husband, that she does not 'like to touch him when he wants [her] to do something for him'. What makes this moment so extraordinary is that it is the closest she ever gets in the film to complaining. And of course it is not a complaint at all. She is the victim of deep and frequent abuse, her husband has grossly violated her and she actually believes that *she* is the one in the wrong.

But is this too strong a way of putting it? It is not just his endless complaining and bullying that is significant but also, more specifically, his behaviour in two earlier scenes in particular. First, the scene in the pub when Mr Thornley boasts to a fellow drinker that he has his meals made for him, his feet under the table. He recommends that the other man, who is going home to a stone-cold bed, get married, so he can have the same benefit Mr Thornley enjoys ('she'll be there beside me'). This pub scene is intercut with shots of Mrs Thornley getting into bed with her hot water bottles and her rosary. And it is shortly followed by the second of the two scenes just mentioned. This is a bedroom scene. Mrs Thornley appears to be asleep but as her husband prepares for bed he does his best – loudly sighing, groaning, vigorously smacking his side of the bed, crying out 'Are you asleep, eh?' – to wake her. The camera is at one point unusually positioned, with Mrs Thornley's face in the lower foreground (she is lying on her side) and little more than her husband's belly visible on the other side of the bed (the camera cutting him off at the chest). By throwing the hot water bottles onto the floor, Mr Thornley makes it clear that his wife will be *his* hot water bottle. Not that this is the only way in which he intends to use her. Behaving like a real brute, he forces her to wake up, and to submit to his lust. He does not even bother to utter a tender word – just 'Come *on*', repeated twice. Leigh does not dwell on the event, and he films it discreetly, with the camera briefly noting their movements beneath the bed clothes.

It is a shocking moment, all the more so because of Leigh's restraint, his refusal to sensationalise it. After all, it is nothing less than a rape, the most difficult kind of rape to prove because it occurs within a marriage. It seems appropriate that, the next morning at breakfast, Ann complains that eating with her father is 'like eating with a pig'. And it may well be that the bedroom scene inevitably conditions the way most of us respond to the later hairy-back scene, in which we get another close-up, this one more extreme, taking us in close to the glistening white hairs that cover Mr Thornley's back. If he was not – as usual with his wife – being such a bully (he has a nauseating way of impatiently emphasising the second syllable as he repeatedly orders her to 'Come *on*') and if we could forget the earlier rape, we might feel differently but, as it is, I would guess that most of us experience a sense of the revulsion we are convinced his wife must be feeling as she performs this task for him.

If Mr Thornley is a tyrant, he is not the only one in *Hard Labour*. Veronica behaves like a tyrant too, especially on the occasion when her mother-in-law turns up – along with Edward's friend Barry and his girlfriend June – for Sunday afternoon tea. In effect, Veronica proceeds to quietly terrorise everyone in the name of 'Good Manners' (a recurring theme in Leigh). As a result, it almost becomes difficult to know which is worse – this or the crude way Mr Thornley behaves at the dinner table. Except that these are not the only alternatives the film presents us with.

Mrs Thornley behaves so selflessly throughout that she could almost be mistaken for an angel. There are times, it is true, when she could also be mistaken for the kind of 'mute and spiritless mate' (quoted in Cavell 1981: 87) Milton thought would justify divorce but she is not 'spiritless' and, though she is often 'mute', there are times when she speaks up to great effect. We have noted her telling Ann about childbirth already but also of interest is the help she gives to the Indian lady in the laundromat and an early moment of ironic affection when her husband gets out of bed late and she refers to him as 'sleeping beauty'. But even so, most of the time, almost everyone takes her for granted and treats her as if she were no more than an object of their convenience.

The nun to whom she gives a plate for the church sale is no exception to this and, when she leaves, she sanctimoniously declares that 'we all have to carry our burdens in this world and hope they'll ease up in the next'. Often, however, Mrs Thornley is placed in the position of carrying *other people's* burdens. And overall there is no doubt that she is the one character in the film on whom life bears down the most. She performs (or has performed) most of the different kinds of hard labour referred to in the film's title – preparing meals, generally looking after her family, cleaning both her own house and someone else's, meeting her husband's sexual needs/demands, birthing two children. Indeed, it is hard to think of a film that more strongly supports the feminist argument that many women deserve more recognition (and reward) for the often invisible work they do than Leigh's *Hard Labour*.

CHAPTER FIVE

Leigh and Lawrence on 'the middle-class thing' and What it Leaves Out

I was born in a working-class part of North Salford, Lancashire, in 1943, into a world that was characterised by its day-to-day ordinariness, its industrial grime, and before the Clean Air Act. My father was a doctor, and we lived over the surgery. I went to the local primary and grammar schools, which were both predominantly working-class. I was, therefore, a middle-class kid growing up in a working-class environment, so I have an awareness of and sensitivity to both those worlds – I suppose I was an insider and an outsider, all at once.

I lived in this particular kind of working-class district with some relations living in slightly leafier districts up the road. So there was always a tension, or at least a duality: those two worlds were forever colliding. So you constantly get the one world and its relationship with the other going on in my films.

– Mike Leigh (Fuller 1995: xi, xxi)

Leigh and D. H. Lawrence? Why do we need to bring Lawrence into the discussion? Since Lawrence is now out of favour, at least in academic circles, it is easy to forget – and some may be unaware of the fact – that, in the early 1960s, when Leigh began to produce his first work (in the theatre), Lawrence's reputation was at its height. *Lady Chatterley's Lover* was published in 1960 and, as Philip Larkin jokingly put it (in his poem 'Annus Mirabilis'), it almost seemed as if sex was invented in the short period between the trial that made this possible and the arrival of the Beatles on the scene. Not that this was by any means the only thing Lawrence was known for. In fact, from the publication of F. R. Leavis' book *D. H. Lawrence: Novelist* in 1955 until late in the 1960s, Lawrence was widely viewed as a major figure and point of reference in the culture-at-large. So much so that, for example, as late as 1981, the BBC was prepared to invest heavily in a splendid (and now scandalously unavailable) seven-episode production of *Sons and Lovers* that was scripted by Trevor Griffith. So it ought not to be surprising to find Coveney being reminded by 'the opening high-angle shot over the Salford back-to-backs' in *Hard Labour* of 'D. H. Lawrence's miner Lambert [similarly returning home] in *A Collier's Friday Night*' (1997: 92).

But still, Lawrence's reputation in the 1960s is hardly a reason to turn to him for help now. Much more to the point is the fact that in an earlier generation, Lawrence also had 'an awareness of and sensitivity to both worlds' in which Leigh grew up. It could be said that (again, like Leigh) Lawrence too 'was an insider and an outsider, all at once'. He was born in the mining community of Eastwood, Nottinghamshire, in 1885. His father was a collier and so, as he explains in the 'Autobiographical Sketch' he wrote in 1929, Lawrence was 'born among the working classes and brought up among them'. But at the same time, his mother 'came from town, and belonged really to the lower bourgeoisie' (1970: 592). So that, like Leigh, Lawrence could also have responded to the question as to whether or not he had a working-class background with a Yes and No. Here is Leigh's response to the question:

> My father was a doctor and I grew up in a very working-class area so the answer is, strictly, no, but yes in many ways because I went to working-class schools and have actually lived in working-class territories throughout my entire life. (Movshovitz 2000: 23)

Of course, Lawrence did not spend the rest of his life living in 'working-class territories'. Whereas, as Leigh explained in 1991, his (now dissolved) marriage to Alison Steadman ('somebody ... from a lower-middle-class background') meant that he had 'always had an ongoing relationship with the very ordinary and prosaic world' (Movshovitz 2000: 23–4), Lawrence married a German and spent his life travelling around the world. And there are other significant differences too, possibly the most important being the fact that, judging simply by the evidence of their work, nature was always much more important to Lawrence (Eastwood being surrounded by beautiful countryside) than it ever seems to have been to Leigh.

I am not interested in trying to make Leigh seem particularly Lawrentian; the differences between them can also be instructive. Yet the main reason for introducing Lawrence here is for the insight he can provide into the ways in which class functions in *Nuts in May* and *Grown-Ups*.

While it is true that the two worlds of the working- and middle-classes are 'forever colliding' in Leigh's films, the collision seems more central to his third and sixth films – *Nuts in May* (1976) and *Grown-Ups* (1980) – than to any of the others (except perhaps *High Hopes*), hence these two films are discussed together in this chapter.

Thus, in *Nuts in May*, the Pratts – Keith (Roger Sloman) (who works in the Social Services 'organising pensioner's holidays, meals-on-wheels, that sort of thing'), and Candice-Marie (Alison Steadman) (who works in a toy shop) – are on a camping holiday in Dorset. The film opens with the two of them in their car, coming off a ferry and then driving along a country road, happily singing one of the songs they have composed themselves. It begins as follows:

> I want to get away, she said, I want to get away.
> I'll take you on a trip, he said. We'll have a holiday.

We begin to understand one of the things they are hoping to 'get away' from when, on the second day, they return to their tent and find another tent close by and its owner up a tree some distance from it, while his transistor radio is on, if not exactly at full-blast, too loudly to ignore. When Ray (Anthony O'Donnell), the owner, refuses to respond to the Pratts's complaint of 'noise pollution', they feel obliged to move their tent some distance away. A bit later on, after they have picked him up in their car during a rain-storm, the Pratts and Ray are brought into a somewhat friendlier if strained relationship. We then learn that Ray is studying at a Teacher Training College in London, so that he is far from being the lout they seem to initially take him to be. Even so, the Pratts soon feel obliged to move their tent again. This time, the arrival on a motorbike of the working-class Finger (Stephen Bill) (a plasterer in the building trade) and Honkey (Sheila Kelley) (a clerical officer in the Civil Service) first leads to a fight and then forces Keith (who looks like an English Pete Seeger) and Candice-Marie to leave the camp-ground altogether. We last see them in another field, on their own.

Grown-Ups opens with Dick (Philip Davis) (who works in the kitchen of the catering department of a hospital) and his wife Mandy (Lesley Manville) (who works in a cafeteria) moving into their new house and, although it is itself owned by the council, they agree with the verdict of Mandy's sister, Gloria (Brenda Blethyn) (a typist), that they 'have come up trumps' because they are situated right on a divide: it is privately-owned housing on their one side, council-owned on the other. As it turns out, the privately-owned house next door is occupied by one of their former schoolteachers, Ralph Butcher (Sam Kelly), and his wife, Christine (Lindsay Duncan).

In *Nuts in May*, we mostly look at things from the point of view of the middle-class couple, Keith and Candice-Marie, who experience what happens first as an invasion of their space and then as their being forced to vacate it. In *Grown-Ups*, on the other hand, we mainly see things through the eyes of the lower-class Dick and Mandy and, though it is true that their world collides with that of the Butchers, it is Gloria who plays the role of invader, invading both worlds.

The intention here, then, is to start off by examining some of the ways in which (what Lawrence called) 'the middle class *thing*' can be seen to be at work in a number of Leigh's films, but the discussion will focus particularly on *Nuts in May*. This is the section in which I shall be drawing most heavily on Lawrence to offer a framework to better understand the significance of what is going on in these films.

The middle-class thing in 'Nuts in May' and other films

> Class makes a gulf, across which all the best human flow is lost. It is not exactly the triumph of the middle classes that has made the deadness, but the triumph of the middle-class *thing*.
>   – D. H. Lawrence (1970: 595)

As we have noted, *Nuts in May* ends up with the Pratts on their own, having an entire field all to themselves. How can Lawrence help us to understand the significance of this?

I propose that we turn first to his review of Edward Dahlberg's novel *Bottom Dogs*, in which we find him claiming that one of the main characteristics of modernity is 'what would have been called in the old language the breaking of the heart' (1972: 268). It seemed to Lawrence that this 'deep psychic change', which he saw taking the form of 'the collapse of the flow of spontaneous warmth between a man and his fellows', was happening 'now all over the world'. Lawrence admits that, while 'the old sympathetic flow' continued, there were 'violent hostilities between people' but he thinks they were not then – as they have now become – 'secretly repugnant to one another'. Here is part of his explanation as to what has occurred:

> It has been said often enough of more primitive or old-world peoples, who live together in a state of blind mistrust but also of close physical connexion with one another, that they have no noses. They … hardly are aware at all of offensive human odours that madden the new civilisations. As it says in this novel: The American senses other people by their sweat and their kitchens. By which he means, their repulsive effluvia … The secret physical repulsion between people is responsible for the perfection of American 'plumbing', American sanitation and American kitchens, utterly white-enamelled and antiseptic. It is revealed in the awful advertisements such as those about 'halitosis', or bad breath. It is responsible for the American nausea at coughing, spitting, or any of those things … And it is this repulsion from the physical neighbour that is now coming up in the consciousness of the great democracies, in England, America, Germany. (1972: 269)

Lawrence's attitude to this phenomenon is not at all moralistic, incidentally. A man cannot, in his view, help it if 'his nose is so sensitive that a stink overpowers him … He can't prevent his senses from transmitting and his mind from registering what it does register' (1972: 270). But even though Lawrence clearly thought that 'the sense of the repulsiveness of the neighbour [is] a condition we are [all] rapidly coming to' (1972: 271), he also thought it is 'displayed by the intellectuals much more than by the common people' (ibid.). He found it especially pronounced, for example, 'in James Joyce, in Aldous Huxley, in Andre Gide, in modern Italian novels like *Parigi* – in all the very modern novels' (1972: 270). And he suggested that this might be because it was the intellectuals in particular (and the middle classes in general) who had been for 'the last hundred years' elevating themselves above their 'baser functions, [rising] superior to their bodies' (1972: 269, 270).

What this can help us to grasp is the other side, as it were, of the Pratts' desire, in *Nuts in May*, to 'get away'. On one level, what they desire to get away from is no mystery. From Keith's first inquiry at the camp-ground (he wants to know if they can get free-range eggs and untreated milk) to the lyrics of the song Candice-Marie is singing at the end ('Black smoke, crisp bags, detergents in a river/Cigarette smoke, it makes me choke/Litter makes me shiver'), it is obviously pollution – in all its myriad guises – that they are trying to flee. But for there to be pollution, there has to be a polluter, who in a camp-ground is more often than not one's neighbour, our proximity to whom virtually defines 'the midst of life' (at least, as noted earlier, for Santner). So, on another level, what the Pratts are trying to escape is precisely their neighbour, who they perceive as a polluter and therefore find repulsive.

As Lawrence saw it, just as one sense ('the sense of the repulsiveness of the neighbour' [1972: 271]) was growing stronger, another sense ('the sense of touch') was growing weaker ('There is plenty of pawing and laying hold, but no real touch' [1999: 45–6].). And I take it that Leigh's own belief in the vital importance of this second sense is what we find conveyed in such absolutely key moments as – to give only three examples – (i) *Bleak Moments*' Sylvia saying to Peter that '[if we] could … ever get around to touching one another, it wouldn't be a bad thing'; (ii) *Hard Labour*'s Mrs Thornley explaining to the priest that she knows she does not love her husband because she no longer 'like[s] to touch him'; (iii) *Secrets and Lies*' Cynthia (Brenda Blethyn) asking her brother to hold her ('Give us a cuddle, Maurice … please sweet'eart!' [Leigh 1997b: 37]) – *the* heart-breaking moment, I am tempted to say, at the centre of Leigh's work. (It is anticipated, incidentally, years earlier in *Grown-Ups* when Gloria – also played by Brenda Blethyn – gets a reluctant Dick to hold her arm at the bus-stop ['Come on, link my arm and call me Charlie'].)

If, in *Nuts in May*, Keith and Candice-Marie – very much like Peter in *Bleak Moments* and Mr Butcher in *Grown-Ups* – all conspicuously lack a sense of touch, this is not surprising since they all elevate themselves above their bodies, even to the point of going without sex. Keith and Candice-Marie sleep in separate beds and, instead of kissing one another before they fall asleep, Candice-Marie hands Keith 'Prudence' – her hot water bottle (shaped like a cat) – to kiss. It is true that they do not go on (as Lawrence noticed the Americans doing in 1929) about plumbing and sanitation in the bathroom and kitchen but, on the other hand, they are just as preoccupied with keeping the insides of their bodies clean, just as compulsive about their diet. As Keith says, 'the important thing of course is to maintain our dietary balance'.

At the end of the film Leigh chooses to return us to a sense of the real by focusing on the least glamorous of animals, the pig.[1] While we see the highly cerebral and ecology-conscious Keith heading into a nearby muddy field to defecate and carrying a spade with him so as to cover it up afterwards,[2] the camera comes to rest on a pig, which gives us the film's last image, that of the animal body in what is widely (and of course conventionally) perceived to be its grossest, most disgusting, form. And this is where we see Leigh making use of the kind of 'grotesque realism' whose 'essential principle', according to Mikhail Bahktin, 'is degradation, that is, the lowering of all that is high, spiritual, ideal, abstract'. It is important to note, however, that Bahktin is not asking us to view this negatively:

> To degrade … means to concern oneself with the lower stratum of the body, the life of the belly and the reproductive organs; it therefore relates to acts of defecation and copulation, conception, pregnancy and birth; it has not only a destructive, negative aspect but also a regenerating one. (1984: 21)

No matter how much someone like Keith would like to escape from, or deny, the body, it has needs that cannot be ignored forever and sooner or later it returns. But while it is not too difficult to appreciate this on the level of theory or in principle, the broad and bawdy and indeed unapologetically crude humour that ends *Nuts in May* is largely at the expense of Keith and Candice-Marie. After all, even if they themselves are blissfully unaware of the fact, they are the ones being 'degraded' – Candice-Marie too, since, even though she is not going to relieve herself, the image of Keith's toilet paper snagged on the barbed-wire fence and blowing in the wind provides an ironic comment on the image moments earlier of her shawl similarly blowing in the wind; in addition to which, the camera is on the pig while she is singing. And this makes the ending rather painful – especially since (regardless of how clearly we see how impossible they are) many of us have nevertheless probably found ourselves partially identifying with them.

Yet what makes both Keith and Candice-Marie – but especially Keith – 'impossible'? To begin with, Keith is tyrannical. But it is not just his bossiness that makes him so aggravating. It is also the way in which he over-plans, over-organises, just about everything he does.[3] When the Pratts erect their tent for the first time, we see that Keith is the one who gives directions and that he proceeds in terms of clearly numbered 'stages'. Similarly, when they visit Corfe Castle the next day, Keith is the one who – despite Candice-Marie's complaint – holds the guide book and he is obviously put out when she tries to draw his attention to anything that is not explained in it. We already realise that he will not be good at handling surprises and the following day, when the Pratts come upon the unexpected in the form of a road diversion, Keith's reaction is to insist that there can be no question of changing their plans: 'there's no point in having a schedule if you don't stick to it'. In much the same way, Keith later makes it plain to Ray that there is little point in exercising unless one does it systematically. Keith himself 'follows the Royal Canadian Airforce system of exercises' and, when he is pressed, Ray admits that he does a basic sort of Rugby circuit training programme. 'Yes', says Keith, 'but is it a *system*? Is it tabulated?'

This last exchange occurs after Candice-Marie has (despite Keith's reluctance) befriended Ray and invited him over to take their photograph. Keith then insists that she show Ray the water-colour painting she has done of Corfe castle, declaring with false modesty that it is just a hobby, one of their 'many interests', which of course suggests that these interests are all tabulated as well. During this sequence, as Ray patiently waits to take their photograph, he is subjected to a brow-beating from both Pratts – obviously (to anticipate something Keith says later) for his own good. They lecture him, for example, on the evils of white sugar and ask him if he eats meat, they themselves believing it is 'inhumane to kill animals for food'. 'It's a well-known fact Ray', says Candice-Marie as she tries to get him to see the light. And of course this is the point: both Pratts have the zeal – and the humourlessness – of true believers, as they try to make a new convert to what is obviously for them a kind of religion. When he politely asks them if they would mind his having a smoke, Ray gets a real earful, with Keith irritatingly explaining that 'air polluted by one person has to be breathed by another' and, in her response, Candice-Marie unintentionally bringing out the ludicrous side of all of this: 'You see ... if I could take one of your lungs now and put it on the table in front of you and cut it in half, I think you'd be absolutely horrified.'

Eventually, after Keith has given him detailed instructions on how to do it, Ray is allowed to take their photograph and to return to his tent. And it is shortly after this that Finger and Honkey arrive on their motorcycle. If the motorcycle itself is enough to incense the Pratts, the sounds Finger and Honkey make on their return from the pub that night are a further irritation.

Getting out of his bed to explain to them that he can hear everything they are saying, Keith is told to go back to his tent. 'And you', he replies, 'go back to your tenements.' But it is not until the following day, when Keith notices Finger gathering wood for a camp-fire, that things turn really nasty. Going, as always, by the book, Keith points out that the first of the camp rules they were all issued on their arrival says no open fires. This is news to Finger, who tells Keith to mind his own business. At which point, clearly believing that this is the kind of challenge for which he has been living, Keith puffs himself up and declares that his 'business is to protect the life of the countryside and our heritage'. Since Finger refuses to back down, Keith then says he will go and tell the camp receptionist. But she is not around and so, when he returns, he ups the ante even further, announcing that he is going to assume 'his responsibility as a good citizen', that he has 'the right to arrest another citizen who is breaking the law', that he intends, in other words, to make a citizen's arrest. And then, when Finger still refuses to back down, Keith suddenly goes berserk, grabs the stick of wood Finger has been holding and threatens to knock his head off. It is as if all the anger he has been repressing for so long suddenly erupts. For a few seconds the two men become enraged little boys, their masculine pride stung, chasing one another around, each ready to do real violence to – perhaps even to kill – the other. Until Keith abruptly breaks down and starts whimpering.

'I was only trying to advise you for your own good', he explains to Finger as he wanders off.

In the end, after they have driven away from the camp-ground and been submitted to the kind of badgering (by an officious policeman) to which they submit others, the Pratts find a field all to themselves, assuring the farmer who gives them permission to put their tent up that they 'always obey the country code'. They tell themselves that they are happy. Candice-Marie notices that the wind blowing through the strings of her guitar makes it sound as if the latter is playing itself and Keith says that it is in harmony with the birds.

It is at this point that Leigh cuts to a shot of chickens in cages and cows in stalls. Ironically, the Pratts are camping in a farm that kills animals, which means that their sense of being at harmony is based on their ignorance of where they actually are. Even so, this is *not*, in my view, the 'relatively merciless attack on a priggish couple's faddish vegetarianism' (Movshovitz 2000: 60) that some have taken it to be. But if not, then what is its target?

As I see it, the satire is mainly directed against the kind of insanity ('nuts') that can be produced by a certain restricted form of rationality, which is something like that 'thin, spurious mental conceit' that Lawrence thought of as typically middle-class and that he claimed 'is all that is left of the mental consciousness *once it has made itself exclusive*' (1970: 596, my italics).[4] If we return to Lawrence's 'Autobiographical Sketch' we find another relevant passage:

> As a man from the working class, I feel that the middle class cut off some of my vital vibration when I am with them. I admit them charming and educated and good people often enough. *But they just stop some part of me from working.* Some part has to be left out. (1970: 595)

I think we can get some idea of what gets left out from the awful poem Candice-Marie has written and that she recites the first time she and Keith are in their tent together:

> A gentle flower
> The bird in spring
> That feels the sun upon its face
> It's free to smile and grin
> It knows no guilt, or hate or sin
> It has no battles it must win
> Oh how I love and envy him.

Whereas, on the other hand, as Lawrence understood it, being in the midst of life is necessarily to be involved – at least from time to time – in battles, in which one inevitably incurs guilt, feels hate, and so on. And, judging by his book on *Happiness, Death and the Remainder of Life*, I take it that Jonathan Lear would agree. Having explained, for example, that, from a psychoanalytical point of view, 'the structural insight that life is lived under conditions of tension' gives us one of the 'senses in which *life is too much*', Lear claims that for 'the mind to discharge all its tension, to achieve a completely unpressured state, is precisely what it is for it to die' (2000: 109).[5] Life, then, being too much, is more than the Pratts can take and they are trying to escape it – by discharging 'all its tension'. (Even though it is also true that – with their energy and principles – they create a lot of the tension themselves). Is it not something like this that Keith must mean when he feels forced to move his tent the first time and he tells Ray that 'everything was peaceful until you came along'?

Perhaps this explains why, despite everything (including his infuriating drawl and her whine), in the last analysis, it is not so difficult for many of us to partially identify with Keith and Candice-Marie. Who does not feel the attractiveness of such peace – such freedom from tension or pressure, especially on holiday – even if its real meaning is death? In addition to this, many of us are likely to share some of Keith's and Candice-Marie's attitudes. Indeed, which of us would *not* be disconcerted to discover that, just when we thought we had found a little solitude, someone had decided to move in right next to us? And with a transistor radio? It is painful to see people hurt and isolate and make fools of themselves and Keith and Candice-Marie certainly do that. They are nut-cases, all right, and there is undeniably something monstrous about Keith. But for all this, they are not entirely unsympathetic.

'Impossible' Gloria: Identifying with the Sympton in 'Grown-Ups'

> Dick is genuinely different from most viewers, as are Mandy and Gloria. It takes effort to get our minds around them and our emotions into a place where we can appreciate them … The world is a world, not of ourselves writ large, our own emotional and intellectual structures flatteringly mirrored, but of genuine 'others' with challengingly 'other' points of view.
>
> – Ray Carney (2000: 144)

In his book on *The Coen Brothers*, James Mottram informs us that *Grown-Ups* was one of ten films 'screened as part of a tribute to the Coens at the Stockholm Film Festival, chosen as personal favourites by the brothers' (2000: 5). Mottram claims that by virtue of its juxtaposing 'the working-class couple with their more affluent neighbors', together with its emphasis on 'the maternal desire to raise a family … Leigh's film pre-empts much of the Coens' work, particularly in *Fargo* and *Raising Arizona*' (2000: 8–9).

This claim is interesting but I do not intend to pursue it here. Instead, I want to try to get at what seems most original in *Grown-Ups* by examining its treatment of Mandy's sister Gloria. Like Keith in *Nuts in May*, Gloria is in some ways an impossible character. But her eventual fate is significantly different from his.

What makes Gloria impossible is that she will not stay away. No sooner have Dick and Mandy moved into their new house than she is there visiting them, having brought a few items with her for a house-warming. It takes her no time at all to discover that they have a spare room and to wonder if it is intended for her. Like Pat in *Bleak Moments*, Gloria lives with her mother and is desperate to get out of her house. Dick and Mandy are both kind to her at first and they are warmly appreciative when she makes them a gift of a new (and much-needed) vacuum cleaner. But she visits them much too often and then will not leave of her own accord. She will not take a hint, and even a blunt word or two is not enough to get her to leave. Eventually, some fifty minutes or so into the film, the situation has deteriorated to the point where a comic montage of shots of an increasingly frantic Gloria knocking at their door or window or visiting Mandy at work makes it seem as if her visits have increased exponentially. Finally, when they are huddled together discussing the problem, she knocks on the door again and, even though they say they are going out for a drink, she is undeterred and manages to leave with them.

By this point they are the ones who are getting desperate; the following night, after they return from the pub (Dick for the first time having been reluctant to take Mandy along), we see the strain Gloria has been placing on their marriage. Having made it plain earlier that (now that they have the new house) she hopes they can start trying to have a child soon, Mandy announces she intends to stop taking the pill at the end of the month. Dick wants to put off discussing it and an argument ensues. It quickly turns ugly with Dick declaring that 'We'll have kids when *I* say so and you'll take the pill even if I have to ram it down your throat!' But if this is vicious, Mandy is uncowed. 'Oh yeah?' she replies, 'I'd like to see you try.'

It is obvious the next day that relations between Mandy and Dick have soured. And they abruptly and dramatically get much worse when Mandy and her single friend Sharon (Janine Duvitski) return home from a shopping expedition and discover that Dick is at the end of his tether – Gloria having 'been sitting here for two bleeding hours.' What then follows is a sequence of fifteen or so minutes in which – as Leigh himself puts it – all of the characters 'go absolutely, totally ape-shit' (Movshovitz 2000: 21). Claiming that her mother has thrown her out, Gloria has brought her nightie and plans to stay the night. Mandy insists that that is not possible. Dick threatens Mandy and Gloria tries to come between them. Amidst screaming and yelling, Gloria goes from the bathroom to the spare room before she is physically forced outside the front door. Appealing, piteously, to Mandy, she then runs around the side of the house and returns through the back door. At which point, she is forcibly ejected a second time. In a moment of utter panic, seeing Mrs Butcher washing her car in the street, Gloria runs down Dick and Mandy's path, past Mrs Butcher, before the latter realises what is happening, and – the front door being open – inside her house and straight up her staircase. Gloria then locks herself in the Butcher's upstairs' bathroom while Dick and Mandy and Sharon join the Butchers in trying to persuade her to come out. Dick threatens to tear the door down and to tear her bleeding head off, but Mandy tries to assure Gloria that he only said what he said because she makes him angry. Eventually, after Dick has agreed to leave and Mrs Butcher has promised to make her a cup of tea, Gloria comes out and allows herself to be led down the stairs. But when she discovers Dick at the bottom, she panics again, runs back upstairs and clings to the railings of the banister. This is the point when they all lose control, as all five characters become entangled in something like a rugby scrum as they try to pry Gloria loose. Only afterwards, perhaps, do we realise that for all the shouting and cursing, there has not really been any physical violence. And after Gloria has had her cup of tea and a nap on the sofa, she finally allows herself to be escorted out of the Butchers' house and into a taxi to be taken back to her own house.

What are we to make of all of this? We can begin by noting that Gloria is not the only impossible character in this film. Mr Butcher is another. This is most obvious when we get a glimpse of him in the classroom earlier on. Ironically, he is the Religious Knowledge teacher. 'Jesus loved his enemies', he instructs the class, 'did he not?' 'Come *on*', he impatiently yells at his young pupils as he gets a number of them to recite the line 'Father forgive them for they know not what they do.' But in his own way, he is impossible at home too. Nor is Gloria the only adult who behaves like a child. Both Mr Butcher and Dick do as well. Think of the ways in which both men have to be humoured by their wives, especially, for example, of the importance both men and Gloria attach to their favourite biscuits. (We might also think here of how much like a little girl *Nuts in May*'s Candice-Marie often seems, in her eagerness and openness as well as in her adulation of Keith.)

In what way then does Gloria stand out? What distinguishes her from the others is the *extent* of her neediness. This, more than anything else, is what makes her so disturbing. I emphasise 'extent', however, because what the film helps us to see is that everyone is needy. The film's originality is mainly to be found in the way it treats Gloria as the kind of 'symptom' the psychoanalytical process would, at least according to Slavoj Zizek, have us identify with. Zizek argues that 'in "going through the fantasy" we must in the same move identify with the symptom,' recognising in its excesses 'the truth about ourselves' (1989: 128). Thus the significance of the position that Gloria occupies at the end of the film is that it shows that the newly emerging family – because Mandy is now big with child – is *identifying* with her, rather than disavowing her. She is, after all, right in the centre of the frame, in between Dick and Mandy, bent almost double as, with her ear up against Mandy's belly, she waits to detect the movement of the new child.

But this is not all. The movie opens with the camera observing Dick and Mandy's moving truck coming along a somewhat shabby-looking street and it then surprises us by having the camera swivel around as the truck moves by until it reveals that the truck is going in the direction of the cathedral, which we can see over the rooftops in the distance and which turns out to be Canterbury Cathedral. The cathedral choir can be heard in the background and it seems natural to expect that the point about to be made will be one of ironic incongruity. The lives the film is about to explore will be entirely cut off from the life of the cathedral. But this is not what happens. Not only do we hear the church bells ringing from time to time – once, for example, when Dick and Mandy are standing in their garden – but the film's last scene is set at Christmas time and it actually has the cathedral choir on the soundtrack singing 'The Holly and the Ivy'. So that it seems quite appropriate to recall the following paragraph from Leigh's piece on *The Tree of the Wooden Clogs*:

There is indeed a holiness about the film, but not a piousness. Olmi allows his characters their state of grace, which is beautifully underpinned by his occasional use of J.S. Bach. (1995a: 117)

This passage of Leigh's certainly seems to apply to the *ending* of *Grown-Ups*.

As I understand it, then, *Grown-Ups* is trying to be as inclusive as possible. So I had better say something about the two uses of the term 'normal' near the end. The first occurs when the Butchers are in bed together. Ralph has just said that 'She's mad that woman, she ought to be locked up, they're all mad, coming around here like that, disturbing people's privacy. It's absolutely outrageous.' 'Well, I shouldn't worry about it', Christine ironically responds. 'We're back to normal now, aren't we?' And when he wants to know what is the matter with her, what she wants, he gets an earful: 'I'll tell you what I want. I want sex and I want love and I want a family, that's what *I* want!'

This prompts us to reflect on the extremely measured way in which Christine Butcher has been speaking throughout the film, as if she has been walking on egg-shells. Which in turn helps us to understand the high price she has paying for the suppression of the anger that her last speech tells us she must have been feeling for some time. The speech leaves her husband speechless (just as Gilbert is left speechless at the end of *Topsy-Turvy* when his wife makes a similar – except much less direct – declaration) and we then cut to Dick and Mandy in bed. Dick is on top of Mandy who is apologising because she forgot to take the pill. He is all tenderness and assures her that he is now OK with this: 'It's what *you* want, in'it?' 'You want to have a baby an' all then?' 'Why not?' he responds. 'It's only normal, in'it?'

I can see how it *could* be argued that this reinforces a heterosexual system that is basically oppressive precisely because it makes those who do not or cannot have children or a family feel left out. That is why I think it is so important that the film is making such an effort to include both Gloria and Mandy's friend Sharon, and to at least make us aware of Christine's loneliness – she, however, remaining on the other side of the gulf that separates the two classes as much at the end of the film as it did at the beginning.

Escaping the middle-class thing: 'The Kiss of Death'

The Kiss of Death is a coming-of-age film and what is so beautiful about it is that two of its central characters – Trevor (David Threlfall) (an undertaker's apprentice) and his friend Ronnie (John Wheatley) (who works in a Co-op food store) – are still at the point of trying to figure out what they want. The film is set in Oldham, Lancashire, and it begins when Ronnie has recently acquired a girlfriend, Sandra (Angela Curran), who has already started to make Trevor feel that three is a crowd. Luckily, when all three of them are in the pub, the unattached Linda (Kay Adshead) turns up and Sandra is able to introduce her to Trevor.

Such as it is, the action mainly focuses on Trevor and Linda getting to know one another. The film ends on the day after Linda has persuaded a very unwilling

Trevor to take her to a disco. Trevor had felt oppressed by the noise and Linda had found herself dancing and semi-flirting (Sandra not seeming to mind) with Ronnie. The following day Trevor attends a marriage ceremony, the bridal car appropriately decked out in white ribbons for the occasion. He gets into a discussion with a little girl who is dressed in white and who assures him, when he asks her, that no, she herself never intends to get married. It is as if this is a question that he is wondering about himself. He then goes to visit Ronnie, who lives nearby and who apologises for his involvement with Linda the previous evening. Trevor says there is no need to apologise, they both laugh and the film ends with their deciding, on the spur of the moment, to take the car and go to Blackpool for the day.

According to Coveney, Leigh's original plan 'was to have a final scene in which they drive to Blackpool and pick up two girls on the motorway, girls with long hair wearing jeans and duffel-coats, girls with whom they could communicate. "That,"' he reports Leigh saying, '"would have told the story of escape from those small-minded, rather bone-headed girls in Oldham and their middle-class aspirations." But he ran out of time' (1997: 112). This strikes me as being uncharacteristic of the kinds of remarks Leigh makes in his published interviews. In two ways: in its lack of generosity and in its inaccuracy. Ronnie seems at least as 'small-minded' and 'bone-headed' as Sandra and, while I can see that Sandra has 'middle-class aspirations', I think it is unfair to Linda to imply that she can be summarised in this way. There is much more to her than that.

But at the same time I find Leigh's remark interesting and provocative because it suggests to me that at the time when he made it (I presume in conversation with Coveney) he may not have quite taken in the full scope of this film's achievement himself. Unlike *Nuts in May* and *Grown-Ups* (both of which climax in outbursts of violence and craziness, even if no one is physically hurt as a result), *The Kiss of Death* is another of those films in which nothing happens – not, at any rate, on the level of what ordinarily counts as significant action in film. Yet something momentous is nevertheless *revealed* – during the scene that takes place inside Linda's mother's house. Without showing any physical nudity, Leigh somehow manages to have two youngsters – Trevor and Linda – discover their sensuality and it is a powerful spectacle, one that can make most of what has passed for the representation of sensuality in the cinema seem the feeblest of pretenses.

I should begin by setting the context for this scene. The previous evening Trevor had stood Linda up on a date and she had angrily gone to where she guessed he would be, at the pub, and there she had hit him. Far from discouraging him, however, this seems to have revived his interest in her and the following day after work he visits her at her mother's house. While Trevor and Linda are talking outside the front door, her next-door-neighbour (the middle-aged Christine) arrives and asks them to help her get her elderly and infirm mother up to her bedroom. At this point the seemingly indecisive Trevor comes into his own and does exactly what needs to be done. Then, when Christine is in another room phoning the doctor and Linda and Trevor are alone with the elderly lady in the latter's bedroom, Linda asks Trevor (who is seated on the bed) if she hurt him when she hit him the previous evening. It is an intimate moment. Linda is shot from underneath and she looks strong and attractive. But Trevor also looks strong. 'Yeah', he tells her. 'Don't do it again.'

This is shortly followed by the kissing scene, which lasts for about ten minutes and begins with Linda inviting Trevor in for coffee and explaining that her mother will be back soon. On first entering the room Trevor puts his foot on the sofa to see out the window and Linda reprimands him for this. They then sit facing one another. He giggles and she asks him what sort of books he likes to read. He produces his copy of *Dracula*. She sits closer but not next to him, takes a magazine and asks him if he thinks one of the women in it (whom we do not get to see) is pretty. He says she is all right. Linda then suggests he fancies Christine (the next-door-neighbour) and he laughs. Linda has already begun her not-at-all subtle process of seducing Trevor. The rest of the scene unfolds as follows:

Linda: You can kiss me if you like. (*Pause.*) Do you want to?
Trevor: (*After a pause.*) Yeah.
Linda: Put your coffee cup down.
Trevor: I haven't finished it yet.
Linda: Well finish it after.
              (*He puts it down. Pause.*)
              Well (*in a silken cooing voice*), come on. (*Pause*) Come on.
Trevor: You're over there and I'm over here.
Linda: Well come over here then. (*Pause.*) Come on.
              (*He moves and sits next to her.*)
              Come on. (*Pause.*) Come on.
              (*He starts moving towards her as if he intends to kiss her and she starts laughing.*)

It seems that for Linda (who is incidentally chewing gum throughout all of this) sex is a fairly straightforward transaction. First, the invitation: 'You can kiss me if you like.' Then, after she has ascertained that he does in fact 'want to' (since of course the invitation has not immediately produced a kiss), she turns her attention to what appears to be holding him back. After she has got him to put his cup of coffee down, she then shifts gears and – adopting a soothing (come hither) tone – she tries again. But it all takes quite a bit of coaxing on her part and so it is not entirely surprising if, when she finally has him next to her moving in for the kiss, the tension that has been building up should result in her succumbing to a fit of involuntary laughter. At this point the situation begins to change quite rapidly.

Trevor's immediate response is to ask what Linda is laughing at. 'I'm not laughing,' she says. 'I'm not...' But then, noticing how stunned Trevor looks, she asks him if he does not 'know how to kiss anybody'. It would seem that the thought has only just occurred to her and so, far from sounding superior or ironical, she asks the question in what sounds like a spirit of genuine curiosity. This perhaps partially helps to explain why, instead of his being embarrassed, it is now Trevor who reacts with spontaneous laughter. Alarmingly, however, once he has started, he does not seem able to stop laughing and, after a while (after she has asked him 'What are *you* laughing at?' and his only answer is to have somehow turned his by now unnaturally prolonged laughter into a deliberate taunt), she strikes him across the face. Even after this he does not stop laughing immediately but when he does stop they move to kiss – only for him then to start laughing again. Finally, he grabs her face rather roughly and kisses her passionately, almost savagely.

What makes the scene exciting is the fact that, because Trevor seems to have never done anything like this before, his reactions are unexpected and they shake the (in these matters) relatively experienced Linda out of her routine way of proceeding. So that it does not take too long before they are *both* out of their depth, in emotional territory that seems to be new for both of them.

This may be why, when Linda abruptly pulls away from the kiss and invites Trevor upstairs ('Are you coming upstairs? Come on'). his only response is to start (it would seem involuntarily) laughing again. As if she has moved too quickly back into the realm of predictability. Or perhaps he sees her move as an attempt to reassert her control of the situation. In any case, she waits for a few moments, looks a bit angry and when he stops laughing she again urges him to 'come on'. At which point he resumes laughing and in a calm, no longer angry, tone she tells him 'You'd better go then, hadn't you?' He gets quiet and puts his hands round his knees. Then he stands up and moves next to her. They are both quiet now but as he prepares to leave she asks him if he 'want[s] to see [her] again. Do you Trevor?' When he says that he does she looks relieved and triumphant, then says she wants to go to a disco and he agrees to take her. She smiles happily.

In part, the film's achievement is to have taken the gum-chewing Linda – an adolescent girl who *might* (cruelly but accurately) be described as being a bit 'small-minded', even 'bone-headed', and having, in her concern for appearances, incipient 'middle-class aspirations' – and shown her spontaneously tapping into a formidable source of erotic power that momentarily transforms her. I say 'in part', because the truth is that it is her interaction with Trevor that – for a few minutes – makes this transformation possible. And he is transformed by it as well. It is an astonishing ten minutes to watch.

Linking this scene to the comparable one between Sylvia and Peter in *Bleak Moments*, Carney claims that they 'are among the most thrilling sequences in all of cinema' (2000: 77).[6] This is not, in my view, an exaggerated description of the scene in *The Kiss of Death*, part of which Coveney nicely describes as follows:

We glimpse, as if in a series of intuitive flashes, an entire catalogue of human emotions in the mating game: anxiety, cruelty, affection, wonder, contempt and playfulness. This is how love scenes are endured in life, not in the movies, but distilled and refined for *this* movie. This sequence, camera tight in on the two faces, with no long shot and no trickery, is one of the highlights in the Leigh canon, and all about the performances, which are fresh, funny, completely original, and entirely truthful. (2000: 111–12)

I would agree that the scene in *Bleak Moments* is also extraordinary – and among the most *powerful* sequences in cinema – but I would myself reserve the word 'thrilling' solely for the scene in *The Kiss of Death*, in which we see Trevor actually respond to Linda.

As for Leigh's reference to an escape from middle-class aspirations, I am glad that he makes it: it is just that, in my view, *this* – the interaction between Trevor and Linda in their kissing scene – is where we already see it taking place.

The Political and the Flaubertian Leigh: On Stupidity, Taste, Anger and Resistance

[*The Kiss of Death*] is about received notions of how to be, and how to behave, both generally, and in relationships. All that upwardly mobile rubbish in *Hard Labour* with Alison's role [as Veronica] is obviously the beginning of all kinds of stuff, and it's all about insiders and outsiders and received ideas.

Characters like Nicola, like Aubrey [in *Life is Sweet*] ... are receptacles of received notions of how they should be...

Is it not the case that people are ... encrusted with layers of indirectness, and received prejudices, and received notions?
– Mike Leigh (quoted in Coveney 1997: 108; Movshovitz 2000: 18, 66)

Though it is actually one of Leigh's Television Studio Recordings and so not, strictly speaking, one of his films, I will begin this chapter with a discussion of *Abigail's Party* (1977). My reason for doing so is that this recently revived play seems to be the source of one of the most persistent and damaging of the received ideas about Leigh, which is that his work is sometimes (some think frequently) patronising and heartless. Here, for example, is the opening of Charles Spencer's *Daily Telegraph* review of the stage production at the Ambassadors Theatre, London, in December 2002:

What a brilliant and hilarious play this is – and what an absolutely vile one too. This is a comedy entirely devoid of magnanimity. It patronises its characters and holds them up to ridicule, pandering to one of the meanest vices of human nature, snobbery. I would guess that even Mike Leigh now feels uneasy about it. His later films, such as *Life is Sweet* and *Secrets and Lies* have revealed a generosity of spirit that is entirely absent here.

It is also worth noting that, since a copy of Spencer's entire review ('A Great But Guilty Pleasure') was on display at the theatre entrance, someone was obviously calculating that it would draw people in – people enticed, presumably, by the prospect of experiencing the guilty pleasure of indulging the 'snobbish contempt' Spencer assures his readers he himself is 'not immune to'. It is, he claims, 'shamelessly entertaining stuff – the modern equivalent of visiting Bedlam to laugh at the lunatics'.

This discussion of some of the issues at stake in (the televised version of) *Abigail's Party* will lead into a consideration of some of the questions raised by Leigh's fifth, seventh and eighth full-length films – *Who's Who* (1979), *Home Sweet Home* (1982), *Meantime* (1983) – and the short film, *A Sense of History*, that he made much later (in 1992). While I readily admit that other films could be used to illustrate what can be called the political and the Flaubertian Leigh, the latter can, in my view, be most clearly seen at work in *Abigail's Party* and (to a lesser extent) *Home Sweet Home* and the former, the political Leigh (about whom more will be considered in subsequent chapters), is the director of *Who's Who*, *Meantime* and *A Sense of History*.

The ghost of Flaubert in attendance at 'Abigail's Party'

Why, then, and in what sense, Flaubert? I am not assuming that Leigh is consciously indebted: he may or may not be. But considering Leigh's preoccupation with received ideas, Flaubert, the author of a *Dictionary of Received Ideas*, would seem to be the obvious point of reference. And it is not as if Flaubert's *Dictionary* – a compilation of the stupidities that he spent much of his life collecting – stood apart from the rest of his work. On the contrary, there would seem to be a consensus among Flaubertian scholars that it is at the centre. By general agreement, the spirit in which he worked throughout his life is clearly revealed in the letter he wrote when he was nine years old: 'there is a lady who visits papa and who tells us silly things, I could write them down'.[1] (I should say that this and the others letters I shall be drawing on are conveniently available in translation in Leo Bersani's edition of *Madame Bovary*.)

For a quick sense of what Flaubert's *Dictionary of Received Ideas* is all about, we can turn to a letter he wrote to Louise Colet on 17 December, 1852. In it he explains that the *Dictionary* 'would attack everything' but in such an ironical way that he 'would be safe from the law'. Among other things, the book 'would contain, in alphabetical order, on all possible subjects, *everything one should say in society to be a respectable and agreeable man.*' Here are some of the examples he provides:

Artists: are all disinterested.
Erection: said only in speaking of monuments.
France: needs to be ruled by an iron hand.

As Flaubert then goes on to say, his aim in putting the *Dictionary* together would be to shut people up:

It would be necessary that in the entire book there not be one word of my own invention, and that once people had read it they would no longer dare open their mouths for fear of unintentionally using one of the expressions that are in it. (1972: 320)

The fear in question would be that of making oneself look ridiculous by uttering one of the clichés Flaubert cites, an example, as he saw it, of typical human stupidity. By way of further explanation, here is an excerpt from another letter to Louise Colet, this one dated 9 October 1852:

I'm working on a conversation between a young man and a young lady on literature, the sea, mountains, music – in short, every poetic subject there is. It could be taken seriously and I intend it to be totally absurd. I believe this will be the first time a book has ever made fun of its leading lady and its leading man. (1972: 319)

Emma Bovary and Leon Dupuis are the young lady and the young man in question and the conversation to which Flaubert is presumably referring takes place over dinner on the evening of Emma's arrival in Yonville-l'Abbaye. Some excerpts:

'I don't think there's anything more beautiful than a sunset,' she said, 'but I like them especially on the seashore.'
'Oh, I love the sea,' said Monsieur Leon.
'Doesn't it seem to you,' asked Madame Bovary, 'that the mind moves more freely in the presence of that boundless expanse, that the sight of it elevates the soul and gives rise to thoughts of the infinite and the ideal?'
'The same is true of mountain scenery,' said Leon.
[...] Emma went on: 'And what kind of music do you prefer?'
'Oh, German music, the kind that makes you dream.'
                              – (Flaubert, *Madame Bovary* 1972: 70–1)

If we are in any doubt as to what is going on here then, as Hugh Kenner has pointed out, two of the entries in Flaubert's *Dictionary* (which Kenner leaves in the French original) can help us:

Mer: N'a pas de fond. – Image de l'infini. – Donne de grandes pensées.
Allemands: Peuple de reveurs (vieux).[2]

We can now turn to *Abigail's Party*. The situation in this play is that Beverly (an ex-beautician) and her husband Laurence (an estate agent) have invited three guests over for a social evening – Angela (a nurse) and her husband Tony (a computer analyst) who have both just moved into the neighbourhood, and Susan, who lives nearby and whose fifteen-year-old daughter Abigail is having a party. Though we hear music from Abigail's party, we never actually get to see Abigail herself. So the play is really about *Beverly's* party, which is mainly characterised by the quarrel between Beverly (Alison Steadman) and Laurence (Tim Stern) that runs and escalates throughout it. The play ends with Laurence dying on stage of a heart attack for which Beverly – another of Leigh's 'impossible' characters – is at least partly responsible.

Apart from the fact that it is set on a lower rung of the social ladder, this is clearly reminiscent of Edward Albee's 1962 play *Who's Afraid of Virginia Woolf?* in which, as Coveney notes, 'the cocktail party of George and Martha becomes a marital wasteland, and their guests, pawns in the struggle' (1997: 124). But the relevance of Flaubert's work seems to me much greater than that of Albee's play. Let us look at a few examples, starting with an exchange on the number of people expected to attend Abigail's Party. Susan (Harriet Reynolds)[3] has just said that the previous night she had noticed that the anticipated number had gone up to twenty-five:

Beverly:	It's creeping up, Sue.
Susan:	I've told her that's the limit. Well, I think that's enough. Don't you?
Beverly:	Definitely, Sue, yeah, definitely.
Angela:	Yeah.
Beverly:	But, this is it with teenagers: okay, they tell you twenty-five; but a friend invites a friend: that friend invites another friend; and it creeps up till you end up with about seventy or eighty. This is it. This is the danger! (Leigh 1983: 22–3)[4]

It is the confidence with which Beverly delivers this last speech (especially those last two sentences), as if she were saying something wise, even profound, that strikes the authentic Flaubertian note. It is there again in her contribution to the brief discussion about Susan's ex-husband. Angela (Janine Duvitski) has just said that his Sunday visits are 'nice – for the kids':

Beverly:	Yeah, well, let's face it, Sue, whatever else you say about him, he is their father, isn't he? (1983: 25)

A bit later, after agreeing with Angela, who has just said she thinks 'more and more people are getting divorced these days,' Beverly adds this: 'Mind you, I blame a lot of it on Women's Lib. I do. And on permissiveness, and all this wife-swapping business' (1983: 27). And while discussing Tony's choice of a Bacardi as his drink, Beverly volunteers the information that it is her 'dream, actually, just lying on the beach, sipping Bacardi-and-Coke' (1983: 40). 'Actually' is of course *exactly* the right word (Flaubert's *mot juste*) in this context and its placement is simply masterly.

Not that Beverly is the only character in *Abigail's Party* who sounds like this. We have already noticed that '*Artists*: are all disinterested' is one of the entries in Flaubert's *Dictionary* and at one point in *Madame Bovary* we learn that Leon's ambition is to 'lead an artist's life! He would take guitar lessons! He would wear a dressing gown, a Basque beret, blue velvet slippers!' (1972: 102; see too 189–90). Here is Leigh's Laurence explaining to Sue his feelings on the subject: 'You know, I think musicians and artists, they're very lucky people: they're born with one great advantage in life. And d'you know what that is? Their talent' (1983: 41).

As noted earlier, it was, according to Coveney, after *Abigail's Party* that 'words like "condescension" and "patronising" started to appear regularly in reviews' of Leigh's work (1997: 119) and we saw that Dennis Potter was particularly incensed by this play. It should be clear by now that Potter is mistaken and that words like 'condescension' and 'patronising' miss the point, which is the same point Flaubert made when he famously confessed that he actually *identified* with his heroine: '*Mme. Bovary, c'est moi.*' Most of us are probably not as different from Beverly and Laurence as we might like to imagine ourselves being. Is this not the real reason we find ourselves wincing with embarrassment when we hear Beverly and Laurence coming out with their platitudes and banalities and wanting them to pass for wisdom? And also, perhaps, when we hear her insistence (echoing that of the liquor store attendant in *Bleak Moments*) that the others enjoy themselves ('go on, Tone, take a little cigar, enjoy yourself' [1983: 38]; 'Laurence, we're not here to hold conversations, we are here to enjoy ourselves' [1983: 56]).[5]

As for Laurence, his interest in 'Art' puts him in a slightly different category, one that might usefully remind us of Leonard Bast in E.M. Forster's *Howard's End*. But it is the differences as well as the similarities that make the comparison useful. Here is Leonard's reaction when he is first exposed to Margaret Schlegel:

> Her speeches fluttered away from the young man like birds. If only he could talk like this ... Oh, to acquire culture! Oh, to pronounce foreign names correctly! Oh, to be well-informed, discoursing at ease on every subject that a lady started! But it would take one years. With an hour at lunch and a few shattered hours in the evening, how was it possible to catch up with leisured women, who had been reading steadily from childhood? His brain might be full of names, he might even have heard of Monet and Debussy; the trouble was that he could not string them together into a sentence, he could not make them 'tell'. (1973: 52–3)

What this shows is that in terms both of cultural aspiration and acquisition, Laurence – who thinks that Shakespeare is 'part of our heritage,' though 'it's not something you can actually read' (1983: 55) – is much less advanced than Leonard, who does, after all have a genuine interest in culture and the arts. Laurence's interest, as is made even clearer in the exchange he later gets into with Sue, is entirely superficial.

Having discovered that Sue has been to Paris, Laurence asks her if ('Talking of Paris') she 'like[s] Art':

Sue: Er – yes.
Laurence: So do I. Beverly doesn't. Of course, you know that Paris is the centre of the Art World. D'you like Van Gogh? (1983: 61)

Apart from anything else, it is obvious that Laurence is interested in 'Art' mainly as a way of demonstrating his superiority over Beverly. When he has pointed out to Susan (what is obvious to her already) that the reproduction he has on his wall 'is a Van Gogh,' and then asked her if she likes the Impressionists, he is clearly taken aback when she says she does and he has no idea how to respond: 'Oh, you do? That's good. Fine. Fine.' Moments later, however, a memory kicks in and he resumes:

Laurence: Of course, you know, Van Gogh was a very unstable man. Not only did he cut his ear off and leave it in a brothel, he also ate paint, and he shot himself.
Beverly: Thank you, Laurence! We don't want all the gory details.
Laurence: I'm talking to Sue, and Sue is interested in all these things.

At this point, it is difficult not to sympathise with Beverly. Not because the details are 'gory' but because talking about 'these things' is a poor substitute for talking about the paintings. No wonder then if Beverley's next move is to enlist the support of Tony and Angela as she moves to the record player in an attempt to 'liven things up a bit'. And when Laurence then switches his attention to Angela and asks her the same question he had asked Sue ('Do you like Art?'), Beverly's response seems the appropriate one: 'For Christ's sake, Laurence, give it a rest!' As she says, 'Nobody is interested.' Then, after he has accused her of being 'ignorant', we get the following exchange:

Beverly: It's not a question of ignorance, Laurence, it's a question of taste!
Laurence: Taste! And what would you know about taste?
Beverly: The trouble with you, Laurence, is if somebody doesn't happen to like what you like, then you say that they've got no taste!
Laurence: That's rubbish!
Beverly: Oh, is it rubbish?
Laurence: Yes!
Beverly: Then what about that picture I've got upstairs in the bedroom?
Laurence: That is cheap, pornographic trash!
Beverly: Laurence, just because a picture happens to be erotic, it doesn't mean it's pornogaphic. (1983: 62–3)

Shortly after this, Beverly defies Laurence by going upstairs to get the painting in dispute and Laurence defies Beverly by putting on Beethoven's *Fifth Symphony*, during the opening of which he has a heart-attack and, in spite of Angela's attempt at reviving him, he dies.

Part of my point, then, is that while it is easy to feel superior to both Laurence and Beverly in *some* of the exchanges above, much of the time – as, for example, in the distinction Beverley wants to make between the erotic and the pornographic – they sound just like the rest of us. And their quarrel ends by raising a question – of taste – that is much more troubling for us than it was for the readers Forster must have imagined for *Howard's End* in 1910. About one thing, at least, readers of Forster's novel are left in no doubt. Both the Schlegels and Leonard Bast are at least sure that they know what culture is and Forster expects us, his readers, to agree with them. But today this agreement can no longer be counted on. We speak, for example, of popular culture and of high culture and we no longer have the same kind of confidence in the latter that Forster had. In many places, furthermore, the university discipline of 'English' has been replaced by 'Cultural Studies'. In this sometimes confusing situation there are many who seem ready to take one truth (that there is often a connection between one's taste and one's class position) for the only truth (with taste then becoming nothing more than a function of class). So that while I, for example, want to say that Laurence is wrong on the 'question of ignorance' (in the sense that he knows virtually nothing about the 'Art' he pretends to be interested in and Beverly at least genuinely likes the pop music she plays for her guests) and Beverly wrong on the 'question of taste' (in the sense that I do not share her belief that – just because they are in some sense personal – all tastes are equally valid), one has to recognise that there are many these days who consider themselves cultured and yet are closer to Beverly's position on this question than they are to mine.

Yet it is still difficult to see any evidence of the 'rancid disdain', 'genuine hatred', 'immense condescension', 'yelping derision' and 'contempt' that Dennis Potter found in *Abigail's Party* and that he thought was all directed at 'the dreadful suburban tastes of the dreadful lower-middle-classes'. But leaving this aside for a moment, what I find most interesting and disturbing about Potter's reaction is the implication that he considers hatred and contempt to be *always* inappropriate responses, always and everywhere. It would seem that he is far from being alone; and it is not just a question of hatred and contempt. In a footnote in which Carney explains why he disagrees with his collaborator Leonard Quart's assumption 'that Leigh's attitude to Rupert and Laetitia [in *High Hopes*] ... is one of anger', Carney gives the impression that he thinks anger is never an appropriate response either.[6]

In the circumstances, then, it might be helpful to briefly recall how it was once thought that the artist and the critic have a right – and, indeed, occasionally, a duty – to express anger, contempt, hatred, derision and disdain.

During the Second World War, D. W. Harding published an article entitled 'Regulated Hatred: An Aspect of the Work of Jane Austen'. It is an attempt at underlining some features of her work that might be appreciated by 'the sort of readers who sometimes miss her – those who would turn to her not for relief and escape but as a formidable ally against things and people that were to her, and still are, hateful' (1940: 362). But 'hateful' is a strong word. Exactly what kind of things or people deserve to be called it? Earlier writers than Austen were in no doubt. Let us consider briefly what Ben Jonson and Henry Fielding had to say on the subject.

According to Ben Jonson, we do not – or ought not to – require in the poet 'mere elocution; or an excellent faculty in verse; but the exact knowledge of all virtues, and their contraries; with ability to render the one loved, the other hated, by his proper embattling them' (1975: 405). In other words, Jonson was quite clear about what we ought to hate: the vices. And just over a century later, in the Preface he wrote for *Joseph Andrews*, we find Henry Fielding similarly insisting that 'Great vices are the proper objects of our detestation' (1973: v). At the same time, since Fielding intended *Joseph Andrews* to be a 'comic romance', his concern was with the 'Ridiculous only' (1973: iv), the source of which was, in his view, to be found in 'affectation', which in turn proceeds from either 'vanity or hypocrisy' (ibid.). So insofar as, against his own rules, Fielding had 'introduced vices, and of a very black kind,' into *Joseph Andrews,* he apologises and explains that at least 'they are never set forth as the objects of ridicule, but detestation' (1973: vi).

If, as Charles Spencer maintains, it were true that in *Abigail's Party* Leigh is indeed 'pandering to one of the meanest vices of human nature, snobbery', Leigh would, in my view, deserve censure. But I do not for one moment believe that he is. And where Spencer sees him patronising the play's characters and holding 'them up to ridicule', I would submit that what the play encourages us to laugh at is the *ridiculous*, the ridiculous as manifested in the kind of language cited. Further, this play encourages the kind of laughter that might help to break (or at least weaken) the hold that certain kinds of 'stupidity' (the kinds embedded in 'received ideas') have on us all.[7]

But, in any case, even if there is no longer any widespread agreement on what constitutes stupidity or good taste or even the nature of the virtues and the vices, we still have the task of trying to distinguish between more or less appropriate responses. At one point, for example, in his book *Orwell*, Raymond Williams maintains that it 'is much easier to despise the ruling class than to hate and break them' (1971: 26). Obviously from Williams' point of view, the appropriate response of a socialist to the English ruling class in 1971 was one of hatred.

This brings us to *Who's Who* and *A Sense of History*, both of which examine aspects of England's ruling class.

England, Whose England?: 'Who's Who' and 'A Sense of History'

Margaret Matheson, who commissioned *Who's Who* for *Play for Today*, said to me, 'You always make films about your background. Why don't you make a film about mine.' So I did, but with the character of the clerk, played by Richard Kane, watching it all and from his voyeuristic, lower-middle-class perspective. *Who's Who* was also a fairly sympathetic look at kids weighed down by their background and their mores and their received ideas.

– Mike Leigh (Fuller 1995: xxiii)

Who's Who begins with Nigel (a young stockbroker) sitting with his back to us in an armchair, smoking a pipe, and listening to a voice on the radio reciting John of Gaunt's 'scept'red isle' speech from *Richard II*. Here is the relevant part:

> This royal throne of kings, this scept'red isle,
> This earth of majesty, this seat of Mars,
> This other Eden, demi-paradise,
> This fortress built by Nature for herself
> Against infection and the hand of war,
> This happy breed of men, this little world,
> This precious stone set in the silver sea,
> Which serves it in the office of a wall,
> Or as a moat defensive to a house,
> Against the envy of less happier lands,
> This blessed plot, this earth, this realm, this England
> – (William Shakespeare, *Richard II*, act II, scene i, 40–50)

This is of course one of the best-known passages in the whole of Shakespeare and Leigh's ironic citation of it here implicitly raises a number of questions, one of which – to whom does this England belong? – was formulated in an explicit allusion to this speech by E. M. Forster at the end of the nineteenth chapter of *Howards End*:

> Does she [England] belong to those who have moulded her and made her feared by other lands, or to those who added nothing to her power, but have somehow seen her, seen the whole island at once, lying as a jewel in a silver sea, sailing as a ship of souls, with all the brave world's fleet accompanying her towards eternity? (1973: 178)

It was asked again – this time with reference to D. H. Lawrence's short story 'England my England' and Part One of George Orwell's *The Lion and the Unicorn* ('England Your England') – by Raymond Williams in a chapter heading ('England whose England?') in his book on Orwell. Whereas Lawrence's 'England My England' seemed to Williams 'an assertion, a declaration of independence, a challenge,' he saw Orwell's 'England your England' as 'a dream. And when it breaks, under pressure, it will,' he prophesied, 'become a nightmare' (1971: 28). In the event, however, I would say that the 'dream' lives on today, in both Orwell's version ('England … resembles a family … with the wrong members in control' [1982: 53–4]) and in John of Gaunt's (as a 'scept'red isle', 'a jewel in a silver sea').

So where does Leigh stand in relation to all of this? My answer comes in two parts, the first of which is with reference to *Who's Who* and *A Sense of History*.

Judging by these two works, I would say that (at least as an artist) Leigh is not sufficiently interested in the English ruling class to hate it.

Alan Dixon (Richard Kane) – the clerk who, as Leigh says, watches everything 'from his voyeuristic, lower-middle-class perspective' – works for a London stock-broker's office. The principal stockbrokers are three young men – Nigel (Simon Chandler), Giles (Adam Norton) and Anthony (Graham Seed) – and one middle-aged man, Francis (Jeffrey Wickham), who particularly impresses Alan on the day when Francis tells him he is off to meet the firm's most distinguished clients, Lord Crouchurst (David Neville) and Lady Crouchurst (Richenda Carey). Such as it is, the film's action is mainly divided between the office, where Alan, his fellow clerk Kevin (Philip Davis), a typist Samya (Souad Faress) and the stockbrokers all work, and live at home, or rather in two homes – the house that Alan shares with his cat-breeding wife April (Joolia Cappleman) and the apartment that Nigel shares with Giles. In the latter, the big event on the horizon is a dinner party that Nigel and Giles are planning to give. When it eventually starts to take place (some forty minutes into the film), it is comically intercut with scenes from Alan's household, which is in a state of chaos because the Dixons have two vistors and Alan cannot stop himself from fawning over them – Mr Shakespeare (Sam Kelly), who has come to photograph April's cats, and Miss Hunt (Geraldine James), who is there to buy one of them.

Whether or not Mr Shakespeare's getting Alan's surname wrong (calling him Mr Dickens) is meant to suggest it, the character of Alan Dixon is reminiscent of Mrs Pocket in *Great Expectations*. When Pip first visits the Pockets he notices that – instead of helping the two nursemaids to look after the seven children, who are tumbling over themselves – Mrs Pocket has her head buried in a book (1979: 209–10). Pip tells us that it later 'appeared that the book [he] had seen Mrs Pocket reading ... was all about titles, and that she knew the exact date at which her grandpa would have come into the book, if he ever had come at all' (1979: 215).

For his part, Alan Dixon's favourite reading is *Debrett's Peerage* and, though he has much less of a sense of his own importance in the scheme of things than Mrs Pocket does of hers, he is every bit as preoccupied with titles. An important difference is that – because of the way in which she relates to her children and her husband and because of her choice of the blackguard Drummle as a friend – Mrs Pocket is contemptible, while Alan is merely pathetic. But either way, contemptible or pathetic, Dickens was surely right to feel that it would be a mistake to give such a character anything more than a minor role. I think Alan plays too large a role in *Who's Who*.

Another way of stating my objection is in terms of one of the ideas touched on in the last chapter (in the discussion of *Grown-Ups*): the importance – from a psychoanalytical point of view – of traversing the fantasy. *Who's Who* can certainly be said to traverse or go through the fantasy of the upper class that Alan shares with Mrs Pocket and no doubt millions of others and the film leaves us facing 'a certain void, lack, empty place in the Other' (Zizek 1989: 74). Where the fantasy had promised plenitude, we see that there is actually nothing there. But, unlike

Carney (whose reference to the 'horrific wit' of Leigh's presentation of Lord and Lady Crouchurst [2000: 127] suggests that he finds the film devastating), I do not find this enough. Dickens does this kind of exposure as well, in incomparably more powerful ways, in both *Great Expectations* and in *Little Dorrit*,[8] but he does so while managing at the same time to make us feel that he is simultaneously giving us a sense of the real. And in *Who's Who* I, at least, get no sense of the real.

The film *is* occasionally funny: it is amusing, for example, to see Lady Crouchurst played by Richenda Carey, the camp manageress in *Nuts in May*. But there is no bite or edge to the humour and, while it may well be that Leigh did his best to offer 'a fairly sympatheic look at kids weighed down by their background and their mores and their received ideas', the 'kids' in question appear obnoxious and also uninteresting.

It might be said that in his depiction of Lord and Lady Crouchurst in *Who's Who* and throughout *A Sense of History* Leigh is closer to despising the English upper class than he is to hating it. But it would be more accurate to say that in these works he is inclined to focus on its affectations and to therefore find it more ridiculous than anything else. This is especially true of *A Sense of History,* which was scripted by the actor Jim Broadbent and is the only one of Leigh's films that he did not write himself. In it Broadbent plays the twenty-third Earl of Leete, who has arranged to tell his life-story to a documentary film crew while walking over his country estate. It is a short film (twenty-eight minutes long). Broadbent's impersonation of the mad and homicidal Earl – who sometimes resembles one of Edgar Allan Poe's narrators – is brilliant and it is interesting to note that, in this film, one of the ways in which Leigh heightens the comic effect is by constantly making us aware of the movements of his usually unobtrusive camera. One gathers that this is supposed to be a rather amateurish documentary.

Unlike *Who's Who*, which is surely Leigh's weakest film (mainly, I suspect, because he is not really all that interested in the material), *A Sense of History* seems perfectly successful on its own terms. It is just that, by Leigh's own high standards, it seems a bit predictable, its target a bit too easy.

It is interesting to note, however, that at least one of the institutions that has helped to keep alive the 'dream' referred to above (of England as 'a scept'red isle', 'a jewel in a silver sea') is the genre that *A Sense of History* mocks – the Earl of Leete being in no doubt that the patch of England on which he stands belongs to *him*. This is the genre that has come to be known as Heritage cinema and that was perhaps inaugurated by the television productions of *Brideshead Revisited* (1981) and *The Jewel in the Crown* (1984). Any list of its highlights would have to include *A Passage to India* (1984), the four Merchant-Ivory-Jhabvala films – *A Room with a View* (1986), *Maurice* (1987), *The Remains of the Day* (1993) and *Howard's End* (1992) – *Sense and Sensibility* (1995) and the television production of *Pride and Prejudice* (1995). And whatever else is to be said about the Heritage films (including some of the ways in which they differ from one another),[9] they invariably focus (whether at home or abroad) on different forms of the conventionally beautiful: on unspoiled country landscapes and buildings that are occupied by attractive-looking people who speak in voices that are refined, polished and well-bred. Think, for example, of Jeremy Irons' voice-over in *Brideshead Revisited*. Even when these people are sometimes shown to be corrupt, they still manage to keep up an impressive appearance. For the most part, they are of the middle- and upper-classes. When the lower-classes appear it is usually as servants who are often at least as groomed and refined in manner as their masters, sometimes – like Anthony Hopkins in *The Remains of the Day* – more so. In short, though some of these films (for example, *The Jewel in the Crown, The Remains of the Day*) certainly offer sharp criticism, it is inevitably muted by the smoothness of their surfaces. They all tend to be extremely pleasing on the eye and ear; they all manage, in one way or another, to leave us feeling soothed, stroked and caressed.

In stark contrast, this is *not* how we feel when we emerge from one of Leigh's films, whose focus is clearly not on the conventionally beautiful in any of its guises. But, even without *A Sense of History's* mockery, it is, I take it, perfectly obvious that Leigh's films have played no part at all in the promotion of the national 'dream'. Not, at least, in its second version ('a jewel in a silver sea'). But what about the first Orwellian version ('England … resembles a family')?

It is true that Leigh's films are indeed preoccupied with the family – or, to be more precise, with families. How should this be understood? With Williams' critique of Orwell's image in mind, it might be helpful to consider Leigh's preoccupation with the family in reference to some of Santner's reflections on the thought of Franz Rosenzweig, for example his claim that for Rosenzweig 'the family is the primary site of the *memic* [or cultural] – rather than *genetic* – replication of Judaism' (2001: 111; see also 107). I am definitely not suggesting that Leigh shares Rosenzweig's kind of interest in Judaism. But his films do give the impression that for him too the family is a 'primary site'. And Santner's claim that what 'makes Judaism different is that it elaborates a form of life around the disruptive, even traumatic, pressures induced in us by the "neighbour-Thing" rather than, under the auspices of the superego, transferring those pressures into this or that national project, this or that construction of "home"' (2001: 117) is especially interesting.[10] This suggests that what makes Leigh distinctive is that he too does not seem all that interested in 'this or that national project', or, finally, in such questions as to whom does England belong? Rather, he seems more interested in celebrating particular, smaller-scale, forms of life that are organised 'around the disruptive, even traumatic, pressures induced in us by the "neighbour-Thing"' and by the family.

Perhaps, in the last analysis, Leigh's radicalism and his basic political orientation are to be found in his implicit answer to the question Who's Who? Which is to say, who *matters*? Who *counts*? If, despite its weaknesses, the film *Who's Who* can help us to get a better grasp of where Leigh stands, it can do so by making us more aware than we might otherwise be of the extraordinary extent to which his entire oeuvre is devoted to putting the phrase that serves as the title of this film into question.

In other words, the most important test as to where Leigh stands on these matters may be found in the answer to the question as to whose stories he thinks are worth telling. Most of the people whose stories Leigh tells could be described – by, for example, some contemporary version of the narrator of *Howards End* – as people whose lives do not count. For example, the opening of the sixth chapter of *Howards End* is as follows:

> We are not concerned with the very poor. They are unthinkable, and only to be approached by the statistician or the poet ... The boy, Leonard Bast, stood at the extreme verge of gentility. He was not in the abyss, but he could see it, and at times people whom he knew had dropped in, and counted no more. (1973: 58)

But of course Leonard Bast is in some ways an exceptional member of his class and, on the whole, Leigh's characters are not exceptional in this way, even though they are certainly distinct from one another. Nor, for the most part, do they belong among the *very* poor. Nevertheless, in the Society of the Spectacle, they might as well be invisible: it is as if they exist in a kind of 'abyss'.

Adultery and Parental Responsibility: 'Home Sweet Home'

> [Leigh's] area is the glory of everyday nothingness which he elevates to great drama. The minutiae of people's repetitive lives becomes of the utmost importance. *And his people are never seen anywhere else*, except when they are destroyed in the tabloid newspapers or in patronising documentaries. If you were to tell me you think Mike's patronising, I'd accuse him of the dead opposite: of elevating, and of making amusing and tragic, what most people in life go through. Which is nothing to do with glamour.
> – Timothy Spall (quoted in Coveney 1997: 160, my italics)

In the critique of Flaubert that he wrote in 1893, Henry James maintained that, when the characters Emma (of *Madame Bovary*) and Fréderick Moreau (of *The Sentimental Education*, 'our author's second study of the "real"') are considered alongside one another, they suggest 'a question that can be answered ... only to Flaubert's detriment': 'Why did Flaubert choose, as special conduits of the life he proposed to depict, such inferior and in the case of Fréderick such abject human specimens' (1968: 263). What would James have made of the inarticulate postmen and their wives whose stories Leigh tells in *Home Sweet Home*?

James' response might well, one imagines, have been similar to that of David Edgar, who, in the course of an essay on 'Public Theatre in a Private Age', devotes two paragraphs to Leigh, whom he uses to point out the weaknesses of naturalism, the tradition within which he sees Leigh working. According to Edgar, then, the main problem with Leigh's naturalism – and he makes it clear that he is thinking specifically of *Home Sweet Home* – is that, 'being only interested in what can be seen or heard, it is bound to imply that a poor environment reveals a poverty of spirit, and a limited vocabulary, a pettiness of mind' (1988: 170). Indeed, though I now consider it a major work, when I first saw *Home Sweet Home*, I too was mainly struck, and dismayed by, what I took to be its depressing 'poverty of spirit'.

The film opens with the camera positioned in a moving vehicle in front of Gordon (Timothy Spall), who looks troubled and who we see driving his motorcycle towards us on his way to work. When he arrives at work we see him and two of his fellow postmen – Stan (Eric Richard) and Harold (Tim Barker) – stacking their letters for their routes. The first time we see Gordon at home, we realise one, at least, of the reasons he is unhappy. Having recently lost weight (four stones) herself, his wife, Hazel (Kay Stonham), now wants to put him on a diet too. And, as many others would do in the same circumstances, he protests. The way in which he does so certainly indicates 'a limited vocabulary'. 'I ain't fat', he insists – not once but a number of times. 'I ain't going on a bleeding diet.' For her part, Hazel tactlessly suggests that he 'look at Stan, he's forty two, you ain't going to look like that in sixteen years time'. Later on, when she has invited Stan and his daughter Tina (Lorraine Brunning) over for Sunday dinner, Hazel calls her husband a 'fat bleeding pig' in front of their guests. And later that afternoon, when they are around at Stan's, Hazel calls Gordon 'a stupid sod'. Finally, when Gordon realises that Hazel has been flirting with Stan and seems to want to begin an affair with him, Gordon calls her a 'bleeding 'ore'. And this too, I take it, is how many men react when they suddenly learn that they're in danger of being cuckolded. It is just that in most fictional representations of the situation, the men and women involved tend to be better educated and know the correct pronunciation of such words as 'whore'.

But then, this is part of the point Leigh's film is making. When Stan is first visited by Melody (Frances Barber), the social worker,[11] she exclaims – on discovering that he has been a postman for thirteen years – that she took her eleven-plus in 1968. 'Passed them, did you?' is his dry response. Of course she did. But presumably he did not pass his. And as for Gordon, when he learns that Tina is fourteen, he recalls that he started work when he was fifteen. The point is that the main characters in this film are educational drop-outs. And to a large degree, the originality of *Home Sweet Home* is to have taken an important subject – adultery, an important subject of the nineteenth-century novel (*Madame Bovary, Anna Karenina, The Scarlet Letter*) – and then explored its impact on the lives of the sort of characters who have seldom, if ever before, been deemed worthy of this kind of attention. We might also think here, by way of contrast, not just of such recent Hollywood treatments of the subject as, say, *Fatal Attraction* and *Unfaithful* but also of Pinter's more serious *Betrayal* (which, in comparison with *Home Sweet Home*, is still glamourised, especially in its film version).

As Ray Carney sees it, it is as if in *Home Sweet Home* 'Leigh set out, not only to choose the most repellent group of figures imaginable (that's relatively easy), but to find ways to allow them to justify their behavior (a great artistic challenge)' (2000: 160). In my view, 'most repellent' is seriously misleading; so too his claim that the characters are like 'horror-movie zombies' who 'have lost their minds' and about his description of Stan, the adulterer, as 'despicable' (2000: 158, 161). However, on the other hand, the latter description is hardly worse than Coveney's view of Stan as being 'attractively valiant and horny', driving 'a wedge of solid integrity through the film' (1997: 162). This strikes me as being too complacent by far. The important point, however, is that this is not a film that tells us what to think of its characters and their behaviour. Like all of Leigh's films, it leaves us with 'work to do, and matters to be faced' (Movshovitz 2000: 121).

As Leigh explained back in 1975, his 'very particular kind of story-telling' takes the form of an invitation to 'the audience to go through a process of identifying [with], reacting to, reacting against, sympathising with, caring for, getting cheezed off with, a complex set of interactions between people' (quoted in Carney 2000: 42). In this process the *sequence* of the main events is clearly crucial. It seems important, in retrospect, therefore, that we see Stan working alongside Gordon and Harold before we learn – some forty minutes into the film – about his relationship with Harold's wife, June. Up until then we have been led to expect that if an adulterous affair is to take place it will be between Stan and Hazel, since she is the one who invites him in for coffee while he is delivering letters and who then starts flirting with him. But we have also been made to realise – when Melody, the social worker, visits Stan and gets him to agree to go and see his daughter, Tina, who has been living in a home ever since his wife left him years earlier – that Stan's life is more complicated than it first appears to be. And when, on the following Sunday, Stan picks up a young woman (Sheila Kelley) in a laundrette and takes her back home to his bed instead of keeping the appointment Melody had pressured him into making to see Tina, we see that the moral issue we are being invited to consider here concerns parental responsibility. The next day we see the moral issue shifting back and forth: first the temptation to commit adultery (with Hazel flirtatiously inviting him in for a cup of tea and behaving like a 'tease'); then the appeal to his sense of parental responsibility (with Melody phoning to reproach him for failing to visit Tina the previous day). So when, shortly after this, Stan visits Harold's wife June and we learn that they have already been having an 'affair', even though he has not been to see her for six months, it is so unexpected that it is difficult to know how to react.

It is clear that June (Su Elliott) sees the 'affair' as the kind of 'romance' she spends so much of her time reading about – like a latter-day Emma Bovary. Whereas Stan takes a more 'realistic' view of it – there is nothing of the gallant, romantic hero about him. He is there for the sex and when June shows initial reluctance he speaks roughly, even brutally, to her. But then he switches to a tone of tenderness: 'Come on,' he says gently, 'don't let's mess about.' In other words, since we both know that we really want the same thing, let's get down to it. But of course June does not want exactly the same thing Stan wants: she would like something more than just sex. And Stan either cannot or will not provide it. When invited to tell her that he misses her ('It's been at least six months'), all he can manage is 'I wouldn't be here if I didn't want to see you, would I?'

The following day, thanks to Melody's prompting, Stan visits Tina at the home and Melody pressures him into inviting Tina to spend the weekend with him. So that, when Stan turns up for Sunday dinner with Hazel and Gordon, he has Tina with him. Which means that Tina is still with them all when – despite Gordon's protests (it means missing his afternoon nap) – they first go for an after-dinner walk and then back to Stan's house for tea. And it is there, in Stan's living room, with her husband sitting next to her and with Tina sitting across from her father, that Hazel starts showing signs that she is sexually aroused by Stan. As is made clear by the eye contact Stan has with Hazel, he has seen these signs and is himself excited by them. And moments later, when the two of them are in the kitchen area – just out of sight of Gordon but not of Tina – Hazel and Stan kiss one another passionately. It is perhaps the one purely erotic and genuinely passionate moment in the film – a striking instance of the eruption of that surplus of the real that we noted earlier. At the same time, it is an obviously impossible situation and made even more so as the two potential lovers are interrupted by the unexpected arrival of June, which turns the proceedings into farce.

We have noted that the subject of this film is adultery and so, on one level, it might seem to invite comparison with the seventh of Kieslowski's *Decalogue* films, but in fact the latter only touches on the adultery theme obliquely. *Home Sweet Home* examines this theme more directly while at the same time making it unmistakably clear that what we ought to be most concerned about is the fate of the young girl. It is of note that each of the main characters (except June) is at his or her most sympathetic in brief interactions with Tina, who seems to play a central role. It is perverse, therefore, of Carney to insist that 'there is no bubbly, hopeful inner Tina waiting to bloom, given the right opportunities or attention' (2000: 158). How can he possibly know?

When Stan visits Tina at the institution in which she has been living for six years, we see in an exchange she has with her room-mate Kelly, that – even if she is unable or unwilling to tell him – she does care whether or not he visits her. 'I told you he was coming', Tina tells Kelly. 'She said you weren't coming', Tina then tells her father, 'because you were with a woman.' Actually, Kelley guessed right: Stan was with Janice, the woman he had picked up at the laundrette. Clearly these girls are used to being disappointed, but Tina has not yet completely given up hope. But, for whatever reason, Stan does not grasp the significance of what his daughter is telling him. Later, when he is with Tina in his backyard, he makes an effort to engage her in conversation. It is not easy. He asks her if she remembers the time when she got lost as a child. She does not respond at first and it seems for a few moments that she has forgotten. Unfortunately, when she eventually reveals that she does in fact remember, Stan again fails to follow through.

In the moving penultimate sequence of the film we see the romance-addicted June trying to get her husband to take in the fact that she has had an affair, trying to get him to see the significance of this fact, and at the same time trying to persuade herself that it *has* some significance. But it is Tina's image – as we see her standing alone and abandoned in the grounds of the home – that the camera focuses and lingers on at the end of the film as Dave (Lloyd Peters), the second social worker, forces a bemused Stan to listen to his lengthy monologue on the evils of capitalism. David Edgar maintains that, while this is exactly how the 'leftist social workers' he knows talk, they would not talk this way in 'meeting with a client' (1988: 170). My own feeling is that the non-naturalistic way in which Dave's words float free is surely intended and effectively conveys the problem. It is not words that are needed here but action: the abandoned youngster needs to be rescued. While Dave lectures Stan, we actually get to *see* Tina: the camera makes her present to us.

The Importance of Naming: Growing into Adulthood in 'Meantime'

In some ways *Meantime* invites comparison with Stephen Frears' *My Beautiful Laundrette* (1985), but the significant difference is to be found in the ways the films treat male friendship. In *My Beautiful Laundrette* Frears opts for the mode of romance, in the specifically American form that focuses on blood-brothers from different races (Huck and Jim, Ishmael and Queequeg, etc.) – in this case, Omar (Gordon Warnecke), a young Pakistani, renews his friendship with Johnny (Daniel Day Lewis), whom he rescues from a life in the National Front. In *Meantime*, on the other hand, Mark (Phil Daniels) has an uneasy friendship with Coxy (Gary Oldman), a dangerous skinhead, but by the end of the film they appear to be going in different directions. If, indeed, Coxy can be said to be going anywhere. As Coveney notes, we finally see him 'rolling around in a tin drum, like one of Beckett's doomed dustbin-dwellers in Leigh's beloved *Endgame*, bashing it noisily in a self-absorbed lather of pointless, energy-consuming bravado' (1997:173–4). Coxy certainly has an attractive side and it would be nice to think of him seeing the light and relinquishing his racism but *Meantime* is not a romance: like all of Leigh's major works, it is grounded in an unmistakable sense of the real.

Yet at the same time, this study of the demoralising effects of unemployment – 'three years into the Thatcher era' (Fuller 1995: xix) – does have a brighter side too since it is also, like *The Kiss of Death* – if in much worsened circumstances – a coming-of-age film. *Meantime* begins with the Pollock family – the parents (Frank [Jeff Robert] and Mavis [Pam Ferris]), and their sons, Colin (Tim Roth) and Mark (Daniels) – on what looks like their once- or twice-yearly visit to see Mavis' sister (Barbara [Marion Bailey]) and her husband (John [Alfred Molina]). (At the end of the visit, the two families agree that they will see one another next at Christmas.) John has a well-paying job and he and Barbara live in a comfortable house with an attractive, tree-lined lake nearby. We see this in the film's opening shot as the camera follows a jogger who is running around it – in contrast to the bleak scenes that make up the body of the film.

All four of the Pollocks are unemployed, which is presumably why Colin and Mark – who are young adults and so really too old for such visits – are with their parents. When we first see these characters, the four men have just returned from the park where they have been kicking a football around and 'the boys' are told to take their muddy shoes off and leave them in the kitchen). 'Yes, Auntie Barbara', says Mark, ironically. 'Good boys, aren't we?' But moments later we see Mark standing up for himself in the only way available in this situation, by acting like a 'bad' boy and sitting on top of the cabinet. He is then able to get in a mocking 'Yes, Uncle John' when he is asked to get off it.

When they leave, the Pollocks return home to their East End council flat, which is the cramped scene of their endless bickering. But what soon begins to emerge is that the heart of the film is to be found in the growing rivalry between Mark and Coxy as role-models for the mentally slow and very shy Colin. So that if, for example, Mark tries to set Colin up with Hayley (Tilly Vosburgh), a young woman they meet in the pub, it is Coxy who later takes Colin with him to Hayley's mother's flat and manages to simultaneously make fun of Colin while claiming that Colin is his mate and recommending that he buy the same kind of boots he himself wears (Doc Martens).

As in so many of Leigh's films, this too is one in which there is – in conventional terms – very little happening. But in these circumstances, Barbara does something that counts as a major initiative. She decides that she will offer Colin a job: she will hire him to help her do some decorating in her house. But Mark sabotages the plan; it is difficult to be sure exactly why. Possibly because the evening before he is to start work, Colin has let it be known that he hopes to be able to buy Doc Martens boots with his pay. But it seems highly possible that Mark himself may not be sure about his reasons. His negative reaction seems instinctive, rather than thought out. At any rate, Mark goes independently to Barbara's and makes Colin feel so uncomfortable that he ends up not doing the job. But before Colin leaves, he asks Mark why he has come if not to steal his job and it feels as if Mark is formulating the answer on the spot. It is a matter, he claims, of 'principles', 'things that don't grow on trees'. After Colin has gone, we see that Barbara is obviously displeased but when she tells Mark that he is Colin's 'minder', this is said not only with understandable ironic resentment but also with a grudging respect.

Mark returns home before Colin and somewhat enigmatically announces 'Mission accomplished'. In a brief exchange with his father, he then manages to articulate the beginnings of an ironic critique:

Mark: You've got to take your hat off to them [Barbara and John] really though, ain't yer.
Frank: You what?
Mark: For getting out of this area. New life. Respectable friends. High standard of living. All you've got to do is look at them together. Picture of happiness.

From this Leigh cuts immediately to a shot of a tearful and drunken Barbara sitting in a corner of her room where we see the impact of Mark's action on her life. Her room is in a state of disarray, as are her hopeful plans for brightening up her own life – because she had, after all, stripped and prepared everything for the decorating project that has now fallen through. Nevertheless, in this unpromising position Barbara musters the courage to confront her husband when he returns from work. In fact, in what turn out to be the last words she speaks in the film, she tells him to 'fuck off' and, judging by the smile on her face after she has said them, these words were ones she had been needing to say to him for some time. It is a moment of genuine resistance and necessary self-assertion, low-keyed but real, a small sign of hope.

When Colin gets back his head is covered by his parka and, after his parents recover from their disappointment on learning that he did not do the job after all, they vent their anger on him. At which point Mark comes to his brother's defense and strengthened by this Colin yells at his parents for the first time, actually ordering them out of *his* room. Whereas up until now, Mark had tended to patronise Colin, often calling him 'muppet', he now treats him more like an equal.

Mark wakes up first the following morning and, seeing that Colin is asleep, he lifts the hood of the parka that is still over his brother's head and discovers that Colin has had his head shaved bald. Colin wakes up at this moment, is clearly terrified at the thought of Mark's reaction and he quickly puts the hood back on. Mark is visibly shocked and says nothing for a few moments. We then get this exchange:

Mark: Who made you do that, Coxy?
Colin: Nothing to do with Coxy.
Mark: What, no-one tells you what to do?
Colin: That's right.

In this way Mark helps Colin to arrive at a new understanding of himself. But the process is not quite over.

Mark: [*Teasingly*] My brother's a skin-head.
Colin: [*Smiling*] No he ain't.
Mark: You sorry you had it done.
Colin: Don't know … Yeah.

At this point, Mark reaches over and strokes Colin's head. He holds it affectionately for a moment, trying to assure Colin that he need not be ashamed of it, that he does not have to keep it covered. And then, as he is going out the door of the room, he has an idea, sticks his head back in, and addresses Colin by the new name of 'Kojak'.

In context, this act of solidarity between two brothers – coming as it does after so much distrust, frustration and impotence – makes for an extraordinarily moving moment. In effect, Mark's loving interpellation of his brother functions here like a christening – especially with the earlier hand-on-the-head moment kept in mind.

Though there are obviously many other things to say about this powerful film, it is well to end this chapter with this hard-won image of hope, hinting as it does of the possibility of growth and change in the least promising of circumstances.

CHAPTER SEVEN

Comedies Celebrating Marriage, the Family and the Pursuit of Happiness

It might be perceived from this book [*Naked and Other Screenplays*] that *High Hopes* belongs with *Life is Sweet* and *Naked*, but if there's a run of any three films I've made that can loosely be described as a trilogy, it would have to be *Meantime*, *Four Days in July*, and *High Hopes*. Each of them took on board a political objective...

– Mike Leigh (Fuller 1995: xix)

I would like to say that in these films [the Hollywood comedies of remarriage] the central pair are learning to speak the same language ... What this pair does together is less important than the fact that they do whatever it is together, that they know how to spend time together, even that they would rather waste time together than do anything else – except that no time they are together could be wasted. Here is a reason that these relationships strike us as having the quality of friendship, a further factor in their exhilaration for us.

– Stanley Cavell (1981: 88)

Let us return to a point made in chapter two, when we noted some of the things that Leigh's *Four Days in July* has in common with Leo McCarey's *The Awful Truth* and the other films discussed by Stanley Cavell in his *The Pursuits of Happiness: The*

Hollywood Comedy of Remarriage. In their own ways, the three full-length films that Leigh made in between *Meantime* and *Naked* – his ninth, tenth and eleventh films (*Four Days in July* [1985], *High Hopes* [1988] and *Life is Sweet* [1990]) – can all be read as works that celebrate marriage, family and the pursuit of happiness. It seems that it ought to be possible to see this without denying the sense in which *Meantime*, *Four Days in July* and *High Hopes* are more *obviously* political than most of Leigh's other films. This is clearly the case, and I do not plan to ignore the politics of the last two films; nor, more specifically, will I be ignoring John Hill's claim that *High Hopes* partly reproduces 'conservative (and, indeed, *Thatcherite*) values regarding the family and women' (1999: 198). I will, however, be trying to show that it can be useful to consider the group of films chosen for discussion in this chapter in the light of some of the terms Cavell uses to analyse the Hollywood comedies of remarriage. The chapter will end by briefly considering *The Short and Curlies* (1987), which is definitely the odd one out here – not just because it is an 18-minute short but also because it draws our attention to the sadness that surrounds marriage.

I am not claiming that only resemblances exist between, on the one hand, Leigh's *Four Days*, *High Hopes* and *Life is Sweet* and, on the other, the Hollywood comedies. That would be impossible. The differences are of course more striking and we can list some of them first: (i) Cavell's comedies focus on *remarriage*, Leigh's on marriage;[1] (ii) Leigh's focus on the importance of having children, Cavell's do not;[2] (iii) Cavell's comedies are *Hollywood* comedies, Leigh's are obviously very far from being that; (iv) though there is a strong comic element in all of them, none of these four films by Leigh is a *pure* comedy.

However, there are four main resemblances. We have already noted (in chapters two and four) that for Cavell the two main distinguishing features of the Hollywood comedies of remarriage are the importance they attach (a) to conversation and (b) to laughter. It will be immediately obvious how important talk and humour are to the central couples in the four films by Leigh that concern us here; but it may still be worth providing a couple of quick examples. Recall, then, the moment in *Four Days in July*, in the home of the Protestant couple, when Lorraine (Paula Hamilton) asks her husband Billy (Charles Lawson) if they can go to her grandmother's that evening: 'Sure it would be good crack [that is, good conversation],' says Lorraine; 'she'll have half the street down there.' And later the same day, in the home of the Catholic couple, after Brendan (Shane Connaughton) and Dixie (Stephen Rea) have just left, Collette (Brid Brennan) refers appreciatively both to Dixie's humour ('he's a tonic, that Dixie fella … if you didn't have a laugh, you'd go mad') and to the 'crack' Dixie and Brendan must have had when they were political internees together at Long Kesh. Or again, take the moment in *Life is Sweet* when Nicola's lover (David Thewlis) explains that what he wants to have with her is 'an intelligent conversation' (Leigh 1995c: 170). As it happens, this is closely followed by her mother, Wendy (Alison Steadman), telling Nicola (Jane Horrocks) that, when she and her sister were born, her parents – Wendy and Andy, who were teenagers at the time – 'came through, laughin'' (1995c: 172), which is pretty much what we see them doing throughout most of the film.

According to Cavell, the third distinguishing feature of the Hollywood comedies of remarriage is to be found in the importance they attach to faith. If, as Cavell hopes, 'a redemptive politics or a redemptive psychology' are to succeed Christianity, he thinks they 'will require a new burden of faith in the authority of one's everyday experience, one's experience of the everyday' (1981: 240). And this, he argues, is precisely what the Hollywood comedies – in which 'redemption by happiness … depend[s] on a faith in something that is always happening, day by day' (1981: 241) – understand. Leigh's four comedies understand this as well and Leigh himself draws our attention to it in the following interview excerpt:

> Obviously what *Life is Sweet* and *High Hopes* have in common, in one way, is faith. You can draw some parallels between Shirley and Wendy: the positive spirit in women who have faith and who trust, and who inculcate that in other people. When Wendy talks about Andy's enthusiasm for the caravan, she's acknowledging that he may be a dreamer, but he still has hope and spirit… (Fuller 1995: xxxi)

Faith, hope, trust and spirit: this is the language of redemption. And, as for the way in which Leigh's films implicitly ask us to understand redemption, I think it is indicated in the fourth resemblance between these two groups of films.

Here I am indebted (again) to Andrew Klevan who asks us to recall *The Music Box* (1932) in which Laurel and Hardy desperately try to carry the box 'up the huge flight of steps' only to have it fall, time and time again, 'all the way back down to the street' (2000: 25). Observing that Raymond Durgnat has likened the structure of this film to 'the myth of Sisyphus', Klevan sees 'the crucial difference' in the fact 'that Sisyphus enacted his frustrating task all alone' (2000: 35). For Klevan, 'Laurel and Hardy's friendship and behaviour [render] the inevitable need for, and yet the difficulties of, human relatedness in the middle of the desperate endeavour to stay devoted to the world of one's life (2000: 26). In short, Stan and Ollie always show 'the willingness to carry on' (ibid.) and in this they resemble the couples in the Hollywood comedies.

My point, then, is that in Leigh's comedies too 'the willingness to carry on' is a key virtue. I think first in this connection of the pride both Collette and Eugene (Des McAleer) take in their refusal to complain: Collette when we first see her waking up and in obvious discomfort from her pregnancy ('I shouldn't be complaining') and Eugene when he treats Brendan and Dixie to a detailed explanation as to how he received his various injuries, all of which are serious. 'Apart from that, you're rightly', says Dixie. 'But I can't complain', says Eugene. 'But he does', Collette adds, giving him a loving smile – the point of which is that this gentle humour is one of the means by which they keep one another on their toes. Another is the traditional method by which one is reminded that there are always others who are worse off than oneself. Eugene considers himself lucky compared to some of the men he has seen in hospital 'who are burned just from the neck down'. 'They'd be better off dead', says Brendan. 'Now don't be saying that, Brendan,' says Eugene. 'Aye, some of them can make more of their lives than we can', says Collette.

In a similar vein, the key moment in *Life is Sweet* occurs towards the end when Wendy delivers the long speech in which she reproaches Nicola for having 'given up' (Leigh 1995c: 173), while making it clear that the alternative is to be 'still out there, fightin'' (1995c: 171), which is what she maintains she and Andy are both doing. And I would say that in *High Hopes* the most striking evidence of 'the willingness to carry on' is to be found in the hitherto reluctant Cyril's last-minute acceptance of Shirley's desire that they should bring a child into the world. In each case, we are made to understand that carrying on is not something that should be taken for granted – it takes faith and courage.

In the light of the foregoing, it might seem that, if any of Leigh's earlier films anticipate the four I have grouped together here, it is not so much *Meantime* as *Grown-Ups*. But if the virtues of faith and the willingness to carry on can be seen to be at work in *Grown-Ups*, Dick and Mandy are not strong on either conversation or laughter. This fact can help us to see that, more than anything else, it may be the energising presence of these two activities that makes these four films so upbeat, so positive, so radiant – that makes them, in a word, Leigh's happiest films.

There is something else that ought to be mentioned here too, the question of setting, which points to both a difference *and* another point of convergence between films like *The Awful Truth* and films like *Four Days in May*. Here is Cavell on the subject:

> In stressing the ascendancy of being together over doing something together, the problem of these narratives requires a setting ... in which the couple have the leisure to be together, to waste time together. A natural setting is accordingly one of luxury, or as [Northrop] Frye puts it concerning romances generally, a setting for snobs. At least the settings require central characters whose work can be postponed without fear of its loss, or in which the work is precisely the following of events to their conclusions (rather than the gridding of days into, say, the hours of nine to five), as, for example, the work of a newspaper reporter. (1981: 88–9)

Obviously none of these four films by Leigh features a luxurious setting, 'a setting for snobs'. But then, it is also true that, apart from Collette and Eugene in *Four Days in July*, Leigh's other couples do not spend anywhere near as much time together as Cavell's. On the other hand, they do spend a lot of time talking and laughing together: that is the main basis of the comparison. But what Leigh's films make us realise is that, given the couples' willingness and ability to find and then take advantage of time together, the setting can be fairly basic.

Far from being a setting for snobs, the house in which Eugene and Collette spend most of their time in *Four Days in July* was supposed to have been demolished years ago. And the reason we see them spending so much of their time together is that Eugene is crippled, a casualty of the Troubles (having been badly wounded by stray gunfire in the street, he has great difficulty moving around and is on crutches), and Collette is pregnant and expecting the arrival of their child any day. But the fact that the 'leisure' Eugene and Collette have 'to be together, to waste time together' (1981: 88–9) is enforced in no way detracts from their keen appreciation of it. And while they certainly exhibit (what Cavell calls) 'a capacity, say a thirst, for talk' (1981: 87–8), what is so wonderful about this film is the way it celebrates this capacity being exercised by others too; for example, the sequence near the middle that lasts for roughly thirty minutes in which Eugene and Collette are visited by two workmen. Brendan, who is a plumber and their neighbour from across the street, arrives first to fix their blocked-up toilet. While he is working on that, Dixie, the window-cleaner, turns up. Soon all four are conversing and exchanging jokes over tea and biscuits in a scene that seems at least worth considering in the context of Cavell's saying that he does not 'know any words on film that seem to satisfy better the thirst for conversation than those exhibited by these Hollywood talkies of the 1930s and 1940s' (ibid.). Furthermore, the playful nature of the talk might also remind us of some of the scenes in which the townsfolk entertain one another around the porch in Zora Neal Hurston's great novel *Their Eyes Were Watching God.*

In *High Hopes*, Cyril (Philip Davis) works as a motorbike despatch rider and we see Shirley (Ruth Sheen) planting trees (for the local council); in *Life is Sweet*, Andy (Jim Broadbent) is a chef in a large industrial kitchen and Wendy (Alison Steadman) works in a kiddies-wear shop. So here we clearly have very different situations to those obtaining in the Hollywood comedies. Yet even so, even if Leigh's two pairs hold down full-time jobs, they still manage to find time in which they can 'play games' and 'have fun together'. For one thing, it is a Saturday when *Life is Sweet* starts so we first see Wendy and Andy (and their two grown-up daughters) on their two days off from work. And indeed a lot of the humour is at Andy's expense, since he seems to be perpetually putting off doing the various jobs that need taking care of around the house. In *High Hopes*, on the other hand, we see more of Cyril at his work, but he and Shirley still manage to enjoy a fair bit of time together, partly perhaps because they do not yet have any children.

At the same time, it could be said that *High Hopes* has other priorities. In some ways, it *is* a political film, after all. As is *Four Days in July*.

An Affirmation of Ordinary Life in 'Four Days in July'

The opening shot of *Four Days in July* faces down a sun-lit, back alley way, which looks a hundred yards or so in length and is approximately twelve feet wide, with brick walls on either side. Three girls come from behind the camera, two of them running, the other on a bike. They are not in a great hurry but look relaxed and playful. They stop after about fifteen yards where the alley is crossed by a road and they wait until two army trucks pass by. They then cross the road and continue further down the alley. After they have gone about forty yards or so we see the same two trucks again crossing the alley, but this time going in the other direction and they are crossing in between us and the girls. All this time, the camera position has not moved. The trucks have come and gone in a matter of seconds, the children continue their play, two dogs pass by.

It is a brilliant opening, which immediately establishes both the political context (the reality of military occupation) and the fact that ordinary life goes on. The next shot shows, from a distance, the two trucks emerging out of the warren of criss-crossing narrow streets into more of an open space and this is accompanied by the commencement of the halting, and haunting, Celtic-inflected musical score. The third shot takes us actually inside one of trucks, allowing us to see the streets through the eyes of the soldiers within.

Letters on the screen then inform us that this is 'Tuesday 10th July' and we next see that the soldiers – who we learn a little later belong to the City of Belfast Battalion of the Ulster Defence Regiment – have set up a road-block and are interrogating the driver of a van, Edward McCoy (John Keegan), who turns out to be unintimidated and quite a joker. The soldier who interrogates him, in a fairly good-natured and respectful way, is Billy, who forms – along with his wife, Lorraine – one of the film's two couples. So in this opening section we see him doing his job, and what could easily have lent itself to melodrama is – thanks to Mr McCoy – treated more like the comedy of everyday life instead.

This is not the last we see of these soldiers. For one thing we see Billy throughout the film, but apart from this, we also from time to time hear helicopters nearby and see soldiers – holding rifles, moving along the street – through Collette's window. Leigh's intention, however, as the film's opening seconds demonstrate, is clearly to celebrate the fact that through all of this ordinary life persists. I take it that this is what he is getting at when he says that in making *Four Days in July* he 'simply wanted to respond to whatever [he] found in [his] investigation of Northern Ireland and all [he] wound up saying, really, was something very fundamental and basic about people' (Fuller 1995: xx). And my point here is that this constitutes one very powerful kind of political statement in itself.

John Hill's case against 'High Hopes': on Leigh's women and 'family values'

High Hopes makes a very different kind of political statement but, as Leigh reminds us, by the time he came to work on it the UK was 'eight years into Thatcherism' and he felt that he 'wanted to express the frustration and confusion that a lot of ordinary socialists like [him]self were feeling' (Fuller 1995: xx). He explains, furthermore, than any 'notion that there's a bias on [his] part in *High Hopes* and that, in some way, Cyril and Shirley are the goodies and Rupert and Laetitia and Valerie and Martin are the baddies is absolutely true' (Fuller 1995: xx).

What makes Cyril and Shirley 'the goodies' is that they embody the kind of caring attitude towards others that – for all its talk 'about "the caring society"' – Thatcherism is seen as attacking. And, as Leigh's quite uncharacteristic use of this sort of language ('goodies' and 'baddies') indicates, they do so in a film that asks to be viewed – to some degree, at least – as a kind of political cartoon, one in which it is OK not just to dislike but even to hate the villain (or 'baddies': the Booth-Braines,

Valerie and Martin all representing 'a particular kind of uncaringness' [Fuller 1995: xx]).

In his book on *British Cinema in the 1980s*, John Hill argues that the way in which *High Hopes* opposes 'Cyril and Shirley's ordinary sense of goodness and concern ... to the selfish temper of the times' makes it 'one of the few films of the period to attempt to give a positive embodiment to traditional socialist values. However, it is a portrait of "practical socialism"', Hill warns, 'that only goes so far' (1999: 196). Hill's critique comes in two parts.

In the first, Hill objects to such things as (a) the fact that Cyril 'isn't actually a member of a trade union' (ibid.); (b) the fact that 'while the film chides the lack of neighbourliness shown by the Booth-Braines towards Mrs Bender, there is no evidence of any "community" in the block of flats in which Cyril and Shirley live (where no neighbours are seen, or identified, at all)' (1999: 197); and (c) the fact that 'Cyril and Shirley would appear to lack any clear sense of connection or involvement with a more broadly based social or political community and tradition' (ibid.). In other words, he wants Cyril and Shirley to be different characters.

Though I am not persuaded by the second part of Hill's critique either, it is more interesting than the first part. It is summarised in the claim that if, as Cyril argues and as *High Hopes* shows, 'families are flawed, they seem, none the less, to be all that the characters have to hold on to, given that other forms of communality extending beyond the family, are either inadequate or non-existent' (1999: 196). The claim that this is the picture *High Hopes* presents us with seems to me certainly arguable and possibly true. It is just that, insofar as it is true, I take this to be a criticism not of the film but of the state of affairs that the film investigates.

But Hill has more to say on the subject than this and, considering my own argument, I need to confront his position in some detail. Here is the opening of his penultimate paragraph and the ending of his last paragraph:

> Cyril ... explains to Shirley how he feels 'cut off' and that he 'don't do nothing' except 'moaning'. The way out of this for him seems to be acceptance of fatherhood [...] In celebrating the virtues of the privatised family as a kind of escape route from political impotence and passivity, the film, for all its apparent 'socialism', appears to end up reinforcing the very scepticism about more collective (or 'socialist') forms of political action that was already such a feature of this era. (1999: 197, 198)

There is, in my view, no question of the film celebrating any form of 'privatisation' at all. But leaving this aside, Hill's mistake here is to assume that the film is celebrating the family as a 'way out' or an 'escape route'. Whereas the celebration is surely more in the spirit of 'At least this possibility still exists, at least there is still this to hold on to, or to try to make something of. It seems unlikely to be able to satisfy Cyril's yearning for greater connection and purpose but it is something.' As for the 'more collective (or "socialistic") forms of political action', it is not, after all, as if they could be *wished* into existence.

Notice that Hill begins by suggesting that Leigh's 'portrait of "practical socialism" … only goes so far' and ends by implying that it is not really socialist ('for all its *apparent* "socialism"') after all. In fact, he ends up by equating this film in particular and Leigh's work in general with Thatcherism. On what grounds? Here is the core of Hill's critique with the italicised words and phrases representing what seem to me the weak links in the argument:

> It is, *of course*, significant that all of the couples are childless in the film and, in the case of the Gore-Booths [the Boothe-Braine's?] and Burkes, this is *associated with* the 'sterility' of the values they represent. *In the same way,* Suzi's revelation that she had an abortion *seems*, for the film, to underscore the fruitlessness (and lack of 'humanity') of her politics. The decision of Cyril and Shirley to have a child, therefore, invests the end of the film with a degree of optimism (or 'high hopes') about the future. However, while the film may, in this way, succeed in expressing values of care and responsibility which cut across the prevailing ethos of Thatcherism, it only does so by partly reproducing conservative (and, indeed, Thatcherite) values regarding the family and women […]
>
> Indeed, *while it is a theme that is not made explicit* in High Hopes, the film *clearly links* Valerie's hysteria and unhappiness (as well as her sexual grotesquerie) with her apparent failure to become a mother. (1999: 197–8, my italics)

Quite simply, since by his own admission the 'theme' he is analysing is 'not made explicit', Hill needs to show how the associating and the linking he claims to find are done. But he still has not finished. Claiming that 'childless women recur in Leigh's films', Hill names three – Valerie (in *High Hopes*), Barbara (in *Meantime*) and Monica (in *Secrets and Lies*) – all of whom he seems to think are portrayed negatively (since two of them get drunk and all three are over-interested in home decoration). On this shaky basis, Hill levels the following charge:

> It is not just that consumerism and social climbing are associated with femininity … but that this is an apparently 'flawed' femininity, characterised by the failure to fulfil the 'proper' or, given the way that mother-to-be Shirley is associated with plants and cultivation, 'natural' female role of motherhood (and it is notable that none of the childless women in these films are offered any alternative kind of fulfilment in the form of work or activity outside of the home). As such, a film like *High Hopes* ends up conforming to a conservative ideology of 'familialism' that is little different from that associated with Thatcherism. (1999: 198)

First, Monica and Barbara are by no means simply negative portrayals. Yes, they do seem preoccupied (Monica especially) with home decoration and this does seem to be an attempt to compensate for the absence of some more vital interest in their lives. Leigh characteristically gives his attention to the kinds of people who get a bum deal in life. There is no implication in his films that anyone's femininity is 'flawed' and it seems ludicrous to suggest that it is the film's business to *offer* these characters alternative kinds of fulfilment. If it were indeed that easy, we would be living in a very different kind of world. As for 'consumerism', Leigh's films show little interest in it. Valerie definitely and Monica possibly are just about his only characters who might reasonably be said to be in its thrall. His films definitely do not associate 'social climbing' with either sex. And, finally, it is bizarre to assume that Leigh's female characters should be measured against Shirley whose interest in 'plants and cultivation' is distinctly atypical. Think of all his *other* strong female characters who work outside the home, from Sylvia in *Bleak Moments* to Hortense in *Secrets and Lies*, to the actresses in *Topsy-Turvy* up to Penny and Maureen in *All or Nothing*.

Why, then, has Hill produced an account of Leigh's female characters that is so clearly skewed and unjust? I suggest three possible reasons, the first of which is that Hill appears to have started off from the assumption that Leigh is a misogynist. Thus, near the beginning of his section on *High Hopes*, we find him claiming that, although 'it is often argued that the representation of misogyny in Leigh's films is not the same as its endorsement, the problem, in the case of *High Hopes*, is that Martin's disdain for Valerie is shared by the film and, thus, runs perilously close to colluding with his behaviour towards her' (1999: 194). This is carefully worded but it is footnoted by the following:

> Michael Coveney, Mike Leigh's biographer, draws attention to the repeated 'eruption of sadistic sexual violence' in Leigh's films but, in his enthusiasm to defend Leigh against all criticism, fails to weigh up how this impacts on the films themselves (irespective of Leigh's own personal attitudes).

This is grossly misleading and it has to be said that Coveney is partly, though not entirely, to blame. In the circumstances, I think we need to see the entire paragraph to which Hill is referring here. It begins with Coveney drawing our attention to a moment in *Abigail's Party*:

> Beverly asks Angela if he [her husband] is violent. 'No, he's not violent. Just a bit nasty. Like, the other day, he said to me, he'd like to sellotape my mouth. And that's not very nice, is it?' 'It certainly isn't, Ang!' It is clear that the eruption of sadistic sexual violence in *Naked* does not herald a new subject for Leigh. Traces of it are discernible in *Abigail's Party* as they are in *The Kiss of Death*, *Goose-Pimples*, *Smelling a Rat* and *Life is Sweet*. And those traces become heavily marked tracks in *Hard Labour*, *Ecstasy*, *Home Sweet Home* and *Meantime*. (1997: 118)

There is the clear implication, to begin with, that Coveney intends the verbal black humour he cites from *Abigail's Party* to count as an example of 'sadistic sexual violence'. Limiting myself only to the films he then goes on to mention, I can find no 'eruption' of any kind of sadistic violence in *The Kiss of Death* or in *Life is Sweet*. It is true that in the latter Nicola does have a masochistic scenario that she persuades her lover to participate in. But though it does involve his tying her up, it involves no violence. As for the 'heavily marked tracks' in *Hard Labour*, *Home Sweet Home* and *Meantime*, I can see not the slightest evidence of them in the last two, which only leaves what I referred to earlier as the marital rape in *Hard Labour*, which it is extremely difficult to imagine any spectator taking any pleasure in. Apart from this, the only other Leigh film that needs to be mentioned in this context is *Career Girls*, insofar as Annie confesses to having masochistic fantasies in it, fantasies that we do not, however, see being acted out. And that's it! This is what is supposed to justify Hill's telling us that 'Michael Coveney ... draws attention to the *repeated* "eruption of sadistic sexual violence" in Leigh's films but ... fails to weigh up how this impacts on the films themselves'. This strikes me as being unfounded insinuation of the worst sort.

I think the second reason Hill has produced such a skewed and unjust account of Leigh's female characters is that he has convinced himself that Leigh has it in for childless women. And here too he is able to take advantage of one of Coveney's comments on *Abigail's Party*. Having just noted that she 'is undoubtedly a monster', Coveney goes on to claim that 'the whole point about Beverly is that she is childless' (1997: 120). As Hill says, Coveney 'fails to consider the implications of this observation' (1999: 198). Yes, but for his part Hill fails to consider that Coveney's observation might be inacurate, that her being childless might not be – indeed, I am sure it is not – the 'whole point' that the play intends to make 'about Beverly'.

Finally, I suggest the third reason is that Hill appears to have fallen victim to right-wing propaganda, which famously claims that it alone speaks for/is concerned about 'family values'. Versions of the family long preceded 'Thatcherism' and, in all likelihood, they will long survive its demise.

In the face of this, it seems important to point out two things: (i) that it is possible to celebrate – as Leigh does in these three full-length films – a mother like Wendy (*Life is Sweet*) and two mothers-to-be like Collette (*Four Days in July*) and Shirley (*High Hopes*), all three of them strong women, without implying as a corollary that those women who do not or cannot have children are flawed in their femininity. And (ii) that it is possible to celebrate certain married couples and certain families without losing sight of the fact that there is of course another, darker side to marriage and the family, one that it seems more appropriate to lament than to celebrate. Thus, for example, after Graham Fuller has noted that several women in Leigh's films 'have loveless, sexless marriages – Beverly, Barbara, Valerie, Christine, Candice-Marie in *Nuts in May*' – Leigh responds as follows:

> Marriage is hard work and it doesn't hold up very easily for a lot of people. Some people marry for the wrong reasons in the first place or it happens for the right reasons and runs out of steam. I think I have dealt with it from various angles. (Fuller 1995: xxvi)

Leigh's celebration of and ambivalence about marriage and the family

As Andy Medhurst sees it, *High Hopes* is one of Leigh's weaker films because it falls

> prey to just the kind of sentimentality about class authenticity that he avoids
> elsewhere. Shirley and Cyril are such snuggly bunnies of socialistic concern,
> all baggy jumpers and shaggy hair, that the dice are irretrievably loaded from
> the start, and the treatment of Cyril's upwardly aspiring sister Valerie leaves
> a nasty taste in the mouth. (1993: 9)

I agree about the 'nasty taste' though I wonder if we could have an embodiment of
(Thatcherite) greed and selfishness that did not have it. Though I do not share it, I
can also understand Medhurst's reaction to Cyril and Shirley. Here is Pauline Kael
on the last two:

> As if to confound the viewer, scenes that our instincts tell us shouldn't work
> – the ones, for example, that show the sound, loving relationship between
> Cyril, the messenger, and his dark-eyed, dark-haired Shirley – are the bedrock
> of the movie … They're believable mates, even though the irony that the only
> true marriage is that of the unmarried pair can stick in your craw, along with
> their spontaneity, their unforced smiles, their open eyes turned to the future,
> and the pot smoking that marks them as good people. (1991: 88–9)

The reason our instincts tell us that the scenes in question *should not* work is that
they risk seeming sentimental. And no doubt we are right to be wary of this. But, on
the other hand, as Kael inadvertently demonstrates, it is possible to allow the need
for vigilance here to blind one to the true nature of what one is looking at. Cyril
and Shirley do dress like 'snuggly bunnies' – as, for that matter, do the irritating,
non-snuggly middle-class couple in *Nuts in May*. But in *High Hopes* neither Cyril
and Shirley's dress nor their pot smoking is intended to mark them as 'good people'.
What does that is the care and concern they show vis-à-vis Wayne at the beginning
and Cyril's mother at the end.

Unironical artistic representations of goodness are of course notoriously difficult
to achieve, much more difficult than representations of badness. But I would say
that in Collette and Eugene (of *Four Days in July*), in Cyril and Shirley (of *High
Hopes*), and in Wendy and Andy (of *Life is Sweet*) Leigh convincingly shows us
kinds of goodness and basic decency in action. As Carney sees it, the 'possibilities of
imaginative flexibility, relaxed intimacy and emotional responsiveness that are only
intermittently realised by Sylvia and Norman in *Bleak Moments*, Ann and Naseem in
Hard Labour, Dick and Mandy in *Grown-Ups*, Colin and Mark in *Meantime*, Carol,
Dawn, Len, and Mick in *Ecstasy* [one of Leigh's plays], and Eugene and Collette in
Four Days in July come to fruition in the interactions between Shirley and Cyril in
High Hopes and Wendy and Andy in [*Life is Sweet*]' (2000: 225). Except for the fact
that I see the possibilities Carney mentions come to fruition in Collette and Eugene

as well as in the two later couples, this seems to me extremely well put. Indeed, Carney's commentary on *Life is Sweet* is exceptionally good; particularly his sensitive analysis of the exchange Andy and Wendy have as they lie in bed and discuss his purchase of the rusty old caravan (see Leigh 1995c: 137–9). As Carney says, what we have here is 'a genuine "conversation" in the root sense of the word: a series of subtle "turnings" as Wendy and Andy keep moving from thought to thought, tone to tone, mood to mood, simultaneously expressing their own points of view and responding to the other's, in their comically stumbling, mismatched, mistimed way' (2000: 214; see too 275, n. 7).

On the other hand, although Carney has a point in saying that Wendy and Andy 'could almost be' Cyril and Shirley 'twenty years later in their relationship' (2000: 225), it seems more important to recognise how different they are. As Wendy is provoked into saying, when she finally tries to get her daughter Nicola to explain why she has given up, she and Andy decided to get married only after they had discovered that she was pregnant – pregnant, as it turned out, with twins, Nicola (Jane Horrocks) and Natalie (Claire Skinner). She was sixteen at the time, doing her A-levels, and Andy was seventeen, 'at catering college, and he was workin' in hotels at night, tryin' to get a bit extra' (Leigh 1995c: 172). So that (in Leigh's own words) whereas *High Hopes* 'focuses on the moral question that relates to having children, and the debate that surrounds that for a lot of people, and the tension between the rational and the emotional', *Life is Sweet* centres on 'a family that happened by accident, but who have gone through with it and have kept doing their best despite all their difficulties' (Fuller 1995: xxvii). In some ways, Cyril and Shirley seem more aware of what is going on in the world than Wendy and Andy. Cyril and Shirley may, for example, be politically confused but Wendy and Andy seem to lack any kind of political awareness at all. It is difficult to imagine *them* wanting to visit Marx's grave, or even knowing where to find it. And then there is the matter of Wendy's slightly irritating giggle, which as Leigh says, 'suggests she's a bit soppy' (Fuller 1995: xxxii), just as Andy's susceptibility to his friend Patsy's (Stephen Rea) influence suggests that he is a bit dopey. In fact, we could go so far as to say that Wendy and Andy *are* at times soppy and dopey.

At the same time, Wendy proudly and justly maintains that she and Andy are 'still out there, fightin'', that they have not 'given up' (Leigh 1995c: 171). But given up on what? On the pursuit of happiness. Wendy and Andy are both engaged in this pursuit. The film opens with Wendy leading a group of about twenty-five little girls in a Saturday morning dance class to the sound ('*cheerful, vulgar and sentimental*' [1995c: 100]) of a tape playing 'Happy Holidays'. When, in the late exchange we glanced at a moment ago, Wendy tells Nicola that Nicola has 'got no joy in [her] soul,' and Nicola asks how she knows, Wendy replies, ''Cos you're not 'appy, that's 'ow I know' (1995c: 170). When Nicola says that her mother has 'accepted Nat as a plumber,' though she 'didn't like that at first,' Wendy agrees that she 'didn't like it. But I can see now I was wrong, because she's happy' (1995c: 171–2). And *that*, Wendy goes on to tell Nicola, is all she wants for her:

I just want you to be happy, that's all, and you're not. I wouldn't care what bloomin' job you did, I wouldn't care 'ow scruffy you looked, as long as you were happy. (1995c: 172)

If this scene ends with mother and daughter both sobbing, it is immediately followed by a cut to Andy's industrial kitchen where we see him slip and break his ankle. But, seconds later, when (still tearful) Wendy receives the news on the phone, she bursts out laughing: 'I'm sorry, I know I shouldn't laugh, but...' (1995c: 174) But, in fact, as she has told Nicola only a few minutes earlier, this is how she and Andy get through life: by laughing. Which is what we see *him* doing when he arrives home with, as Wendy explains to Nicola, 'his tongue hangin' out,' expecting 'a bit of tea and sympathy' (1995c: 179). 'I'll tell you what, Andy,' she says when they are going to bed, 'Good job you're not a horse.' 'Why?' he asks. 'They'd 'ave shot you,' she tells him. At which point they both laugh and she gives him a painkiller.

We might usefully be reminded here of the moment in John Keats' famous 'Negative Capability' letter (21 December 1817) in which he tells his brothers that the men he has recently dined out with 'only served to convince [him], how superior humour is to wit in respect to enjoyment – These men say things which make one start, without making one feel' (1969: 308).

But the film does not end there. The key exchange between Wendy and Nicola followed on from the one in which Nicola's lover had made known his desire to have 'an intelligent conversation' with her.[3] When the mother–daughter exchange ends, Wendy says she hopes that Nicola will one day ask for help so that they can then 'start talkin'' (1995c: 173), and we realise that Wendy has been instinctively trying to create the conditions that will make that possible. The film ends with Natalie and Nicola talking together, in effect taking advantage of the opportunity their mother has created by engaging in the first real conversation they have had in the entire film. In the process, Natalie expresses solidarity with her twin sister, making it clear that, even if their parents do not know her sister is suffering from bulimia (not even at the end), she herself knows, so that at least Nicola now shares her secret with one other person, who is being sympathetic and supportive.

In one respect, the ending of *Life is Sweet* resembles the ending of *Meantime*, in which we see the two brothers – Colin and Mark – bonding. But, whereas in *Meantime*, the two brothers come together in opposition to their parents, in *Life is Sweet* we are made to see that Natalie's gesture is not only made on her own behalf but that it is also made on behalf of the family, just as Wendy's was earlier. There is a sense in which the ending of *Meantime* also anticipates the ending of *Four Days in July*, in that both endings focus on the significance of the naming process: in the latter, on the names that Collette and Lorraine are planning to give their newly-born children. Collette will call her daughter Mairead (the Irish name for Margaret) after her mother, Lorraine will call her son Billy – 'after his Daddy', she says in the film's eloquent last words. They are also troubling words insofar as they remind us, in the most understated way possible, of just how deeply entrenched the political conflict is.

Caught by 'The Short and Curlies'

The Short and Curlies (1987) is an eighteen-minute short that was made two years after *Four Days in July* and one year before *High Hopes*. It has four characters, three young adults – Joy (Sylvestra Le Touzel) who works in a chemist's, Clive (David Thewlis) and Charlene (Wendy Nottingham) – and Charlene's middle-aged mother Betty (Alison Steadman), who works as a hairdresser ('Cynthia's Hair Stylist'). The pace is rapid as the film moves quickly through (by my count) eighteen scenes. It begins with Clive entering the chemist's and asking Joy if she has something for a sore throat. It looks as if they have not met or set eyes on one another before. We then jump to Betty going 'the whole hog' with Joy's hair, cutting six inches off it. Then back to the chemist's, where we see that Clive has returned and is now clearly trying to chat Joy up. It was apparent on their first encounter that Clive's idea of conversation is to offer a seemingly endless series of jokes. So far, however, Joy has barely cracked a smile. But she does so when Clive notices her new hair-cut and compliments her on it. In the next (fourth) scene, we see him waiting for her after her work and then accompanying her home.

The rest of the film covers the various stages of their courtship, all of which are intercut with her frequent visits to the hairdresser, and it ends with Joy getting her hair done one last time, in preparation for her marriage to Clive.

Yet the tone of this beautiful little film is far from being unequivocally cele-bratory, for two main reasons: the first of which concerns the relationship between Clive and Joy. Coveney calls Clive 'another of Leigh's bad-joke merchants' (1997: 188). The problem is that, though his jokes are much better, his joke-telling often seems as compulsive as Harold's in *Home Sweet Home*. It is also often at Joy's expense. As, for example, when he tells her, after they are engaged, that 'My Dad says he did not know what happiness was until he married my mam ... and then it was too late.' Or again, moments later: 'I'm going to marry the most beautiful girl in the world ... I'll bring her around.' But perhaps more seriously, when in the next (eleventh) scene Joy is asked by Betty if she is courting, she says that she is and that the man in question is 'a very quiet type. He doesn't say much. He's serious.' If this is her ideal, Clive seems like the exact opposite. But if this does not augur too well, we also see moments of real tenderness between them. It is just that, on balance, what we see makes us apprehensive on their behalf. There are moments when both Clive and Joy seem trapped, caught – by the short and curlies, as it were – in a ritualistic progression that might end in happiness but that could just as easily produce misery. In short, this is a marriage that could easily go either way. Like most marriages, perhaps.

The other reason this film seems far from celebratory is the sad presence in it of Betty and Charlene. I think especially of the tenth scene, in which, as she looks at herself in the mirror, Betty tells her daughter she (Charlene) 'should have a boyfriend.' 'I don't want a boyfriend', says Charlene. Which leads to the following exchange:

Betty: Course you do. I know I do.

> (*At this point, the camera pulls back from the previous close-up on Betty's face so that we now see she is in bed.*)
>
> Man about the house. Didn't you talk to no boys tonight, Charlene? Didn't nobody ask you to dance? 'Cause you were a gorgeous little girl Charlene. You were a gorgeous baby and you're gorgeous now. I can't understand how they're not queuing up for you. 'Cause I know they were for me.
>
> Charlene: Yeah, look what happened to you.
>
> Betty: Your father was a gorgeous man, Charlene Flank. That was his mother turned him against me.

Betty has difficulty breathing and, as she speaks these words, we see her clearly struggling. At the same time, as we then cut to the next scene, in which she is again doing Joy's hair and telling her that she will 'be the belle of the ball tonight', we realise that Betty is still just as addicted to the dream of romance as she ever was. And the film ends with her chattering away to Joy about the latter's up-coming wedding, while her own daughter – whom we have only moments earlier discovered to be now visibly pregnant – sadly goes out of the salon on her own.

This resonates with Pauline Kael's reaction to the scene in *High Hopes* in which Mrs Bender has to explain to her next-door neighbour that she has lost her key:

> This passage combines cabaret humour (the unfeeling Laetitia) with kitchen-sink realism (the tired, confused mum), and even though the disparity between the two modes is funny I kept waiting for the modes to come together – for the old woman with her wandering mind to score off smug young Laetitia. A skit like this might be liberated if it were in a revue. The way Leigh uses it, it has a significance that curdles it. Almost everything in the movie that's jokey and distorted and grotesque plays off the 'reality' of the failing old woman's misery. (1991: 88)

What seems so good about this is the sharpness of Kael's perceptions and the honesty with which she records them. Yet, at the same time, if Leigh had allowed *this* old woman 'to score off smug young Laetitia' he might have created a lively effect but it would have been a lesser film as a result. Of course, we would prefer to forget Mrs Bender's 'misery' just as we would prefer – most of us, most of the time – to forget Charlene's and her mother's: the real is difficult to bear. But relief does eventually come for Mrs Bender, who becomes animated and (to use Kael's word) scores at *exactly* the right moment, the last moment of the film.

Mrs Bender and Gloria are eventually taken in and taken care of by the members of their own families. Taking care of their own is something that families sometimes manage to do. But what about Betty and her daughter (the soon-to-be unmarried-mother herself, Charlene)? The film proposes no answer to this question but ends by acknowledging the force of their sadness. Without partners, *this* mother and daughter seem incapable of achieving the happiness that we see a different mother (Cynthia) and her two daughters (Hortense and Roxanne) achieving at the end of the later *Secrets and Lies*. Nor does Betty seem anywhere near as interested in looking after Charlene as Maureen does with her pregnant daughter Donna in *All or Nothing*. Though it is easy to overlook, *The Short and Curlies* reminds us of the truth that in the pursuit of the dream of marital and familial happiness many casualties are left by the wayside.

PART THREE

The Films (II)
From *Naked* (1993) to *All or Nothing* (2002)

CHAPTER EIGHT

'Are you with me?': Leigh's 'Traumatising Seducer'

Socrates' fundamental question – how shall I live? – looks so innocent but is in fact traumatic. Socrates rips open the fabric of Athenian life and creates a gap which no one can fill, for as yet there is no established way of taking one's whole life into account in everything that one does. In Freudian terms, Socrates is an incarnation of the death drive: an aggressive puncture in the established modes of life and thought, an occasion for forming new ways of living and thinking.

The Athenians react to this trauma by trying to kill it off ... Socrates *is* a traumatising seducer: he is guilty of the repetitive introjection into life of a message that life cannot contain.

– Jonathan Lear (2000: 102)

After making the claim noted in the last chapter – that *High Hopes* (1988) and *Life is Sweet* (1990) both display 'the positive spirit in women who have faith and who have trust, and who inculcate that in other people' – Leigh immediately went on to say this:

In discussing *Life is Sweet*, the character that tends to be neglected the most is Natalie, the plumber. In her own quiet way, she's as much a nonconformist as Nicola. The difference is that the nature of her nonconformity doesn't preclude getting on with living and working and in some way fulfilling herself, within limited parameters ... what is important to me about her is that she is out there, rolling up her sleeves, getting on with it. (Fuller 1995: xxxi)

Judging by the evidence of the films he made before *Naked*, this gives us a fairly clear idea of what Leigh values: faith, trust, a positive spirit and 'getting on with living and working'. In the light of which we ought not to be too surprised to find that when he offers to tell us what his films are actually about – 'things like work, surviving, having an aged parent or whether it's a good idea to have kids' (1995: xxi) – it is 'work' that heads the list. This is more or less what one might expect of the kind of 'ordinary socialist' (1995: xx) Leigh describes himself as being, of someone who claims that his films 'are primarily motivated by a sense of how we should behave toward each other in terms of sharing and giving [and] 'by a compassion for people' (1995: xl).

On the other hand, in the same interview Leigh can be found expressing sympathy for 'the anarchist' (1995: xxxi) and claiming that if, on the one hand, he has not 'made a film, including *Naked*, that doesn't include moments of warmth and compassion and sharing and giving', on the other, he also has not 'made a film that does not include plenty of the opposite' (1995: xxxiii). Which perhaps partially explains why, 'after completing several films from a more positive perspective', he felt that 'it was time to [make *Naked*]', a film with 'a more anarchist view of the world and maybe deep down, along with layers of 1960s conditioning, one [he] feel[s] with more conviction' (Movshovitz 2000: 64), one that expresses his 'deepest feelings' (Fuller 1995: xl).

Yet the fact remains that this does not come close to preparing us for the sheer explosive force of *Naked*, all of which resides in the powerful way in which it relentlessly calls into question some of Leigh's own basic values, values that we will find him reaffirming in *Secrets and Lies*, the film he made next. In my view, these are both great films, each of which stands on its own but is even more impressive when considered alongside the other.

One further proviso. Just how powerful an achievement *Naked* actually is is only likely to become fully clear to someone who takes the opportunity provided by the published screenplay to study the dialogue with the kind of close attention it deserves. This does not mean that the experience of reading the screenplay can *substitute* for the experience of being exposed to the film: it obviously cannot. It simply means that this film's dialogue deserves the kind of scrutiny that used to be (and sometimes still is) given to literary texts, to a play by Shakespeare or Beckett, for example – the main difference being that in this case constant reference to the experience of seeing the film is absolutely essential, whereas in the case of any theatrical piece, reference to any particular performance of it is optional. In short, it means that *Naked*'s dialogue is, by any standards, exceptionally rich.[1] As can be seen, for example, in the following excerpt:

Johnny:	So ... I dunno ... Would you describe yourself as a ... happy little person?
Sophie:	Yeah ... I'm the life and soul.
Johnny:	Have you ever thought, right ... I mean, you don't know, but you might already 'ave had the happiest moment in your whole fuckin' life, and all you've got to look forward to is sickness and purgatory?
Sophie:	Oh, shit! Well ... I just live from day to day, meself. (*She takes back the joint.*)
Johnny:	I tend to skip a day now and again – you know what I mean? I used to be a werewolf, but I'm all right NOW!!
Sophie:	Oh, fuckin' 'ell!! I bet they're 'appy, eh? All they gotta do is sit round, howlin' at the moon.
Johnny:	It's better than standin' on the cheesy fuckin' thing. Know what I mean? I mean, tossin' all these satellites and shuttles out into the cosmos – what do they think they're gonna find up there that they can't find down 'ere? They think if they piss high enough, they're gonna come across the monkey with the beard and the crap ideas, and it's like, 'Oh, there you are, Captain! I mean ... are you busy, because I've got a few fundamental questions for you!' Are you with me? (Leigh 1995b: 9)

The topic being discussed is happiness and, if Johnny (David Thewlis) opens on an unpromising note of slight condescension, Sophie (Katrin Cartlidge) immediately disarms him ('I'm the life and soul'). She then neatly deflects his mock-gloomy follow-up suggestion that perhaps she has already experienced the happiest moment of her life, by claiming that she 'just live[s] from day to day', and this generates one of the happiest *exchanges* – of spontaneous wit and collaborative invention – in the film. The questions 'you know what I mean?' and 'are you with me?' recur throughout *Naked*, and the exhilaratingly rapid and delightful associations we witness Johnny and Sophie both making here are made possible by the fact that Sophie *does* know what he means, that she demonstrably *is* with him.

As Graham Fuller pointed out, in his interview with Leigh, the latter is 'economical with camera movements in [his] films'. In response to this, Leigh says that, though he has 'always been resistant to doing so if it wasn't necessary', and though his 'instinct is for the camera to be unobtrusive', he has nevertheless 'started to *track* more recently' (Fuller 1995: xxvii, my italics). Leigh then gives three examples from *High Hopes* and *Life is Sweet*. But it seems that none of these is of any great significance and that his first truly significant uses of tracking shots occur in *Naked*, starting with the highly dramatic opening shot, in which a hand-held camera rushes us up a dark alley to witness the last seconds of a '*rough fuck [that is taking place] under a streetlamp*' (Leigh 1995b: 5). Not that this and the other tracking shots in it are the only striking – or obtrusive – features of the film's *mise-*

en-scène. Two other features are just as important – the lighting and the musical score.

Much of the film takes place at night and it often has the look of a *film noir*. Asked by Fuller how he managed to get the 'coarse quality' of the image, Leigh responded as follows:

> *Naked* was shot using the bleach bypass process; it's mostly been used for period films in the past. You miss out the bleaching in the lab and it gives you a saturated quality. Tarkovsky used it a lot, Michael Radford used it on *1984* (1984), and Terence Davies on *The Long Day Closes* (1992). It takes much longer to light, but it paid off, all credit to Dick Pope [Leigh's cinematographer]. (Fuller 1995: xxxix)

Also contributing to the film's darkness is the fact that (as Coveney nicely puts it) Johnny is throughout 'wrapped like Hamlet in a black and inky coat (and one that has seen better days)' and Sophie is dressed – I would say for a carnival – as a 'punky Goth in black leather' (1997: 21). As for the music, it is by Andrew Dickson, who also produced the music for *High Hopes* and for *Meantime*. But *Naked* is the first (and so far the only) film in which the music is used to generate excitement and suspense.

The first thing we see is Johnny, the protagonist, shot from behind, having sex with a woman, standing up against a wall in a dark alley, in Manchester. Judging by the soundtrack, the sex seems consensual at first but then the woman protests and shouts out – Johnny is hurting her, in the words of the stage directions he is '*pushing her head back, his hand under her chin*' (Leigh 1995b: 5). The next thing that happens is that Johnny is running off and we are accompanying him as the woman is promising to tell her Bernard about him ('You're fuckin' dead!' [ibid.]). We then see Johnny run into his house and almost immediately run out again with a canvas shoulder-bag. As he runs through the streets, he notices a car with its boot open and its ignition keys in the boot-lock. So he takes it, drives away and before long we see him on a motorway, where he spends most of the night driving.

In the Fuller interview, Leigh claims that '*Naked* begins by showing Johnny in the most negative light possible, so that you then have to make a journey from there and confront yourself with the fact that you may actually find him charismatic, as well as loathing him' (1995: xxxii.) I think this is accurate. There are other moments later on when Johnny appears in a negative light but the opening is especially disturbing. Mainly because of two things: (i) the fact that what Johnny does to the woman in the street is not entirely clear – all that is clear is that it obviously causes her pain; (ii) the way in which we get caught up in Johnny's haste – first, as we see through the lens of a hand-held camera rushing along beside him and then, as we find ourselves trapped in the position of back-seat passengers in the stolen car – all to the accompaniment of a suspense-engendering musical score. We are plunged, in other words, right into a tension-building and guilt-inducing situation, as we find ourselves having to accompany – and therefore virtually having also to identify with – a man whom we have just seen hurting a woman, a man who has more or less deliberately got himself into trouble and who seems to be heading for more trouble.

Arriving in London the next morning, Johnny dumps the stolen car and walks to the address of his ex-girlfriend Louise, who is house-sharing with Sandra and Sophie. When Johnny turns up no-one is in: Louise is away at work, Sandra is on holiday in Zimbabwe, and Sophie is out somewhere. Sophie gets back first, discovers Johnny – whom she has never met before – sitting on the doorstep, and invites him in for a cup of tea. Louise does not return from work until the evening, which means that Johnny and Sophie spend the day together – spend it, it would seem (from the little we glimpse), joking and flirting and smoking a joint or two. They can do this because – unlike Louise, who has (in Johnny's mocking words) got herself 'a posh job in the big "shitty"' – they are both 'on the fuckin' dole'. Having invaded her space and then spent the day flirting with one of her house-mates, Johnny does not even try to appear glad to see Louise when she turns up: instead, he is openly rude and sarcastic to her.

So how are we to understand Johnny's behaviour? We are obviously not going to get very far with the film until we arrive at a satisfactory answer to this question. It is not an easy question to answer and it is surely impossible to answer it on first viewing, if only because Johnny is constantly surprising us.

Unemployed negativity

What will 'unemployed negativity' *become*, if it's true it becomes *something*? I keep track of it in the forms it creates, not first in myself but in others.
                                                    – Georges Bataille (1988: 124)

Critics have already noted echoes of Renoir's *Boudu Sauvé des Eaux* in Leigh's film. While I agree that there are indeed resemblances, my first suggestion is that it is more important to see *Naked* as belonging to the more literary genre of the Saturnalian dialogue. More specifically, I think it should be seen as extending what Michael André Bernstein has identified as a 'negative and bitter strand at the core of the Saturnalia itself' (1992: 17).[2] Though he traces this strand back as far as such classical satires as Horace's Seventh and the works of Rabelais, Bernstein is particularly interested in the emergence of 'the Abject Hero' whom he considers 'essentially modern', making 'his first full appearance in [Diderot's] *Le Neveu de Rameau*' (1992: 18). Bernstein explains that 'the Abject Hero seeks to exploit … a double authority deriving from a double ancestry. The first is the freedom of the King's fool … The second role model is the archetypal "wild man from the desert" whose imprecations and prophecies proved true when all the philosophies professed by the officially sanctioned sages were revealed as hollow'. The Abject Hero developed, in other words, out of the 'licensed clown' and 'the holy fool of religious parables' (1992: 30). It is suggested, then, that Johnny should be seen as the latest in an impressive line of Abject Heroes and that *Naked* reinvigorates a tradition that

Bernstein himself thinks has grown hopelessly corrupt and that is indeed in some ways problematical; not least, for example, in its recurrent misogyny. Consider Wayne Booth's reassessment of Rabelais' Saturnalia in the light of the feminist challenge, especially his comments on the episode featuring 'the trick Panurge plays upon the Lady of Paris', his sprinkling 'her gown with the ground-up pieces of the genitals of a bitch in heat' (1988: 400). Consider too the Underground Man's cruel and humiliating treatment of Liza, the young prostitute, in Dostoevsky's novella.

A second suggestion concerns something Johnny says to Sandra about Sophie near the end of the film:

> She's got this kind of, er, irritatin' proclivity for negation – I suppose she thinks it's progressive or somethin'. (Leigh 1995b: 94)

I think that we will be better able to understand Johnny's behaviour – and therefore to grasp what *Naked* has to offer us – once we recognise that, much more even than Sophie, Johnny himself has a marked 'proclivity for negation'. And, however unlikely it may at first appear, I suggest that this proclivity of his can usefully be seen in the light of some of the things the French writer Georges Bataille had to say in a letter he wrote in 1937 to Alexander Kojève.

Kojève is now best known for having introduced Bataille's generation of French intellectuals to the philosophy of Hegel and to the (counter intuitive) Hegelian argument according to which history has come to an end. I am *not* suggesting that either Leigh or Thewlis had any of these figures in mind. It has to be admitted, furthermore, that *Johnny's* references to the end – 'The end of the world is nigh, Bri. The game is up!' – are not to the end of history (in the Kojève-Hegelian sense of this phrase) but to the end of the world, and they are allusions to the biblical notion of Apocalypse. But, in any case, Johnny's behaviour begins to make much more sense when seen in the context of the terms Bataille provides in the following excerpt from his letter to Kojève:

> I admit – as a likely assumption – that as of now, history's finished (except for the wrap-up) ... The experiences I've lived through and been so concerned about have led me to think there is nothing more for me 'to do'...
>
> If action ('doing') is (as Hegel says) negativity, then there is still the problem of knowing whether the negativity of someone who 'doesn't have anything more to do' disappears or remains in a state of 'unemployed negativity'. As for me, I can only decide in one way, since I am exactly this 'unemployed negativity' (I couldn't define myself with more clarity). (1988: 123)

Having, in other words, been persuaded by the argument that History has come to an end, Bataille has come to the conclusion that there is no longer anything worthwhile for him 'to do', which presumably means that he thinks none of the available forms of work are worth doing. It is easy to see why some might find this highly offensive, the kind of reflection that could only come from someone who is at least relatively privileged and well-off. Try reading it out to those who are desperately looking for a job – to the young heroine of the Dardenne Brothers' *Rosetta* (1999) for example. But, on the other hand, if we allow no one to raise the kind of questions Bataille is raising here, then we effectively tighten the hold that the system we are all caught up in has over us. And it seems to me that what Leigh has done in *Naked* – having in his earlier film *Meantime* (1983) sensitively explored the demoralising effects of unemployment – is create in Johnny, who is of course something of an autodidact, a character who can raise these questions in such a way as to force us to consider them.

Seen in this perspective, then, what the film's opening scenes show is Johnny moving from one state (of employed negativity) to another (that of unemployed negativity). If *employed* negativity is the kind that finds expression in action or doing (like labour or work-in-general, for example, or, in Johnny's case, theft – at the end of the film as well as at the beginning), then *un*employed negativity is the kind whose main outlet – at least, where Johnny and Bataille are concerned – is language. And whether or not he would share Bataille's preference for the former (if it were available) – Bataille explaining that, in *his* case, his own negativity 'gave up being employed only when it couldn't any longer be employed: it's the negativity of a man who has nothing more to do, not of a man who prefers speaking' (1988: 124) – Johnny also seems to be convinced that it is *not* available; that, like Bataille's, his negativity can no longer be employed either, even if he wanted to be. Like it or not, it would seem that speech is all that is left.

At the outset, Johnny is, as we have noted, literally unemployed (on the dole). But what is more important is that he seems to share Bataille's feeling that there is nothing more for him 'to do' either – in the sense, that is to say, of meaningful and productive work, a job worth doing and not merely as a way of earning one's living. Except, in Johnny's case, for one thing, which is the main thing we see him doing throughout the film: attempting to engage others in dialogue and then challenging them – most of them, at any rate – to provide justifications for what *they* have decided 'to do', for the ways in which they spend their time.

If the reference to a 'proclivity for negation' provides us with one hint as to how we might most profitably understand *Naked*, the film offers us other useful suggestions of particularly rewarding ways in too: for example, Brian (Peter Wight), the night watchman's parting words to Johnny – 'Don't ... waste ... your life' – and Johnny's ironical but also affectionate description of the homeless Scotsman, Archie – 'He's a wonderful exponent of the Socratic debate'. From one commonsensical – basically utilitarian – point of view, Johnny is, of course, precisely, wasting his life. But from another point of view, which we are invited to share while watching *Naked* (and drop or suspend while watching *Secrets and Lies*), he is not wasting his life at all, but rather spending his time in the most profitable way possible. He is trying to draw people into a kind (often, admittedly, an initially-difficult-to-recognise kind) of 'Socratic debate' that is clearly designed to get them to question their basic assumptions – with a view to possibly transforming their lives. Like Diderot's

Rameau, in other words, Johnny appropriates the Socratic role of the 'quirky gadfly, needling a pompous or rigid opponent' (1992: 67). Though he certainly does not say so explicitly, what Johnny is effectively urging his interlocutors to do (at least those of them who seem capable of hearing what he has to say) is to start attending to what is most important in life – in other words, to start taking care of themselves. And this is precisely what Socrates was after, a point made especially clearly in Pierre Hadot's *Philosophy as a Way of Life*. To put it simply, from this point of view, philosophy is a form of therapy for the soul. Hence, the appropriateness of the fact that the first poster the poster-sticking man puts up is for 'THERAPY?'

I disagree, therefore, with the view that 'Johnny doesn't use his intellect to engage with other people; [that] he uses it as a buffer to his own near-psychotic condition and as a weapon of subordination, just as Hamlet uses his own wit as a stalking horse under whose cover he shoots at others (that's everyone) less witty than himself' (Coveney 1997: 28). If, when Johnny and Louise (Lesley Sharp) meet up again, at the beginning of the film, he is very rude to her, it is because she is refusing, at this point to engage with *him* – at least on the unconventional terms he proposes. As we can see, for example, in the following:

Johnny:	So how's, um … work?
Louise:	It's all right.
Johnny:	It's all right.
Louise:	Yeah.
Johnny:	What did you hope it would be?
	(*Pause. Louise exhales some cigarette smoke.*)
	I'm sorry – did you [*now addressing Sophie*] get that? It's everything she hoped it would be, but she doesn't fuckin' know what she hoped it would be! (1995b: 12)

And it seems that, on this occasion, at least, his rudeness is intended not to keep her at a distance but to provoke her into a reaction that is more than merely rote and non-committal.

If so, it obviously fails. Johnny had more luck in the exchange (on happiness) with Sophie, in which we see him doing what he loves to do best – putting things into question – and Sophie entering right into the good-natured spirit of it. Not, as we have already seen, that Johnny is always good-natured. Far from it. But it may be that he is *more* good-natured than would seem – in view of his undeniably nasty outbursts elsewhere – to be possible. Consider, for example, the late exchange with Sandra (Claire Skinner) that follows Johnny's asking her – while she is reversing a decorative fire-screen, which has been facing the wall – what would happen if, at birth, the umbilical cord was never cut:

Sandra:	Why do you feel the need … to take the piss?
Johnny:	I'm not takin' the piss. It's nice that [*the firescreen*] – where's it from?

Sandra:	I don't know, it's something my dad…
	(*They look at it.*)
Johnny:	Now you see, Sophie just turned that to the wall. She's got this kind of, er, irritatin' proclivity for negation – I suppose she thinks it's progressive or somethin'.
Sandra:	What is your problem?
Johnny:	Nothing. What's your problem?
Sandra:	All these silly questions and…
Johnny:	Well, look, I've never met a nurse before, and I'm just interested in, er … well, in life. I mean, d'you think it's worth savin'? (1995b: 93–4)

In addition to his good humour, this reveals two other things: (i) the extent to which Johnny is naturally curious about the life around him; and (ii) the fact that, though they are often couched in humour, the questions he poses are invariably (to use his own word) 'fundamental' ones, and not at all 'silly'; for example the last question (as to whether or not life may be 'worth savin'') but also the earlier one concerning the umbilical cord – in view of the references Johnny elsewhere makes to his mother, this question also seems to be seriously intended.

It seems possible, incidentally, that if Johnny is a bit gentler in his dealings with Sandra than with almost anyone else he meets, this might be because her job is one he actually has some respect for. We can perhaps detect a note of slight regret when, as he is looking through a large anatomy volume much earlier in Sandra's bedroom, he tells Sophie that he 'could've been a doctor'. And, the subsequent exchange can be seen to constitute a significant turning point, at least for Sophie:

Sophie:	D'you wanna examine me?
Johnny:	You don't believe me, do you?
Sophie:	I believe everthink you say.
Johnny:	I've got A-level Psychology.
Sophie:	You 'aven't!
Johnny:	'Resolve is never stronger than in the morning after the night it was never weaker.' What d'you think of that?
Sophie:	It's a load of bollocks. (*She giggles.*)
Johnny:	I thought of that. D'you not agree with it?
Sophie:	Dunno…
Johnny:	Yeah, well, that's 'cos you weren't fuckin' listening, were you? (*Sophie sits up.*)
Sophie:	What's this? A test or somethin'?
	(*She fondles Johnny's hair. They kiss, gently.*) (1995b: 22–3)

In retrospect, we can see that this *was* indeed a kind of test – not the kind you consciously set for someone, but the kind we sometimes find ourselves taking anyway – and that Sophie failed it. Johnny was not asking her – nor does he ask anyone else – to believe everything he says. What he wants from others is something he is prepared to give in return: the willingness to listen, to think for oneself, and to carry the thought forward. As opposed, for example, to either the total compliance that Sophie quickly proceeds to offer him or the attitude he complains of in his later encounter with the poster man – a determination to 'blank it all out' – and that Louise seems to be exhibiting on the second evening when she insists on watching television and refuses (for perfectly understandable reasons) to pay any attention to him.

Not surprisingly, however, it is precisely here that Johnny decides to leave the house, and, when he returns, he only does so – two nights later – out of necessity, after he has been badly beaten up and is in serious need of help.

Onto the streets

> He [Socrates] was a street person.
> – Hadot (1995b: 152)

During this vitally important sequence we see Johnny on and off – and largely at the mercy of – the streets. He spends the first night out with a young Scots couple, Archie (Ewen Bremner) and Maggie (Susan Vidler). He first notices Archie, who has lost Maggie and is calling out her name. Johnny asks Archie if he is 'lookin' for somebody?' to which Archie's response is first the exclamation 'Fuck off, cunt!' and then, moments later, a request for a cigarette. Clearly more amused and intrigued by Archie's roughness than bothered by it, Johnny engages the young man in conversation and soon learns that he has cracked his father 'on the nut wi' a poker' and is therefore 'on the run' – an admission that prompts Johnny to confess he is on the run too.

Gradually we realise that Johnny has befriended Archie, whom he eventually persuades to ''ave a little wander round and go look for the wee lassie' while he, Johnny, waits where he is – and 'if she turns up, I'll keep 'er 'ere till you get back'. When she does turn up, Johnny has difficulty getting her to understand that he has been in touch with Archie and again, he is as undaunted – indeed, as amused – by her response to his invitation for her to come and sit with him, as he was earlier by Archie's:

Maggie: Fuck off, you dirty cunt!
         (*She walks away.*)
Johnny: (*Laughing*) Yeah, well, I know I've not 'ad a bath for a good
         few seasons, but there's no need to 'urt my feelin's. 'E'll be
         back in a minute!
         (*Maggie turns around.*) (Leigh 1995b: 32)

In this way, Johnny starts to befriend her too, learns that she has spent the previous night sleeping in the park, is clearly concerned that that must have been cold, and admits that on this particular night he too plans to sleep 'wherever I drop'. A bit later Archie appears and we understand that – without his taking any credit for it – Johnny has helped make it possible for them to find one another again. And though the language they use with one another – 'Archie: Where the fuck 'a you been?/Maggie: Where the fuck 'a you been?' – is just as violent and obscene as the language they use with others, it seems obvious that, in their own determinedly unsentimental way (Maggie [to Archie]: 'Fuck off! Fuckin' leave us alone!/Archie [to Maggie]: 'Kick your fuckin' cunt… [*They disappear into the darkness*]' [1995b: 35]), they are lovers. A bit like Punch and Judy, or – to mention two comedians Johnny later confesses to liking ('although apparently,' he tells the poster man, 'they didn't get on in real life, you know – another illusion shattered') – Laurel and Hardy. Or again, like two characters out of Samuel Beckett ('Nothing to be done' being the relevant-seeming opening line of *Waiting for Godot*).

In any case, like Johnny himself, these two tramp-like figures are unemployed, homeless and on the run. But whereas he is exceptionally quick-witted, they appear to be mentally impaired and are barely articulate. When Johnny meets up with them, one after the other, there is only one thing they are interested in 'doing': finding one another. Except, of course, that, strictly speaking, from an Hegelian point of view, their desperate attempt to find one another does not really involve any 'doing' at all. Nor – or so Johnny seems to feel – does it require any justification. Hence, perhaps, his willingness to go out of his way to help them.

We jump next to the following night when we see Johnny '*huddled in the doorway of a modern office block*' and '*reading his pocket Bible*' (1995b: 37). A security guard (Peter Wight) comes out to investigate – or, perhaps, out of simple curiosity, just to look Johnny over. At any rate, instead of doing what Johnny half-expects him to do – either asking him to move on or 'stick[ing] the boot in' – Brian, the guard, surprises Johnny by asking if he does not have anywhere to go. Johnny replies that he has 'an infinite number of fuckin' places to go. The problem is, where you stay. Are you,' he then wants to know, 'with me?' And, again to his surprise, Brian *is* with him: 'Indeed, yes.' So that, moments later, after he has returned inside to get on with his work, he is out again, this time Johnny is sure, to get him to leave ('Yeah, all right, pal. I appreciate you've got a job to do, an' it's MOVE ON! MOVE ON! MOVE ON! But it's fuckin' freezin' out there, an' I was a Caesarian.'); instead of which Brian invites him in out of the cold.

In Brian, Johnny has finally met someone who, if not exactly his match, at least shares his interest in reflecting on and arguing about 'fundamental questions'. And since for Johnny, as we have already seen, the *most* fundamental is the question as to what, if anything, at the end of time, is still worth 'doing', it does not take long for him to announce that Brian has 'succeeded in convincin' [him] that [he] do[es] 'ave the most tedious fuckin' job in England'. At first, Brian agrees ('Yes! It is a boring job! Bloody boring, actually') but he then has second thoughts and starts to mount a defence. He claims that Johnny can only see the 'present', the 'tedious here and now'. What Johnny does not realise is that the job secures Brian's future, which means that 'it's not a boring job' after all.

Poor Brian has just given Johnny exactly the sort of opportunity he loves: first to point out that 'there's nothing wrong with the present' – except for the fact that 'the bastard doesn't exist'; and secondly to argue, with reference to the future, that Brian does not 'even 'ave a fuckin' future. I don't 'ave a future. Nobody 'as a future. The party's over'. But, however much he likes an intellectual contest (and also, it has to be admitted, however much he likes – in unsocratic fashion – to show his intellect off), Johnny never loses sight of the fact that his self-imposed task is not simply to win arguments: it is to strip his interlocutors of their illusions and false hopes, thereby helping them to confront – by making it more difficult for them to avoid – the real.[3] Thus, after arguing that it is a mistake to place any hope in God – 'that God is a hateful God' so 'there's no hope [to be found there]' – Johnny notices that Brian has got into the habit of watching a woman (Deborah Maclaren) who dances alone every night in a lighted apartment across the street. In response to Johnny's questioning, Brian admits that he has once seen her naked, and he wonders aloud 'what's her game, taunting people in the middle of the night, eh?' When Johnny suggests that she 'probably gets a kick out of it. Like you get a kick out o' watchin' 'er,' Brian denies doing any 'such thing'. The clear implication is that Brian is deluding himself about this and so – no matter how harmless such a delusion might seem to be – Johnny's next step is to take it upon himself to expose it.

He crosses the street, knocks on the woman's door and manages to charm his way inside and up to her room. From Brian's vantage-point across the street, she had seemed (in Johnny's words) a 'good-lookin' young girl' and the following morning, when Johnny and Brian discuss what happened (or did not happen) over breakfast in the nearby Jubilee Café, Brian cannot believe what Johnny has to report, which is that she is actually older than he is. Then, as if to demonstrate that he still has one resource or dream left intact, Brian shows Johnny a photograph of a cottage in Ireland by the sea where he's 'gonna live'. And it is immediately after Johnny has pronounced his uncompromisingly cruel and heartless verdict – 'Fuckin' shit-hole, innit?' – that Brian utters his last words to him, urging or warning him not to waste his life.

When Brian moves on, Johnny turns his attention to the waitress (Gina McKee) who has served Brian breakfast. And later that day, he charms his way into *her* place. Unfortunately for him, however, just when he seems assured of a room for the night, she throws him out – even though (in his own words) 'it's like a fuckin' Eskimo's grave out there'. And so later that night, we once again find him '*sitting, huddled in a doorway*' (1995b: 71).

But he is not alone for long: a young man (Darren Tunstall) turns up and starts to put up a large poster. As we might expect by now, Johnny's interest is instantly aroused. He first tries a joke ('Is this a stick-up?') and then asks if this is the man's 'job, or a nice little hobby [he's] got for [him]self?' The next thing we know Johnny is enjoying a lift in the man's van and is asking the driver how much he earns 'for doin' this' – 'I mean, is the pay as substantial as say, er, the wages of sin? You know what I mean? Are you with me?' Though the poster man says, on the one hand, that what he earns is 'none of [Johnny's] fuckin' business', on the other, he does give Johnny a lift and, when they arrive at the next '*illicit billboard site*', he also allows him to "ave a go' at putting up a poster himself. So, on one level, at least, he might be said to be 'with' Johnny. But we have seen that Johnny does not usually make it easy for his interlocutors, and he soon manages not only to deliberately make a mess of the poster he had asked to put up, but also to get heavily sarcastic ('does it take like thousands of years of like state-subsidised government training to do this clobber, yeah? ... It's a wonderful career opportunity for me'). Yet the poster man ignores the sarcasm, tells Johnny to get out of the way and continues his work. This leaves both of them facing the wall but Johnny with nothing to do and so he improvises a brilliant free-associational monologue on walls ('the Great Wall of China, and, and, the Wall of Jericho, and the Berlin Wall, and the Wailin' Wall'), in the midst of which he vigorously head-butts the wall in front of him.[4] At which point, noticing that the poster man has been hanging up a number of 'Cancelled' signs, Johnny turns to a more direct form of attack:

> Johnny: What are you doin'? Cancel everything. In the beginnin' was the Word, and the word was 'CANCELLED'. D'you get like satisfaction out of this? D'you think you're makin' a contribution? You're like sort of publicly promulgatin' vacuities? Are you with me?
> (*The Man walks off briskly.*) (1995b: 73)

Faced with the inescapable fact that the poster man is now definitely *not* 'with' him, Johnny, still refusing to give up, follows him to his van and practically invites the beating up he finally receives:

> Johnny: Oh, that's it! Blank it all out! Blank it all out till you just atrophy and die of fuckin' indifference!
> (*The man is closing his back doors.*)
> Can I show you somethin', pal? You see that at the top of your legs? That's your arse and that's your fuckin' elbow! D'you wanna write it down, or s-
> (*The Man assaults Johnny. He knees him in the crutch and knocks him down. Then he kicks his arse very hard.*) (1995b: 74)

If ever anyone asked for it...

Yet what perseverance! Of course, this could be read simply as a prime example of just how self-destructive Johnny can be, as a case of his being on auto-pilot, unable to control himself. But without denying the element of truth in this, I would say that it should also be interpreted as further evidence of the fact that, in his own often perverse-seeming way, Johnny *cares*, cares about the people he comes into contact with, and is doing his best to wake them up, to prevent them from 'just atrophy[ing] and [dying] of fuckin' indifference.'

But does this apply to the women Johnny meets as much as it does to the men? Or does he maintain a double standard? One thing is certain: Johnny's treatment of women deserves to be examined separately. Let us take his relationship with Sophie first. As we have already seen, it starts off promisingly and continues that way through the first bout of vigorous love-making. The description of the action that Leigh is careful to provide in the screenplay seems to me accurate and reliable. The love-making begins on the sofa ('*They kiss passionately, with a hint of sexual aggression, which is mutual, though initiated by Johnny*'), moves to the stairs ('*No sexual aggression from Johnny*') and ends up on the floor in Sophie's room ('*Sophie is on top. It is passionate and loving. No aggression from Johnny. Ecstatic moans from Sophie*') (1995b: 17).

This is followed, however, by the sequence in which Sophie appears more intent on flattering Johnny ('I believe everythink you say') that in engaging with him. After which their sex-play no longer seems so playful and is not at all loving. Thus, after she tells Johnny that she likes him and he maintains that she does not know him, we get the following:

Sophie:	I think I do.
Johnny:	You don't fuckin' – (*He pulls her abruptly down to him by the hair.*)
Sophie:	Oh, shit!
Johnny:	– know me!
Sophie:	Fuckin' hell!
	(*He pins her arm behind her back.*)
Johnny:	D'you still like me?
Sophie:	I love you.
Johnny:	What?
Sophie:	I'm in love with you, Johnny.
	(*He laughs.*)
	Don't laugh – I'm serious, uh!
	(*Grasping her hair very tightly, he forces her head upwards, then down into his chest. She gasps for breath.*)
	I understand you, Johnny ... I do.
	(*Minutes later, still fully clothed, they are having a fuck at the other end of the sofa. Johnny is on top. He is holding Sophie's face roughly. She gasps and whimpers and struggles. He starts to bang her head against the arm of the sofa.*) (1995b: 23–4)

This is reminiscent of some of the passages in *A Midsummer Night's Dream* – of such moments as the one in which Helena tells Demetrius that the more he beats her, the more she 'will fawn on [him]' ('Use me but as your spaniel, spurn me, strike me,/Neglect me, lose me; only give me leave,/Unworthy as I am, to follow you' [II, i, 204–7]). But if this is painful enough in Shakespeare, at least Demetrius does not actually strike Helena. No wonder then – since Johnny is not just verbally but *physically* cruel to Sophie, and when she is most vulnerable, in the sexual act – that it is so much more painful to watch the scene in *Naked*.

What are we to make of this? We can start by noting that it fits into something of a pattern. Thus, for example, in the course of the '*rough fuck*' Johnny is having at the beginning of the film, the woman he is having it with first '*seems enthusiastic*' but then begins to protest ('You're hurting me!') when he starts to push '*her head back, his hand under chin*' – while '*his other hand pins down her wrist*' (1995b: 5). And there is a similar moment in his encounter with the older woman who dances alone in her room late at night, at least partly for the benefit of Brian's voyeuristic gaze across the street:

Johnny: 'Ow old are you, love? It's funny, 'cos from over there you look a lot younger. I think me big brother's quite taken with you.
            (*She takes a sip of vodka.*)
            'E's up there every night, 'avin' a bit of a wank about yer. Are you with me?
            (*… He kisses her on the mouth, gently at first, but his grip on her hair becomes gradually tighter. He starts to jolt her head a little. He is hurting her. She grabs his wrists to try to pull his hands off. She gasps with pain. Suddenly, he stops the kiss, but he keeps hold of her hair.*)
            What's the matter?
Woman: Don't do that.
Johnny: What, that? (*He jolts her head.*) Or that? (*He jolts it again.*) Don't you like that? (*He jolts it back.*)
Woman: You don't 'ave to 'urt me.
            (*He brings his face close to hers.*)
Johnny: I'm sorry.
            (*He jolts her head, then lets go of her hair…*) (1995b: 53–4)

These two scenes are also difficult and painful to watch. But *why* does Johnny behave in this way? Why is he so vicious, so mean, so cruel? And what – apart from calling it by its proper name: sadism – are we to make of this appalling behaviour?

One possibility is that Johnny can only perform sexually if his partner allows him to hurt her. So that a bit later, when the dancing woman '*adopts a "sexy" pose*', Johnny is obliged to tell her 'I can't, love. You look like me mother.' And if we reflect on the sequence that ends up with Jeremy (Greg Cruttwell) raping Sophie – her '*whipping him strenuously with her long hair*' and his first instructing her not to '*give up*' and then forcing her to wear Sandra's nursing uniform – then it would seem that this is a problem (of arousal) that Johnny has in common with Jeremy. Though it is also worth noting that when Sophie asks Louise if Johnny ever hurt her ('when you were fuckin''), Louise does not seem to know what Sophie is talking about. Could it also be that this is one of Johnny's ways (undeniably one of his least attractive ways, to put it mildly) of teaching a lesson? There is probably an element of this, at least in the cases of both Sophie and the drunken dancer, both of whom appear to be either indifferent to or trying to blank out uncomfortable truths. But if so, the idea that Johnny should have taken it upon himself to bring these truths home, as it were, is surely grotesque, cruel and outrageous.

It seems likely that these are the scenes in which some viewers will lose whatever sympathy for Johnny they have had. But is his use of physical abuse evidence of misogyny? Of course, *one* of the characters in this film, Jeremy, is unmistakenly a misogynist. But it does not therefore automatically follow that Johnny cannot be one too. Johnny *could* be one, but I do not think he is – not consistently, at any rate, even if he does sometimes express misogynistic attitudes and does sometimes treat women badly. After all, he also occasionally sounds misanthropic and his treatment of Brian and the poster man is not exactly delicate either. In addition to which, it could be argued that the person he is hardest on is himself.

I think that Jeremy's case can help us to make some of the difficult but necessary distinctions. If *Naked* generates a considerable degree of suspense, if it is often frightening, this is mainly due to Jeremy's obnoxious presence. And it is not just that we are frightened by the thought of what he might do next, it is also that our growing awareness of the sickness of which *he* is capable in his treatment of women deepens the sense of apprehension we feel whenever Johnny is alone with a woman. This effect is largely achieved by the way Leigh cuts back and forth. Here, to begin with, for example, is how the happy exchange between Johnny and Sophie that we looked at earlier continues:

> Sophie: Yeah ... 'cos let's face it, right, what are rockets? I mean, they're just ... big metal pricks! You know, I mean, the bastards aren't satisfied with fuckin' the earth up – they've gotta fuck space an' all.
> *(Johnny takes back the joint.)*
> Johnny: Will you tell me something, love? Are you aware of the effect you have on the average mammalian, Mancunian, x-y-ly-chromosome, slavering, lusty male member of the species?
> Sophie: Er ... yeah.
> Johnny: I thought so. (1995b: 9–10)

But this good feeling quickly evaporates as Leigh immediately cuts from it to a brief scene in a gym, in which we see Jeremy – who has a sneer on his face that we later realise is part of his permanent expression – exercising his arm muscles and then being massaged, in the course of which he asks his masseuse first if she would like to have dinner with him and then if she thinks 'women like being raped?'

Johnny and Sophie's bout of happy love-making occurs not long after this. It is preceded by our getting a glimpse of Jeremy and the masseuse having dinner in a restaurant; intercut with a brief scene that shows him being dumped by the masseuse and switching his attention to the waitress, who has been serving them; and immediately followed by a scene in Jeremy's *'cold, trendy bachelor flat'*, to which he has now returned with Giselle (Elizabeth Berrington), the waitress. Soon he is telling her to kiss him and, as the screenplay puts it, *'she does so, with great feeling'*. But then something happens that we do not see, we only see the effect it produces. Presumably he has bitten her because, *'after a few moments, she screams with pain and sits back. Jeremy sniggers. She manages to smile bravely and nurses her lip.'* Moments later Jeremy is using a stuffed lizard to increase Giselle's discomfort, first rubbing it on her bare arm, then making it *'"bite" her left breast'*, and finally making it *'go for her neck'*. And the sequence comes to an end in his bedroom where we see his throwing Giselle *'roughly on to the bed'* and then *'grasping her wrists and pinning them down'*. Ignoring her protest ('You're hurting me!'), he asks her if she has 'ever thought of committing suicide', explains that he intends to do so himself on his fortieth birthday, and then proceeds – in vampire-like fashion – to fall *'violently on her neck. She screams out loud in pain and fear'* (1995b: 20).

This is creepy and becoming increasingly sinister. It is made clear, furthermore, when – in two of the scenes already discussed – we next see Johnny roughing up first Sophie and then the drunken solo-dancer, that the level of sexual violence is escalating. And it reaches its high point when – just after Johnny has persuaded the waitress from the Jubilee Café to take him home with her – we see Jeremy ruthlessly raping Sophie. She clearly states her desire to stop ('I just don't think I can go through with this') and the screenplay graphically describes what happens:

> (*She attempts to go. Jeremy grabs hold of her. He throws her back on to the bed and jumps on top of her. He goes for her neck. She screams.*)
> Oh ... no! No!
> (*Shortly after this, Jeremy has Sophie forced into a kneeling position on the bed. He is gripping her hair. She is wearing the uniform. He is naked. He is taking her from behind, aggressively, violently, horribly. He is grunting. Sophie is screaming desperately.*) (1995b: 61)

This gets it exactly right: it is indeed horrible, grotesquely so, and would be even if we did not know the character involved. But it is made even more unbearable by the fact that we have come by this point to care quite a bit for Sophie. The awful spectacle of her humiliation and pain is not easy to continue watching.

There is no ambiguity about this scene, and it leaves us with an extremely uneasy feeling that something even worse might be about to happen as Leigh cuts to the interior of the house to which Johnny has been brought by the waitress. But in fact, up until the moment when she rather abruptly orders him to leave and he curses her, he behaves quite gently, even tenderly, towards this young woman. This may be partly because, judging by her 'very sad face', which Johnny confesses to finding 'attractive', she, at least, unlike most of the other people he has been encountering, does not seem engaged in '[b]lank[ing] it all out'. It is true that after she has ordered him to leave he does curse her – in what Coveney is right to call 'a grim echo of the womb-curse in *King Lear*' (1997: 28) – and he does so violently. But there is no hint of any physical violence – and he does leave.

Aggression: in theory and practice

What can we deduce from this? First, that the juxtaposition of Jeremy's behaviour with Johnny's forces us to admit that there are of course degrees of viciousness. And that, in itself, may be relatively uncontroversial. After all, even when he is being physically most abusive, Johnny does, at a certain point, pull back – at least in his dealings with Sophie and the dancer (and it is really not clear how far he has gone with the woman in the opening scene). But while it is relatively easy to agree that this should surely affect the way we think about his behaviour, it is not so easy to decide by how much or in what way. In any case, the same juxtaposition raises questions concerning aggression that are genuinely disturbing.

'How comfortless', says Adorno, 'is the thought that the sickness of the normal does not necessarily imply as its opposite the health of the sick, but that the latter usually only present, in a different way, the same disastrous pattern' (1984: 60). Perhaps this is true, *usually*. But how, if at all, does it apply here? No doubt, from the perspective of 'normality', Johnny is simply sick. But do we have to accept this view?

If we need help in resisting it, we can find it in Adam Phillips' book on *Winnicott* which makes it easier to look at Johnny's aggression as a sign *more* of health, than of sickness. I stress the *more* of health because I do not want to deny that in some of his dealings with women (especially in the film's shocking opening scene) Johnny's aggression seems an undeniable manifestation of sickness. And I realise that it is by no means easy to distinguish a 'good' form of aggression from a 'bad' one. But I think it is worth trying to do so for a number of reasons, not the least important of which is that it is difficult to imagine a possible future for any kind of emancipatory politics without some form of aggression. To take just one example, think of Virginia Woolf's insistence (in her 'Professions for Women' paper) that the women writers and intellectuals of her time needed to kill off the figure of Angel in the House.

As Phillips explains, then, vitality 'and the sense of being really alive are clearly bound up for [Winnicott] with the aggressive component. In fact, he … suggest[s] that what we refer to as aggression is sometimes more accurately described as sponta- neity, for Winnicott the cardinal virtue of the good life' (1988: 111). In a somewhat similar vein, Phillips also notes Winnicott's view that 'creativity is bound up with a capacity for ruthlessness' (1988: 113) and that – from a psychoanalytical point of view – the problem is not so much aggression, which is vital to the 'experience of aliveness', as the 'sense of futility [that is] born of compliance' (1988: 127), the strat- egies of which construct 'the False Self' (1988: 133). There is, I take it, no doubt about Johnny's spontaneous vitality, his aliveness, his bubbling creativity. And, by the same token, it might be difficult to think of someone less compliant.

Admittedly, it is one thing to give one's assent to Winnicott's reflections on aggression on the level of theory and another to contemplate the particular *acts* of aggression that Leigh stages for us in *Naked*.[5] But it is important to keep in mind that the two worst – and easily most violent – of these acts (both of them entirely unprovoked) are the rape of Sophie (by Jeremy) and the savage beating Johnny receives from a passing gang of youths shortly after he has already been beaten up by the poster man. Not, obviously, that Johnny's later status as a victim himself in any way excuses his earlier cruelty to Sophie and the drunken dancer – in which he manages to both physically abuse and also psychically humiliate these two women. Those scenes remain painful to contemplate. Nevertheless, they certainly involve a lesser degree of violence than the rape and the beating up and they therefore encourage us to see that we have a responsibility to make discriminations. And not just between different kinds and degrees of physical violence, but between physical and non-physical (or verbal) violence (or aggression) too.

I am thinking of Johnny's abrasive manner here. Of such things as, for example, his reaction to the kiss Louise gives him when she has just got back home from work and – to her complete surprise, since he has given her no prior warning – has discovered him there with Sophie:

Louise: What are you doin' 'ere? You look like shit.
Johnny: Just trying to blend in with the surroundings.
               (*Louise leans over and kisses him.*)
Johnny: (*Sings, to the tune of Handel's 'Hallelujah!'*) Halitosis! Halitosis, Halitosis! (1995b: 11)

Perhaps it could be argued that in this case Johnny is giving back as good as he gets ('You look like shit'). But what excuse is there for his response to Brian's claim that, since he knows he was 'here in the past, before [he] was born', he also knows he is 'gonna be here in the future after [he's] died':

Johnny: I see. And in this alternative existence, did you still 'ave the same noxious body odour? (1995b: 46)

Surely this is simply unpleasant, gratuitously so, the bad manners of an especially difficult adolescent. But it is worth noting that, even though Brian does tell Johnny that 'there's no need to to be personal', neither Brian here, nor Louise earlier, seem really offended by Johnny's rudeness (not, at any rate, for very long). On the contrary, in fact, they both seem to feel that it has a place in the kind of thrust and parry (Laurel and Hardy-style) that all three of them seem to think of as being necessary to a lively exchange.

Reflect, in this connection, on the significance of the fact that, while (in his interview) Leigh strongly objects when he is 'accused of being patronising', he claims he does not 'mind people saying that [he is] merciless' at all (Fuller 1995: xxiii). The point is not just that there are far worse things than a lack of politeness (including being patronising), but that a refusal to allow oneself to be constrained by the obligation to be nice might – at least in certain circumstances – be one of the essential preconditions for liveliness, or for avoiding the kind of deadliness that Johnny complains of (to Louise) early on: 'I've seen more life in an open grave.' I think it ought to be possible to grant this point without losing sight of the fact that in *other* circumstances a lack of kindness can shut down the 'liveliness' of some people entirely.

As Brian shares his sandwich lunch with Johnny, we get the following exchange:

Johnny: Did you make these yourself?
Brian: I did, yeah.
Johnny: I thought so. (*He glances down the street.*) Well, listen, I might
          be back in a couple of minutes.
          (*Brian laughs briefly.*) (1995b: 50)

Instead of being offended by Johnny's pointed refusal to do the expected thing – express gratitude for the sandwich and compliment Brian for having made it himself – Brian is amused. Because, to recall what Johnny says to Louise earlier ('whatever else you can say about me, I'm not fuckin' bored!'), besides his not being bored, Johnny is not boring either. His brief comment on Brian's sandwich is another instance of the cheekiness that Johnny cultivates and prides himself on. 'I know,' he tells the dancing woman, 'it's a bit cheeky [his having knocked on her door – 'I said I'd come and say 'ello to Isadora Duncan'] but, er … I'm a cheeky young monkey!'

Certainly, as Thewlis says, 'Johnny is not complacent' (Coveney 1997: 26). Nor, as Leigh insists, is Johnny cynical:

One of the most naive things that has been said about him is that he's cynical. He's not cynical. He's sceptical about some things but he has a sense of values. (Fuller 1995: xxxv)

But if, on the one hand, it has to be admitted that Johnny never comes close to doing anything that would remotely justify Louise's threatening *him* in the way she eventually (and quite magnificently) threatens Jeremy – first inviting him to undo his fly; then, when he has done so, suddenly producing a large kitchen knife in her hand and asking him if he wants her 'to slice [his] prick off and shove it up [his] arse'; and finally, as '*he slinks towards the door*', exclaiming 'Maggot dick!' – on the other hand, it also has to be said that there *ought* to be something insufferable about him. After all, what Pierre Hadot has said about Socrates – that he 'harassed his interlocutors with questions which put *themselves* into question, forcing them to pay attention to and take care of themselves' (1995a: 89) – can be said about Johnny too. And harassment is seldom welcomed, especially when, as here, it can so easily seem to smack of self-righteousness. Hadot notes, furthermore, that while the Stoic philosopher Epictetus, praised the Socratic method, he also 'emphasises that, in his day, it is no longer easy to practice it: "Nowadays, especially in Rome, it is not at all a safe business." Epictetus pictures a philosopher trying to have a Socratic dialogue with a consular personage, and ending up receiving a fist in the face' (1995a: 117).

But if Johnny is sometimes difficult to take, much of the time he is irresistible. This is especially the case when he is giving free rein to his strong sense of humour. As when (in one of his throwaway puns) he explains to the waitress from the Jubilee Café that he is not 'homophobic. I mean, I like *The Iliad*. And *The Odyssey*. (*Laughs*.) D'you get that?' (63) Unfortunately, she does not, which does not stop him, however, moments later, from exclaiming, when he notices a '*muscular ancient Greek discus-thrower, part of a table lamp*,' 'Oh, hallo … it's, er … Pizza Deliveryman'. Indeed, Johnny is even funny when he is complaining that everybody is 'so bored':

> You've 'ad nature explained to you and you're bored with it. You've 'ad the living body explained to you and you're bored with it. You've 'ad the universe explained to you and you're bored with it. So now you just want cheap thrills and like plenty of 'em, and it dun't matter 'ow tawdry or vacuous they are as long as it's new, as long as it's new, as long as it flashes and fuckin' bleeps in forty fuckin' different colours. (1995b: 21)

What is not so funny, however, is Johnny's treatment of Louise at the end of the film. Put simply, she takes him back in and, since he has been badly hurt, she looks after him. We have learned earlier, in an exchange she has had with Sophie, that Louise and Johnny 'went out for a year'. And there is an especially touching scene towards the end, which nicely reveals an at least partially shared past, when Louise and Johnny lie next to one another on a bed and sing a song about Manchester. It ends up as follows:

> Oh, I don't want to roam.
> I want to get back 'ome
> To rainy
> Manchester…

It is obviously a sentimental song – one apparently that 'Leigh used to sing … with his friends in Habonim ('The Builders'), the international socialist Jewish youth movement he joined as a schoolboy' (Coveney 1997: 29) – and so Johnny adds the sentimentality-puncturing remark: 'I've got an 'ard-on', after which Louise's smile and tender gesture by which she '*touches his cheek with the back of her hand*' (1995b: 79) suggest that she at least is now convinced they can start again.

It seems clear to her, shortly after this, that they have an understanding: she will go into work and hand in her resignation; they will then return to Manchester together, as a couple. So what are we to make of the fact that, after allowing her to go ahead and quit her job, Johnny then pockets the £380 Jeremy has left behind (it is unclear for whom it is intended) and takes off himself, effectively leaving Louise in the lurch?

After claiming that the problem he 'present[s] the audience with is whether to like or dislike [Johnny]' (Fuller 1995: xxxix), Leigh goes on to say something that applies just as much to the problem how should we think of aggression or violence? as to the question how should we think of Johnny? He says that, 'if the film works, you go away from it locked in debate' (ibid.). But if we apply it just – as Leigh intended – to Johnny, how, then, in the light of what he does to Louise in the end, can we possibly continue to *like* Johnny?

Perhaps Johnny can be seen at the end as having helped to liberate Louise – or, better yet, as having helped her to liberate herself. By her own admission, she finds her job boring, so perhaps she is better off out of it, and also better off – since she clearly prefers it to London – returning to Manchester, even without Johnny, who never actually said he would go with her anyway. Possibly. But the fact remains that he has betrayed her trust and this is shocking and not at all likable.

At the end of the film, we see Johnny hopping down the road, making off as fast as he can on one good leg and without a stick to support the other leg, the one with the badly bruised ankle. He is presumably heading back to the streets. Here, it is worth recalling a bit more of what he said earlier, since it so vividly evokes a sense of just how cold it can get out there. When the waitress from the Jubilee Café orders him to leave her place, Johnny says:

> An', er, listen, love ... I hope that when you're tucked up tonight, all snug and warm underneath your tear-sodden fuckin' duvet in your ankle-length Emily Bronte windin'-sheet, that you spare a thought for me, with me head in a puddle of cold dog's piss. An' I hope that you dream of me. An' I hope that you wake up screamin'. (1995b: 70)

The two things about the film's ending that seem reasonably certain, then, are (i) that Johnny is going to get cold and (ii) that he is necessarily going to be doing what Lear recommended, and what most of us manage to avoid doing – for whatever combination of reasons, he is going to 'expose [him]self to feel what wretches feel' (*King Lear* II, iv, 34).

Finally, what is most admirable about *Naked* is the intensity with which Leigh manages through Johnny to convey the kind of concern for 'the meaning of life' that the critic F. R. Leavis referred to in his essay on Bunyan's *The Pilgrim's Progress*:

> Such a concern, felt as the question 'What for – what ultimately for?' is implicitly asked in all the greatest art, from which we get, not what we are likely to call an 'answer', but the communication of a felt significance; something that confirms our sense of life as more than a mere linear succession of days, a matter of time as measured by the clock – 'tomorrow and tomorrow and tomorrow...' (1967b: 46)

Naked does not propose any answers but it does pose the question in a particularly challenging and memorable way.

CHAPTER NINE

In Search of the Missing Mother/Daughter

We're all in pain. Why can't we share our pain?
                        – Maurice in *Secrets and Lies* (Leigh 1997b: 100)

If, as Leigh states, *Naked* 'is about rootlessness, where everyone is detached from everybody else and a kind of family exists only by default' (Fuller 1995: xxvii), *Secrets and Lies* is about the forging of ties, the making of connections, the re-establishing of roots and the reinforcement of the family. And if *Naked* offers, through Johnny, a scathing critique of the kinds of work performed by Brian, the poster man, and Louise, *Secrets and Lies* movingly celebrates those who roll up their sleeves and get on with whatever job they have been able to find for themselves.

To take the related questions of family and roots first, *Secrets and Lies* has not just one but two major plot lines, which involve (i) Maurice and Monica wanting to re-establish contact with their niece Roxanne, and (ii) Hortense, after the death of her adopted mother, searching to find her biological mother. Though Maurice and Monica have not seen Roxanne for two-and-a-half years, they seem to think of her as the closest they are going to get to the daughter they cannot have and they decide to invite her to their home to celebrate her twenty-first birthday. As for Hortense, she discovers her biological mother, who turns out to be Cynthia, Maurice's sister and

Roxanne's mother. Maurice and Monica have meanwhile recognised that, if they want to invite Roxanne, then – however reluctantly – they must also invite Cynthia, who has not yet seen their new house. And once Cynthia has met Hortense, she decides that she wants to take her along to Roxanne's birthday party too. So, in the event, the party turns out to be a much bigger family reunion than Maurice and Monica intended it to be. To a large extent, then, the film is organised around the kind of rituals that bring people together: not only Roxanne's twenty-first birthday, and the house-warming celebration it forms part of, at the climax, but also the funeral (of Hortense's adopted mother) with which the film opens and the various weddings we see Maurice photographing throughout.

As for its treatment of work, is there any other film that attaches as much importance as this one does to the different kinds of jobs or tasks we see its characters undertaking? We see all of the main characters at work: Maurice the photographer most often, but also Hortense the optometrist, Cynthia at work in a box factory and Roxanne working for the council as a road-sweeper. We see the social worker, Jenny, at work, displaying a wonderful mixture of intelligence, sensitivity, delicacy and tact, as she helps Hortense find Cynthia. The official that Hortense sees at the Office of Population Censuses and Surveys is helpful, polite and respectful. And we hear about the work (scaffolding) Roxanne's boy friend, Paul, does – and about how impressed Maurice is to hear this ('It's very well paid'). Monica is the only major character who does not have a paying job but she has done a lot of work on her house ('It's about time you showed it off', Maurice tells her, 'I mean, you've done a lovely job') and now spends a lot of time stencilling, which is what she is doing when we first see her.

In various ways, all of these characters can be said to be 'getting on with living and working and in some way fulfilling [themselves] within limited parameters' (Fuller 1995: xxxi). In some cases, admittedly, the parameters are considerably more limited than in others: 'Still', Cynthia tells Roxanne, 'I suppose there are worse jobs. Gotta laugh, ain't yer, sweet'eart? (*Pause.*) Else you'd cry.' And Maurice has not given up hope that Roxanne (who he says has 'got a good brain') may still go to college. But the attitude conveyed by the film is not only non-condescending, it is that anyone working is worthy of our respect. And this even includes Monica stencilling, which would of course be the easiest thing in the world to make fun of, if Leigh was so inclined. As for those who have lost their jobs – like the beauty consultant whose face was badly scarred in a car accident ('I lost my job – I was good at my job!'), or like Stuart Christian, the ex-photographer, whose business Maurice took over and who has fallen on hard times – the film's attitude towards them can be inferred from Maurice's parting comment on Stuart: 'There but for the grace of God.'

'You've drawn the short straw, mate,' Maurice tells his wife when she is suffering from particularly heavy period pains. It seems likely that it is connected to her inability to have children. As Maurice says later on, to the former beauty consultant, who lost her job after scarring her face in a car accident: 'Life isn't fair, is it? Someone always draws the short straw.' The world of *Secrets and Lies* is delicately positioned on the edge of an abyss and one's position in relation to the abyss is largely determined by luck.

This, I would argue, is why the movement from the darkness of *Naked* to the (relative) colour of *Secrets and Lies* does not entail any lapse on the film's part (as opposed to that of Maurice's assistant, Jane) into the unreal or sentimental. It is true that it covers some of the territory that might well remind us (for a moment or two) of some of those films – Irving Rapper's *Now, Voyager* (1942), Josef von Sternberg's *Blonde Venus* (1932), King Vidor's *Stella Dallas* (1937), George Cukor's *Gaslight* (1944) and Max Orphuls' *Letter from an Unknown Woman* (1948) – that Stanley Cavell thinks of as forming the genre of 'the melodrama of the unknown woman', a genre he sees as negating that of the comedies of remarriage. After all, from Hortense's point of view, what is Cynthia if not the unknown woman – certainly up until the point when Hortense makes contact with her. But, at the same time, *Secrets and Lies* covers this territory very differently, as we can quickly see by noting Linda Williams' comment on the scene that depicts the resolution of *Stella Dallas*: 'that moment when the good-hearted, ambitious, working-class floozy, Stella, sacrifices her only connection to her daughter in order to propel her into an upper-class world of surrogate family unity. Such', Williams adds, 'are the mixed messages of joy in pain, of pleasure in sacrifice – that typically resolve the melodramatic conflicts of "the woman's film"' (2002: 299). There is no such sacrifice at the end of *Secrets and Lies*, since Hortense voluntarily travels (in class-terms) downwards, rather than upwards, in order to be with her mother. So that, if there is a sense in which it could be said that their reunion in the last scene (along with Hortense's sister, Roxanne) makes this 'a woman's film' (with the scene resolving the drama of the heterosexual couple – Maurice and Monica – taking second place), it is obviously very different to the kind of 'woman's film' that Williams recalls.

As for melodrama, if, as Thomas Elsaesser states, in the 'dictionary sense, melodrama is a dramatic narrative in which musical accompaniment marks the emotional effects' (2002: 50), then this – still, in Elsaesser's view, 'the most useful definition' (ibid.) – would make *Secrets and Lies* a melodrama. But the title of Elsaesser's classic essay on the subject – 'Tales of Sound and Fury: Observations on the Family Melodrama' – explains why it is not one. Though it does offer 'drama + melos (music)' (Nowell-Smith 2002: 70), and does focus on the family, it is definitely not a tale of sound and fury.[1]

We shall now examine the opening twenty minutes of *Secrets and Lies*, which are broken down (somewhat arbitrarily) into thirteen scenes.

The mise-en-scène during the opening scenes

While *Naked* begins with violent sex in a dark alley, *Secrets and Lies* begins in daylight with a funeral ceremony in a cemetery. From a stationary position among the Victorian graves, the opening shot records – to the sound of Andrew Dickson's sad and dignified musical score – the arrival of the funeral cortege some distance away. This is then followed by a tracking shot, but a very different kind of tracking shot to the one that opens *Naked*, serving a dramatically different purpose. Instead of rushing towards the action, the camera is positioned some distance (fifty yards or so) away from it and it moves slowly – behind some tombstones – at an angle to the black-suited mourners, whom we hear singing (the hymn, 'How Great Thou Art') before we actually see them and realise that they are almost all West Indian. After having been kept momentarily at a distance, which establishes an appropriate sense of respect and dignity, we are then allowed in closer. A series of shots – some of the group, some of individuals in close-up – eventually settles on one young woman in particular, who we later learn is called Hortense (Marianne Jean-Baptiste). As the camera holds Hortense's composed but tearful face in close-up, Dickson's score seems to be giving us access to her special sadness, while the communal hymn can still be heard more quietly in the background. The scene comes to an end when – in a shot from up above, looking down on the mourners circling the grave – a wreath, forming the word 'MUM' is placed on it.

This opening scene accomplishes three main things: (i) it introduces us to Hortense (even if we do not learn her name until later); (ii) it makes it clear that, while race is going to be an important element in this film, it will be treated with a minimum of fuss (the music, the setting and the voices makes this feel like a very English funeral, but in actuality this is a faithful representation of a typically *West Indian* funeral in an English setting); and (iii) the combination of the formality of dress and demeanour with the loving familiarity of the word MUM ensure that for many of us this is a film that begins by making us weep. And, in fact, as the film continues, many of us are likely to find ourselves on the edge of tears. In this sense, it can be said to be a tearjerker. Even though, at the same time, it also frequently makes us laugh and smile.

The next three scenes focus on Maurice (Timothy Spall) and his wife, Monica (Phyllis Logan). From a sad occasion (a middle-class funeral, the burial of a mother, whom we later learn is Hortense's adopted mother), the film then abruptly cuts to a happy one, an upper-class marriage ceremony – or, more precisely, it cuts to the bride's session with Maurice, the photographer, which precedes it. But it seems likely that the older man hovering behind Maurice is the bride's father and this may have something to do with the fact that the bride seems close to tears. It suggests to me, in any case, that we have moved from one daughter (Hortense) to another, the second one about to get married. From this introduction to Maurice at work, we cut to a quick shot of Monica, his wife, who is at home but also working, '*stencilling leaves on to a blue Art Nouveau umbrella stand*' (Leigh 1997b: 2).

The fourth scene follows almost immediately but takes place some time later, again in Monica and Maurice's house. It begins with Monica, standing at her bay window, watching some children playing outside. We then see that she and Maurice, who is sitting in an armchair, have changed from their work clothes into something more relaxing and that they are each enjoying a drink of red wine. After Maurice compliments Monica on her clothes, Monica's attention is caught by a framed photograph of a smiling little girl that has evidently been prominently displayed on their mantelpiece for many years. She comments on it now because, as she says, the girl in question – Maurice's niece, Roxanne (Claire Rushbrook) – is going to be twenty-one in August. So this is when they decide to invite Roxanne (the daughter/child they never had) for her twenty-first birthday. The scene ends with Maurice confessing that he is 'really proud of that portrait', which we then see in close-up, Roxanne *'grinning cheekily'* (1997b: 4). 'I reckon', Maurice adds, 'that's the last time she ever smiled'.

By this point the alternating pattern – back and forth, between smiles and tears (or grimness, or sadness) – has been clearly established so that, as we turn to the next three scenes, which introduce us to Roxanne and her mother, we turn *away* from that cheeky grin. Scenes five and six are extremely brief. We quickly cut first to a shot of Roxanne at work, sweeping the pavement and looking glum, and then to a shot of her sad-looking mother, Cynthia, at *her* work, *'operating a machine that cuts slits in sheets of cardboard'* (ibid.).

In the seventh scene we see Cynthia and Roxanne spending an evening in front of the television, which is tuned to a tennis match. Cynthia comments that Roxanne has been looking unhappy for some time and she wants to know why:

Cynthia: You've been sitting there for a month with a face like a slapped arse.
Roxanne: Well, what's there to smile about? (Leigh 1997b: 5)

Before long, Roxanne's refusal to satisfy her mother's curiosity leads to Cynthia complaining that her 'downfall' was getting 'saddled' with Roxanne. This produces the following exchange:

Roxanne: I didn't ask to be born!
Cynthia: No, an' I never asked to 'ave yer, neither.
Roxanne: Well, you should've thought about that before you dropped yer knickers!
           (*Roxanne glares at the tennis, and Cynthia glares at Roxanne.*)
           (Leigh 1997b: 6)

In other words, when we finally get to see an actual mother and daughter interacting in the flesh, they are miserable together.

This is followed by the two scenes in which we learn the identity of the young woman the camera singled out in the churchyard ceremony at the beginning. The eighth scene shows Hortense, the optometrist, at work, testing the eyes of a very sweet – almost angelic-looking – little girl. After the sourness and rudeness of the previous exchange, it is a definite relief to watch the *'friendly and cheerful'* Hortense, who is clearly as good with her clients – at putting them at their ease – as Maurice is with his. We then see Hortense leaving her office and saying goodbye to a junior colleague. Hortense plans to go to her 'mum's house, and sort through her things', and the colleague will be attending a 'christening' (1997b: 7). So here, too, we realise, the focus is still on children (the christening) and, more specifically, daughters (not just Hortense as daughter but also the little girl she is testing for new glasses).

In the ninth scene, we first see Hortense in her mother's bedroom sifting through various things (letters etc.), while she overhears her two brothers and sister-in-law arguing downstairs about what to do with the house. We then – in scenes ten and eleven – first get a glimpse of Hortense later that night looking thoughtful and putting a form into an envelope, which we see her posting the following morning. Only later do we learn that this shows her having just decided to begin the process of trying to discover the identity of her biological mother.

Finally, the next two scenes (which could be separated out into four or five) return us to Maurice and take the form of a long sequence showing him at work, which is broken up twice by glimpses of him and Monica trying to cope as best they can with her extremely painful condition. Thus, scene twelve is made up of a montage of the sessions in which we see Maurice taking the photographs of a variety of people – before the first break, a family group, a prize boxer, a nurse, a young mother with her new-born baby, a shaggy brown dog and its owner, a cheerful elderly lady and her cat, a young Asian man, a man in a tuxedo and a fez, three youngish women, three identical little girls (triplets) and their mother, a small boy and his mother, a middle-aged woman in 'sexy' lingerie and five businessmen in poses. In each case, we see him trying to get them to smile for the camera – occasionally a client will refuse to do so.

In the first part of scene thirteen, Maurice returns home and finds Monica hoovering. She is in a foul temper and obviously feeling awful. This part ends with Monica breaking down in tears and rushing out of the room, slamming the door behind her. We then cut back to scene twelve and in quick succession see Maurice doing some more studio portraits – of a young woman graduate, a young couple, an uneasy black woman with an uneasy older white man, an unsmiling old lady with her smiling, middle-aged daughter and finally a jolly couple in their forties. This last pair 'laugh uproariously and endlessly' (Leigh 1997b: 16) and it is from them that we cut back to scene thirteen, this time finding Monica first in some pain on the toilet and then, a bit later, in bed with Maurice making a hot water bottle for her and finally managing to get her to chortle by making a joke about the chicken she says is waiting for him in the freezer ('Be a bit cold, wouldn't it?'). Then back for the end of scene twelve as Maurice tries to take the portrait of a respectable Greek couple in their thirties. They squabble throughout but he finally tricks them (as he has tricked so many others, partly, it would seem, against their will), into a smile. 'A flash, and Maurice has captured their Happy Moment; the photograph over, they dissolve into an embarrassed pause' (Leigh 1997b: 19).

Immediately after this, we see Hortense receiving an answer in the mail to the letter enquiring about her birth mother she sent off earlier. And a few days later, she is meeting and being interviewed by the social worker, Jenny (Lesley Manville). At this point, near the beginning of the interview, we are twenty minutes into the film. But let us back up for a moment to comment on the twelfth scene (the long interrupted sequence of studio portraits), which seems to be crucially important.

The significance of the studio portraits sequence

In order to see what makes this sequence so remarkable, we need to start by noting that at least eight of the actors who turn up in the extremely brief parts of Maurice's sitters are recognisable to those of us who have seen them in more substantial parts in Leigh's earlier films. Peter Wright (the father in the family group) was the spacey estate manager in *Meantime* and Brian, the night foreman, in *Naked*. Alison Steadman (the dog-owner) first appeared as Veronica in *Hard Labour*, then as Candice-Marie in *Nuts in May*, as Beverley in *Abigail's Party*, as Betty in *The Short and Curlies* and as Wendy in *Life is Sweet*. Liz Smith (the cat-owner) was Pat's mother in *Bleak Moments* and Mrs Thornley in *Hard Labour*. Sheila Kelley (the triplet's mother) was Honky in *Nuts in May* and Janice in *Home Sweet Home*. Angela Curran (the little boy's mother) was Sandra in *The Kiss of Death* and she had brief appearances in *Who's Who* and at the beginning of *Naked* (it is her car that Johnny steals). Philip Davis (one of the men in suits) appeared as Kevin in *Who's Who*, as Dick in *Grown-Ups* and as Cyril in *High Hopes*. Wendy Nottingham (the glum wife) was Charlene in *The Short and Curlies*. Ruth Sheen (one half of a laughing couple) was Shirley in *High Hopes*.

Of course, this is by no means the first film in which Leigh has made use of the same actor for the second (or third, or fourth) time. But it is the first and only time in which he has drawn attention to his actors in quite this way. And part, at least, of its effect is to momentarily weaken the illusion – which, as we have seen, in every other way he works so hard to create – that this is real life we are watching. Up to a point, in other words, this might be seen as Leigh's version of the Brechtian alienation or distancing device. Only up to a point, however, because while it certainly makes us aware of the fact that this is art, it does so without really forcing us to relinquish (even if it slightly weakens) the illusion that it is simultaneously real life. In my view, this makes it all the more effective. And, furthermore, it seems that this sequence encourages us to look back (and forwards) on all those occasions when Leigh is reusing the same actor as other examples of the same distancing device, which Leigh effectively redefines so that in his hands it both distances us and draws us in at the same time. The three main examples in *Secrets and Lies* would be that of Brenda Blethyn as Cynthia (formerly as Gloria in *Grown-Ups*), Timothy Spall as Maurice (formerly as Gordon in *Home Sweet Home* and Aubrey in *Life is Sweet*, and to be Richard Temple in *Topsy-Turvy* and the cab-driver in *All or Nothing*), and Lesley Manville as Jenny (formerly Mandy in *Grown-Ups* and Laetitia in *High Hopes*, and later as Gilbert's wife in *Topsy-Turvy* and the cab-driver's wife in *All or Nothing*).

In addition to this, for those familiar with Leigh's work as a whole, other forms of repetition – which often take the form of correction or revison – can function in this (distancing) way too. Think, for example, of how one's memory of the ways in which the two social workers are portrayed in *Home Sweet Home* affects one's sense of the social worker in *Secrets and Lies*.

The point about the Brechtian distancing device is that it is supposed to facilitate reflection. And, in its own quiet and subtle way, this is precisely what the studio portraits sequence does: it encourages and helps us to reflect – in this case, on Leigh's art and what it is trying to do. Most importantly, I think it encourages us to see that Maurice himself is an artist and that – whatever Johnny (in *Naked*) might have thought of it – his project deserves to be taken seriously. Considering how impressive and central to the film Maurice is, it may, in this connection, be worth noting that Leigh's paternal grandfather, Mayer Liebermann, who came to England from Russia in 1902, opened and operated in Manchester 'a small factory built around his own work as a portrait miniaturist, colouring in people in family photographs and framing them' (Coveney 1997: 37). But, even without our knowing about this possible real-life model, it is clear that Leigh's artistic project in some ways resembles Maurice's, most strikingly, of course, in its preoccupation with those aspects of life that give cause either for lamentation or celebration, that make us either sad (and tearful) or happy (and smiling).

One further suggestion: we might be better able to appreciate what is going on in this key sequence if we consider it in the light of Jonathan Lear's recommendation that 'we need to go back to an older English usage of "happiness" in terms of happenstance'. This, Lear explains, is 'the experience of chance things working out well rather than badly':

> Happiness, on this interpretation, is not the ultimate goal of our teleologically organised strivings, but the ultimate ateological moment: a chance event going well for us – quite literally, a lucky break. Analysis puts us in a position to take advantage of certain kinds of chance occurrences… (2000: 129)

It does not seem too far-fetched to say that Maurice puts his clients in a somewhat similar position. Of course, this means that these are not at all chance events from *his* point of view. On the contrary, he works to make them happen: his aim is to capture these '*Happy Moment[s]*'. But it does seem that there is a sense in which, from his *clients'* point of view, these events do nevertheless have an element of chance about them, that they are indeed 'lucky break[s]'. And what helps to make them so poignant is the possibility that it may be, as Lear puts it (in an admittedly different context), that it is precisely 'in such fleeting moments [that] we do find real happiness' (ibid.).

In addition to which, there is no doubt that, in *Secrets and Lies*, such moments derive a large part of their power to haunt us from the fact that we experience them against a background of sadness and pain. Or to put it another way (while recalling again what the social worker tells Hortense, as the latter prepares to begin her search to locate her birth mother): the journey we embark on as we watch this film is a traumatic one.

The 'shock experience': 'a traumatic journey'

If in *Naked* Johnny rails against those who would prefer to 'blank it all out' (so they can 'just atrophy and die of fuckin' indifference!'), in *Secrets and Lies* Maurice instructs Roxanne – when she has just learned that she has a sister, and is waiting at a bus stop ready to flee the scene – that she has 'gotta face up to it!' The scene in which Maurice leads Roxanne and Paul from the bus stop back to his house is one of the high spots in the film. As Cynthia noted to Maurice earlier on, Paul walks 'like a crab' and it looks very much as if all three are marching, crab-like, to a showdown, which in a way they are, so, in the circumstances, if it feels almost like a comic version of the lead into the last scene in *The Wild Bunch*, this seems oddly appropriate. And, as always in this film, rather than being at the expense of the characters, the humour somehow manages to reinforce our sense of their courage and dignity. Once back in his house, Maurice launches into his powerful 'secrets and lies' speech, thus ensuring, in effect, that they *all* 'face up to it'. And since it is Hortense, whose initiative has, in a sense, made this truth-telling session possible, Maurice pays her the compliment she deserves – first calling her 'a very brave person' and then, when she denies that she is one, explaining what he means:

Maurice: You wanted to find the truth, and you were prepared to
              suffer the consequences. I admire you for that. I mean it.
              (Leigh 1997b: 100)

The language is simple but it is also, in context, extremely effective.

What is particularly admirable about Hortense is her clear-sighted, intelligent determination, which is perhaps easiest to see during an exchange with her friend Dionne (Michelle Austin) that takes place just over two months after her adopted mother's funeral:

Dionne: You're getting better, though.
Hortense: It's a nice day.
Dionne: (*Looking out the window.*) Yeah.
              (*Pause.*)
Hortense: I dunno. My 'ead can't contain it all – it's too soon. There's
              nothing rational about grief. Maybe you're crying for
              yourself.
Dionne: Have you been out much?
Hortense: No, I can't. Some days ... I'm completely vulnerable – I can
              feel everything; other days, I'm numb.
Dionne: You wanna come out with me?
Hortense: No! I've got stuff to sort out.
Dionne: What?
Hortense: Life. (Leigh 1997b: 29)

This gives content to the phrase, facing up to it. Especially since it follows on from the earlier scene, in the office of the social worker, in which we have seen how '*bewildered, shocked, [and] shaken*' Hortense was – '*Tears well[ing] in her eyes*' (1997b: 23) – when browsing through the folder Jenny had handed her (one paper in it being headed 'The National Adoption Society'). In fact, it was in the immediate aftermath of this that the social worker had issued her warning, telling Hortense that she is embarking on 'a very traumatic journey' – 'and there may', she then added, 'be other people's feelings to consider, too'. So that, when Hortense later tells her friend that she has 'stuff to sort out', she clearly knows how painful a process this is likely to be.

To put it simply, then (with reference to Freud's classic text on the subject), a traumatic journey would be one in which one encounters the kind of shocks that break through our 'protective shield', it being understood that '*protection against stimuli is*', in Freud's view, 'an almost more important function for the living organism than *reception of* stimuli' (1963: 53). Furthermore, Walter Benjamin quotes and discusses these lines in his essay on 'Some Motifs in Baudelaire'. He does so because he is arguing that 'Baudelaire placed the shock experience at the very centre of his artistic work' (1973: 17–18). I would argue that this experience is also at the centre of Leigh's work.

If Hortense undergoes the first exposure to shock in *Secrets and Lies*, it is Cynthia's turn next. And not surprisingly, since in her case the discovery that she is speaking on the phone to the daughter she has never seen or spoken to before comes completely out of the blue, the shock is much greater. After all, Hortense had had some time to prepare herself and, as Benjamin says, the 'more readily consciousness registers these shocks, the less they are likely to have a traumatic effect' (1973: 115). But when Hortense first calls her birth mother on the phone and identifies herself to her, the revelation is (in Jonathan Lear's description of the traumatic effect) 'so overwhelming that [it] simply break[s] through the protective shield and flood[s] the mind' (2000: 71). When she realises that Hortense is her long-lost daughter, Cynthia is rendered speechless:

> (*Cynthia is horrified and terrified.*)
>
> Hortense: Look, I'm sorry, I know this must be a shock to you –
> (*Cynthia hangs up abruptly, and rushes out to the scullery, where she vomits into the sink.*) (Leigh 1997b: 47)

And a couple of moments later, when Hortense rings again, Cynthia '*turns in horror*' (ibid.). It is as if she has heard a ghost come back from the dead.

Nor is this the only ghost Cynthia finds herself having to deal with. As we realise when we see her – during the café scene – trying to explain to Hortense why she cannot possibly be her mother:

> Cynthia: Listen, I don't mean nothin' by it, darlin,' but I ain't been with a black man in my life. No disrespect, nor nothing. I'd a' remembered, wouldn't I?
> (*Hortense looks at Cynthia. Cynthia thinks about things. Long pause. Suddenly, something comes back to her.*)
> Oh, bloody 'ell …!
> (*She looks at Hortense.*)
> Oh, Jesus Christ Almighty!
> (*She bursts into uncontrollable tears, and turns away from Hortense.*)
> I'm sorry, sweet'eart … (*Sobbing.*) I'm so ashamed.
> (Leigh 1997b: 52–3)

In ordinary circumstances, she would have remembered, so presumably her encounter with Hortense's father was not ordinary at all, was so traumatic, in fact, that she has completely repressed it until this moment. She was only sixteen at the time and, judging by her willingness, at the end, to identify Roxanne's father but not Hortense's – Hortense: Was my father a nice man?/Cynthia: Oh, don't break my heart, darlin'! (*After a few moments, she breaks down, sobbing uncontrollably...*) (1997b: 101) – it seems likely that he was a stranger who raped her.

Once again, however, though the expression on Hortense's face leaves us in no doubt that she finds this moment extremely painful, she is not physically overwhelmed and shaken, as both Cynthia and Roxanne are. So that it does not seem at all melodramatic to speak of their experiencing 'a rip in the fabric of life ... a rip in the world itself', which is what Lear finds happening in what he calls 'moments of break' (2000: 92, 119). But the marvellous thing about such moments is that, though they certainly do not guarantee it, they create 'a possibility for new possibilities' (2000: 118), for a break*through* rather than a break*down*. Which is of course precisely what we see happening in this film – in the case of each of the five main characters, Hortense, Cynthia, Roxanne, Maurice and Monica.

Missing what they never had: Maurice and Monica

If most of the power of *Naked* comes from Johnny's inventive use of the language – or from his impatience with the cliché, whether used by others (Guard: Waste not, want not./Johnny: And other clichés' [Leigh 1995b: 37]) or by himself (Johnny [to poster man]: Is this a stick-up? Sorry – you must get that all the time, yeah?' [1995b: 71]) – some of the most powerful moments in *Secrets and Lies* are either silent, or very close to it. For example, the visit Maurice pays to his sister Cynthia to invite her and Roxanne to his home to celebrate the latter's birthday. 'Twenty-one', he exclaims, at one point, and this leads into the following exchange:

Cynthia:	I can't believe it, Maurice. I was carryin' 'er when I was twenty-one, wa'n' I? (*She smiles.*) You was good with nappies.
Maurice:	(*Laughing.*) Those safety-pins, though!
Cynthia:	Never stabbed 'er, though, did you, darlin'?
Maurice:	Stabbed meself a couple o' times.
Cynthia:	Seventeen, wa'n't yer?
	(*Pause.*)
Maurice:	I was.
	(*They share unspoken memories.*) (Leigh 1997b: 36)

If the dialogue in this touching little scene is minimal, it is even scantier in the next four moments, the first of which occurs soon after this one. Cynthia has suddenly asked her brother for a cuddle ('please sweet'eart!') and, without his saying anything at all, we see, from the expression in his eyes, as he rather reluctantly holds her in his arms, how terribly uncomfortable and lost this makes him feel. Not long afterwards, Cynthia asks Maurice if he is not 'gonna make [her] an auntie now' and, as the screenplay puts it, he is '*overcome*'. So much so that he starts to tell the truth about Monica's inability to have children – 'Listen, Cynth...' – before abruptly deciding that it would be better to leave. This he soon does and we next see him alone, in an empty Victorian pub. We first see him in long shot – sitting alone with a pint of lager under a *'huge antique portrait of a forgotten dignitary'* (1997b: 40) – and then in close-up. He looks absolutely forlorn and these two shots might well remind us of the portraits Maurice takes – except, of course, that these are without any smile. We then get a quick cut to a shot of Maurice and Monica sitting at their kitchen table, and this shot also momentarily resembles a portrait.

Like the rest of their home, the kitchen is kept spotlessly clean and the framing of this last shot conveys a strong sense of the aching sadness at the centre of this couple's life. The ensuing exchange goes a long way towards explaining it. Having recently been with Cynthia in his father's room, Maurice begins by asking Monica how her mother reacted when Monica's father died. Maurice then confesses that he hated his dad for the fact that he 'never said a word about [his] mum after she'd died.' Now, however, he thinks that his father 'must've been in real pain' and that 'maybe he just couldn't share it'. A little later, he wonders if Roxanne 'ever misses' her father and the scene ends as follows:

Monica:	You can't miss what you never had.
Maurice:	Can't you? (*Pause. He chuckles sadly.*) I was gonna kill 'im. Poor Cynthia!
Monica:	Saint Cynthia!
Maurice:	She tried her best.
Monica:	Did she?
Maurice:	Yeah. Yeah, she did. She gave me a lot of love. (*Overcome, he gets up and goes to the end of the garden. Monica watches him. Tears appear in her eyes.*) (Leigh 1997b: 41–2)

Once again, Maurice is overcome, as is Monica who has of course temporarily forgotten that she and Maurice permanently miss the child they are unable to have.

Saint Cynthia?

When they are on the phone trying to set up their first meeting and Hortense asks Cynthia what she is 'doing this Saturday coming', Cynthia pathetically replies that she is doing 'Nothing – I'm never bloody doing anything.' This can put us in mind of Johnny's 'unemployed negativity' and of his determination to make everyone he comes into contact with explain whether or not, in effect, *they* are 'doing anything' – anything worthwhile with their lives. From this point of view, *Secrets and Lies* is about Cynthia's discovery of something to *do*: she can and eventually does face up to the truth. As, of course, do the other major characters in this film.

And though none of them change as dramatically as Cynthia does, they all become more alive as they get caught up and carried along on the same traumatic journey. The film ends in Cynthia's cramped back garden with the following exchange:

Cynthia:	Cor ... Oh, this is the life, ain' it?

Hortense/Roxanne: Yeah.
(... the three of them enjoy the afternoon together.)

There is obviously some irony here but it is a gentle irony that leaves us with a sense that Cynthia is right after all. Yes, this *is* one version, at least, of what, patting her brother's belly, Cynthia had earlier called 'the good life'. Or, as she said during the drinking of toasts around Roxanne's birthday cake, 'this is livin', ain' it?'

The film's last scene, which celebrates the mother together with her two daughters, is shot from above, which can take us back to the film's only other shot from above – of the wreath for Hortense's adopted mother at the beginning. Furthermore, it can also usefully remind us of the comment made by the triplet's mother (Sheila Kelley) as her three little girls pose for their photograph: 'I never thought I'd have any. Fertility treatment. It's a miracle.' Given the nature of the film's preoccupation with children – the way in which it works to make it difficult for us to take them for granted – this declaration deserves to be read as one of a number of instances when *Secrets and Lies* is making us aware of (what we have seen Eric Santner call) 'the Psychotheology of Everyday Life'. There are two other such instances: (i) Hortense's reluctance to hear her friend Dionne's confession and of Dionne saying that she needs to 'cleanse [her] soul'; and (ii) Monica's reference to 'Saint Cynthia'. Neither of these is without irony, and the second especially is fairly drenched in it,[2] but it seems that it would be a mistake to simply dismiss their surface meaning out of hand.

When Graham Fuller told Leigh that it had occurred to him that Jeremy in *Naked* 'represents the Devil', Leigh responded by admitting that 'that's true on a certain level'. Though all of his films, including *Naked*, are 'exercises in realism', he often has 'a metaphor ... on the go':

> In *Naked*, it seemed appropriate, at a level which shouldn't be taken too seriously but nevertheless exists, that Johnny is implicitly, internally, on a descent into the Inferno, and here in Jeremy is the Devil! It's as straightforward as that, for what it's worth. It informs the texture of the piece. But if you made it literal or self-conscious then it would be crass and irrelevant, and it would turn into another kind of film entirely (Fuller 1995: xxxvii)

So perhaps something similar might be said about the theological language found in *Secrets and Lies* – not that it should be read literally but that, instead of using the irony as an excuse to disregard it, we should allow this language to resonate, to raise questions and to keep certain possibilities open.

Both 'Naked' and 'Secrets and Lies'

> I've spent my entire life trying to make people 'appy...
>   – Maurice in *Secrets and Lies* (Leigh 1997b: 100)

Whatever else is going on in *Secrets and Lies*, it constitutes a resounding reaffirmation of some of those values that *Naked* had put in question. Imagine what Johnny would make of Maurice's job! What, from Johnny's point of view, could be more puerile than Maurice's endlessly renewed effort to get people – if only for the brief moment they are having their photograph taken – to smile!

What then ought we to make of such a radical incommensurability – between these two characters and the two different worlds they represent?

Judging by the 'Best of the Nineties' *Cinemascope* poll mentioned in chapter one, it would seem that for many filmgoers it is a question of either/or, one or the other. So that, while *Naked* was ranked fifth out of eighty-four on the main list (and, solely within Canada, second out of twenty), *Secrets and Lies* was ranked sixty-fifth on the first list and did not even get on to the other one. Given a choice between the kind of affirmation *Secrets and Lies* makes and the exploration of the dark side that we find in *Naked*, this group, at least, would seem to have a definite preference for the latter.

But what makes Leigh's work so extraordinarily impressive is precisely the fact that he can do both of these things: on the one hand, for example, working so hard to persuade us to resist any urge we may be experiencing to feel superior to either Monica's efforts at transforming her environment (her stencilling, the miniature fences in the garden, the master bedroom, and so forth) or Cynthia's laughing decision that her two daughters – together and sitting beside her for the first time – look 'like a couple o' garden gnomes'; while, on the other hand, investing himself just as fully in Johnny's scathing criticism and wit.

CHAPTER TEN

A Meta-commentary on Leigh's Art and an Exploration of Female Friendship

Ricky: Come, er, to 'ave a laugh, 'ave you? Take the piss?

Annie: No!

Hannah: Oh, yeah – seven hours on a coach for a laugh! We're not that desperate!

Ricky: Come to lead us on a bit more, 'ave you?

        (*Annie rushes off.*)

Hannah: You've upset 'er now!

Ricky: She's not the only one 'oo's upset!

Hannah: Well, all right! That's why we've come up 'ere – 'cos we care about you!

        (Leigh 1997a: 77)

While I agree with Ray Carney that – from Sylvia in *Bleak Moments* through Naseem in *Hard Labour* and Mark in *Meantime* up to Cyril and Shirley in *High Hopes* and Wendy and Andy in *Life is Sweet* – Leigh imagines his 'most interesting characters to be artists of life' (2000: 243), I also believe, as discussed in the last chapter, that in the studio portraits sequence in *Secrets and Lies* we see Leigh's art becoming more *overtly* self-reflexive than it had previously been. *Career Girls* takes this development much further; as does *Topsy-Turvy*, the film that follows it. So that, in this respect at least, these three films might be thought of as forming a trilogy. To say this is not to deny the fact that, at the same time, over and beyond the ways in which they draw attention to their own status as works of art, these three films explore their own different kinds of subject matter, with *Career Girls* being primarily about friendship, the friendship of two young women, Annie and Hannah, who meet up again (Annie visiting Hannah in London) after having last seen one another six years earlier when they moved out of the flat they shared as students attending North London Polytechnic.

In her brief but thoughtful review of this film in 1997, Stella Bruzzi makes the following claim:

> *Career Girls* offers the ultimate meta-commentary on the Leigh method. Like a Richard Rogers building, in which normally internal structures are displayed on the outside, *Career Girls* flaunts its own artifice, deliberately announcing itself as a deeply implausible tale. Not only do Annie and Hannah meet by chance (over a single weekend) the three characters featured prominently in the flashbacks of their undergraduate days, but they discuss (and laugh at) the improbability of these freak encounters. This self-conscious narrative technique is liberating for the audience, who are invited to collude in and enjoy their own gross manipulation.

It is probable that Bruzzi is referring here exclusively to the 'method' Leigh employs in this particular film, if only because this is the first (and so far the only) film in which we find the coincidences on which she bases her claim. (It is also, incidentally, the first of Leigh's films that makes extensive use of flashbacks and it stands out as well because of the frequency with which the film utilises tracking shots and a hand-held camera.) But the claim to be made here (and I am not assuming Bruzzi would necessarily disagree) is that *Career Girls* offers a meta-commentary not just on the 'method' Leigh used to make it but on the very substance at the core of all of his films.

In support of this, we can note Leigh's own claim that his films take the form of 'a lamentation and a celebration of human experience' (Fuller 1995: xxxiii). It seems, indeed, that *Career Girls* is organised in such a way as to help us better understand why this is so: why, in other words, a movement back and forth between lamentation and celebration so often seems to be the most appropriate response to human experience. To put it simply, then, *Career Girls* is largely organised in terms of arrivals and departures and, in so far as arrivals are understood as humans coming together, then they can be seen as opportunities, at least, for celebration – just as, insofar as departures are seen as humans-who-care-for-one-another separating, they are occasions for lamenting. Obviously not all arrivals and separations are of this kind so that, for example, as far as the latter are concerned, the person leaving and the person left often experience them differently.

It is tempting to say that the film opens and ends on the platform at King's Cross station, which is both where Annie (Lynda Steadman) arrives and is met by Hannah (Katrin Cartlidge), and also where we last see them saying goodbye to one another as Annie leaves on the return journey to her home in the north, in or near Wakefield. But this would be inaccurate because we first see Annie on the train, still on her way to London, and, in three flashbacks, we see her as a young student – first examining a college notice-board in the hope of finding accomodation; then arriving at an address that had advertised a vacancy and being met and interviewed by Hannah and her flat-mate, Claire (Kate Byers); and then moving in with Hannah and Claire. So that before Annie arrives at King's Cross in the film's present, we have already seen her arrive in her first college digs ten years earlier. Nor are these the only two arrivals we witness in the film's opening minutes.

After picking Annie up at the station, Hannah then drives her through London to the Victorian house in which she has her flat: 'Here we are', she tells Annie as they enter, 'Home Sweet Home. Welcome to my humble abode, and other domestic clichés.' We have not seen them in Hannah's flat for more than a minute before we get two more flashbacks, the first of which shows their arrival in the other flat they shared together as students (this one, after they had dumped Claire, over a Chinese takeaway); the second, their departure from it, when they move out at the end of their four years in college.

At this point, we are just over ten minutes into the film. And in the next quarter of an hour we either see or hear about a number of other arrivals and departures. Thus, in flashback we see Hannah and Annie getting out of their arrangement with (or separating from) Claire while, in the present, we hear Annie explaining how she ended a one-and-a-half-year relationship with a man who had turned out to be 'a dickhead', and Hannah confessing that her 'problem' is that 'none of them [last] a weekend with [her]' – she 'just can't hack it'. In another flashback, we then see Annie wearing kitchen goggles as she prepares to cut up onions in the kitchen of the flat they shared with Claire. Hannah finds this very funny but she quickly takes over the job herself because onions do not bother her. As she explains, she 'can't cry': she has not 'cried since [she] was nine years old'. Annie then admits that she has 'been crying ever since [she] can remember – well, since [she] were eight, 'cos ... [she does not] remember anything before that' – 'it's just, like, one big blank'. And this prompts the following exchange:

Hannah:	(*Mock tragic*) My dad ran off with another woman.
	(*Annie lights the gas.*)
Annie:	So did mine. Coincidence, eh?
Hannah:	Synchronicity.
Annie:	Yeah, but what is synchronicity, and what's, you know like, er, coincidence? 'Cos like Jung says that synchronicity is when two different things happen at the same time, you know like, one's, er, bein' a normal state, and the other, you know, is a psychic one. (Leigh 1997a: 25)

Claire enters the kitchen at this point and – as she makes Annie upset by complaining about the fish she is preparing for their meal – Claire inadvertently helps us to understand why Hannah and Annie decided to move out on her.

This (kitchen) memory is followed by a quick cut to the present, just to inform us who has been remembering this (Hannah, now in bed) and to let us know that

Annie in the next room is also awake in her bed and recollecting the content of the next scene, where she is sitting, as a student, in a tiered lecture theatre. The lecturer is explaining how, in 1920, in *Beyond the Pleasure Principle*, Freud 'enlarged his first theory of dreams to cover the recurrent nightmares of shell-shocked soldiers in the First World War, what we refer to today as post-traumatic stress disorder'.[1] Here the lecture is momentarily interrupted by the entrance of a *'tubby, scruffy male student'* (Leigh 1997a: 26) and when it resumes the lecturer explains that the soldiers' 'dreams show the compulsion to repeat, and by doing so, to try to master actively what was done to the person as a passive agent of trauma'. After another quick cut to the present, which reminds us that it is Annie who is remembering this, the next flashback – on approximately the twenty-five minute mark – shows the same male student, Ricky (Mark Benton), moving with his belongings in with Hannah and Annie, to share their flat over the Chinese takeaway. And within the next ten minutes we see all three getting to become friends, a process that culminates in Ricky's first confessing his love for Annie, then in his being devastated by her rejection (which she tries to make as kind and tactful as possible), and by his abrupt departure, both from the flat and also from the college.

Back in the present – now approximately thirty-five minutes into the film – we see how painful Annie still finds this recollection and it is quickly followed by another memory in which we see how Annie and Hannah felt so badly about Ricky's departure that they actually took a seven-hour coach ride to the north of England to see him (though this flashback breaks off before they have done so – his Nan (Margo Stanley) tells them that he is not in).

One other thing to mention here is that, soon after she and Annie had arrived in her flat, Hannah had explained what she had in mind for the following day's entertainment: first a visit to check out some high-priced accomodations ('Seein' 'ow the other 'arf lives. I thought it might be fun for you ... We'll 'ave to look as though we can spend that sort of money') and then a meal in an 'unusual' Chinese restaurant in the evening. So when we cut from the memory of their trip north back to the present, it is now the second day of Annie's visit and we see her and Hannah being shown first around a luxury penthouse apartment overlooking the Thames by a Mr Evans (Andy Serkis) and then around a flat in a large Victorian house by Adrian Spinks (Joe Tucker).

It turns out that Hannah and Annie knew Adrian at college, that Annie was in love with him and, as she later confesses to Hannah, that she has not 'stopped thinking about him for the last ten years'. So if we exclude the fact that Hannah and Annie both experienced the loss of their fathers when they were eight years old (on the grounds that it happened long before they got to know one another), this meeting is the film's first major coincidence – the first of its *staged* coincidences. And perhaps, on its own, it would not seem entirely unbelievable. But the following day – the third and final day of Annie's visit – they see both Claire (who runs by without noticing them in a park) and, when they decide at the last moment to visit their old flat, they encounter Ricky, who is sitting on the doorstep of the Chinese takeaway, which is boarded-up. And, as Annie says, after Claire has gone by: 'The chance of that happening is one in a million. You know, seeing two people like that in the same weekend.' So that when they then bump into Ricky, it is (again in Annie's words) 'too much, isn't it?' 'I mean', says Hannah, 'a coincidence is one thing, you know, but, er, this is a joke, innit?' So what ought we to make of all of this?

(a) *Departures/Separations*

In the first half of *Career Girls* we hear about two departures (of Hannah's and Annie's fathers, both of whom – as already noted – left when their daughters were eight years old), we see two (Ricky's after his unsuccessful declaration of love for Annie, and Annie's and Hannah's departure from their flat over the Chinese takeaway), and we see Hannah and Annie disentangling themselves from Claire (though we do not actually see them saying goodbye to her). Of these five departures, the only one that seems to involve no pain at all is the last one. And the reason is simple: neither Hannah nor Annie cared much for Claire, nor so far as one can see did she feel particularly close to them. Which is why it seems fitting when (in the present) Claire fails to recognise them in the park and they make no effort to call after her. On the other hand, because they did care about their fathers, about Ricky and about their flat, these four departures are traumatic – the first two presumably having a lot to do with Annie's memory loss and Hannah's inability to cry.

As for their moving-out of their flat at the end of their four years in college, this is so important a memory that it gets two flashbacks, the second in the midst of their meal in the Chinese restaurant on Annie's second day in London. And of course it is not just that they are leaving the flat: it is that they are leaving one another. So that on this occasion they *both* cry, Hannah for the first time in many years.

When, after Ricky has told Annie that he loves her and she has done her best to let him down gently ('I think you're lovely. You're really smashin', but, er...'), he is the one who is devastated but there is no doubt that it is painful for her too. This, of course, is why she and Hannah go north to see Ricky. And again, the significance of this memory is indicated by the fact that it too gets two flashbacks. As already noted, the first one breaks off when they visit his house and his Nan tells them he is not in. The second flashback occurs near the end of the film, immediately after they have (in the film's present) left Ricky sitting outside the Chinese takeaway. They have just explained that they have to go because Annie has a train to catch and they have departed to the sound of Ricky showering them with abuse:

Ricky:	... You never liked us, anyway!
Hannah:	(*Crying*) I did, actually!
Ricky:	Shite!
Annie:	I thought a lot about you.
Ricky:	You don't think! Selfish. Talk, talk, RABBIT!
Annie:	That's not true!
Ricky:	Ah, tittle off! (*They leave him.*)
	Rancid! (*He shouts after them.*) Rancid! Go on – fuck yer!
	(*They walk towards the car. Hannah touches Annie.*)
	LESBOS!!! (Leigh 1997a: 76)

This immediately leads into the second half of the flashback devoted to their trip north. Ricky's Nan has told them that Ricky might be on the seafront and this is where they find him. But he is still hurt and not pleased to see them. Instead of expressing gratitude for their having taken the trouble to visit him, Ricky curses them. As they walk away from him, '*RICKY rants in the distance*':

Ricky: FUCK OFF! FUCKING … NOSY PARKER!
            (*Hannah and Annie head towards the town. Ricky strides
            angrily along the empty promenade, as the wild North Sea rages
            in the distance.*) (Leigh 1997a: 78)

And since this in turn is almost immediately followed by Hannah and Annie taking their leave of one another at King's Cross, it can be said that the film ends with a series of departures.

There is another separation that seems particularly important. In flashback, in the second half of the film, we see how Adrian took his leave of Annie. They are sitting on a park bench. Adrian has his arm around her, they are kissing, and then Annie asks him why he 'split up with [his] ex-girlfriend'. Adrian says it was because 'she wanted to whisk [him] up the aisle' and we then get the following exchange:

Annie: Was it 'cos o' her … or, because you don't like commitment?
Adrian: It's a load o' bollocks, all that shit. (*He takes his arm away, and
            sits up.*)
Annie: What?
Adrian: Commitment.
            (*Pause.*)
            Vagina. Nice place. Wouldn't wanna live there.
            (*And he gets up and walks off. Shocked, Annie watches him go. She
            starts to cry.*) (Leigh 1997a: 63)

(b) *Repetition, Confession, Healing*

Considering the sheer number of departures and arrivals in *Career Girls*, the college lecturer's words on repetition seem strikingly relevant here, especially in their insistence that 'the compulsion to repeat' that was evident in the recurrent nightmares and dreams 'of shell-shocked soldiers in the First World War' should, according to Freud, be understood as an attempt 'to master actively what was done to the person as a passive agent of trauma'. It appears that, as Annie and Hannah relive some of these painful memories and discuss what they have learned, this is precisely what they are doing – actively mastering what has been done to them as passive agents. But it is also obvious that they have both grown stronger and learned a lot over the preceding six years that they spent apart.

Consider, for example, in the Chinese restaurant conversation, Annie's response to Hannah's pointing out that Adrian 'was a shit':

Annie: Oh, yeah, he was a shit. But when you're in love with a
            bastard, you just can't help yourself. You see, psychologically, I
            look up to my father – you know, I see him as strong. In spite
            of everything he's done. But he doesn't respect women, and
            he's never given me the love that I deserve. And that's why I
            have this … need, you know, to – to crave his respect. And
            seek his approval. That's obviously why I choose the men I do.
            (Leigh 1997a: 67)

This restaurant conversation that the two friends have on their second evening
together is obviously crucial and worth looking at more closely. It begins with
Hannah confessing that the time just after Annie arrived in her life was 'the worst
for [her]'. She 'was right on the edge' and actually told herself 'You've either got to
change, or you're going to go under'. Perhaps emboldened by this, she also confesses
that she has 'always envied' Annie and 'admire[d]' her 'innocence'. Annie wants to
know what she means by this and we get the following exchange:

Hannah: You're a very … sort of … trusting person.
Annie: I trust people too easily. That's why I get walked over. You
            see, I envy your ability to stand on your own two feet.
Hannah: Yeah, but that's just self-protection, innit?
Annie: And the way you deal with men.
Hannah: That's all I ever do is deal with them. I mean at least you're
            able to fall in love with them. Even though you are a walking
            open wound.
            (*They gently laugh together.*)
            I'm not strong enough to be as vulnerable as you.
Annie: But … I see that vulnerability as a weakness. You're the strong
            one.
Hannah: Well, you see, if we could be a combination, we'd be the
            perfect woman, wouldn' we? Unfortunately, we can't.

Moments later, Hannah is pointing out that Annie has 'changed more than [she]
think[s]' ('you've stopped bumping into things, and you can look me in the eye')
(1997a: 66). And from this the conversation shifts to Annie's feelings about Adrian
and the speech quoted above, which we can now note elicits the following response
from Hannah:

Hannah: I don't respect my father at all. He's weak. Look what he's
            done to Thelma [Hannah's alcoholic mother]. I don't ever
            want to end up like her – not ever. And when I look at men,
            all I see … is dangerous weakness. I don't want it to be that
            way. I just can't help it. It makes me feel lonely.
            (*She is on the edge of tears. They are both reflective…*)
            (Leigh 1997a: 67–8)

Clearly, then, with this confession of loneliness (added to the confessions that precede it) we see that Hannah has grown 'strong enough' to be vulnerable. And, as if to underline the point, this confession is immediately followed by the flashback to '*that moving-out occasion*' when Hannah cried for the first time since she was nine years old.

What the Chinese restaurant conversation also makes clear is the understanding Annie and Hannah now have as to why they like one another so much. Elsewhere in the film we see that Hannah often seems (in Ricky's words) 'not very 'appy' and that she is frequently 'very aggressive'. 'D'you wanna fight?' she says on different occasions to Claire and to Adrian, each time clenching her fists. 'Sometimes', she tells Annie at one point (in flashback, by way of explaining her sarcasm at Ricky's expense), 'I get the devil in me.' In fact, like Benjamin's Baudelaire, the student Hannah seems perpetually to be in 'an attitude of combat'. So that what Baudelaire wrote of his friend Constantin Guys – 'he is combative, even when alone, and parries his own blows' (quoted in Benjamin 1973: 118) – seems to apply equally to her. Of course, it might also remind us of Johnny (in *Naked*) and, indeed, Hannah's word-play sometimes sounds exactly like his. As, for example, in her self-conscious follow-up to the expression 'Welcome to my humble abode' – 'and other domestic clichés'. The conversation Annie and Hannah have in the restaurant helps us to see why they are so drawn to one another. And it does this, while simultaneously serving, like the three coincidences already mentioned, to draw our attention to Leigh's art: in this case, to the fact that nothing characterises it so much as the way in which it manages to combine and keep in play the opposing qualities the two friends manifest – achingly vulnerable Annie and combative, abrasive Hannah.

(c) *The idea of 'true happiness' and the film's ending*

If Leigh's work typically involves both lamentation and celebration, individual films sometimes lean more in one of these directions than in the other. But one can say that *Career Girls* is pretty evenly balanced between them.

On the one hand, the film is a strong and moving celebration of Annie and Hannah's friendship. So that while there are tears when they part, there is also laughter and a sense of fun – their friendship has been strengthened and it seems more than likely that they will meet again. But, on the other hand, this is not to say that there are no longer any problems on the horizon. For one thing, we have only just been exposed to Ricky's sad plight and, as Bruzzi says, like 'Annie and Hannah, we are left bereft in the knowledge that we feel for Ricky, but are ultimately powerless to help him'. Apart from this, we also need to reflect on the two brief exchanges the friends have in the last seconds.

When they are on the platform, and all that remains is for them to say goodbye and for Annie to climb on the train, Hannah announces she has a little present, which turns out to be the copy of *Wuthering Heights* first seen in a flashback at the beginning of the film, when Hannah had introduced Annie to the ritual of asking 'Ms Brontë' a question.[2] In this ritual, after the question is asked, Hannah '*does a "magic spell" gesture over the book*', opens it at random, and tries to find an answer in the first words that catch her attention. On that original occasion, Annie's question was 'Ms Bronte, Ms Bronte, will I ... er ... will I find a feller soon?' On the railway platform at the end her question is 'Will I find true happiness soon?' And after Hannah performs '*the searching ritual*', the only word she comes up with is '"Pang". Load o' rubbish!' she declares. 'Always was.'

Then, after Annie has got into the train and Hannah begun to walk away, Annie leans out of the doorway and calls out 'D'you think there'll be any more coincidences on the train?' 'I dunno!' says Hannah. 'Maybe you'll meet the Man o' your Dreams!' And though this is said amiably, without the slightest hint of any malice, it can cause us – if we remember Annie's dreams and fantasies – to think twice.

Consider first the dream Ricky heard Annie relate in a seminar and that he brings up in an early conversation we see him having (in flashback) with her and Hannah:

Hannah:	What dream?
Ricky:	Oh, erm, she 'as, er, this dream about, er, this big, er, dark feller in 'er bedroom.
Hannah:	Yer, I know.
Annie:	Dark figure.
Ricky:	With a stick. (Leigh 1997a: 30)

Then the later scene (again in flashback) in which we see Annie '*who is standing against the wall, playing with a blue chiffon scarf*' and '*very tense*', as she takes the risk of trying to explain something to Adrian that is obviously very important to her:

Annie:	(*Sighing*) I've got this, er ... recurring fantasy about ... em, well ... in this fantasy, er ... (*She bites the scarf.*) I'm having sex – well, actually, I'm being *forced* to 'ave sex ... with somebody. (*Pause.*) And the thing is that ... there's a lot o' men, you know ... watchin' us. (*She sighs, she looks at him, and she clears her throat.*)
Adrian:	Oh?
Annie:	Don't get me wrong, it's only a fantasy – it's not reality. It's a myth that a lot o' men believe, but ... it can lead to rape. You know, the idea that ... a woman means 'yeah' when ... like, em ... she means 'no'.
Adrian:	I could bring me mates back after five-a-side to watch if you want. (*Annie is devastated by this. She covers her face with the scarf.*) (Leigh 1997a: 61)

For one thing, then, far from being the 'Sir Lancelot' she thinks of when Hannah says the estate agent they are going to meet is called Lance ('he sounds like a gentleman'), the man of Annie's dreams would seem to be something of a sadist. Apart from that, Hannah's remark (the film's last words) can remind us of something Annie had said on the first evening of her visit, that she is hoping her 'luck might change', that she 'might meet somebody'. So however much Annie may have changed in other ways (most obviously, of course, in her appearance, her skin condition having completely cleared up),[3] we see that she has not given up on her desire, however problematical she herself may now realise it to be. It would seem, furthermore, that she still believes in the idea, first, that 'true happiness' is attainable and, secondly, that it has for her to take the form of sharing a home ('Home Sweet Home') with a partner of the opposite sex.

In light of our reflections in the last chapter on the often fleeting nature of happiness (of happiness in the form of lucky breaks), and also in light of the intense happiness this film shows Annie and Hannah enjoying together, it is easy to feel *some* sadness at the end of the film, as these two good friends again go their separate ways.

CHAPTER ELEVEN

Work as Play: The Utopian Element

'People must be amuthed, Thquire, thomehow,' continued Sleary ... 'they can't be alwath a working...'
> – Charles Dickens (*Hard Times*, 1969: 82)

Topsy-Turvy is a film about all of us who suffer and strain to make other people laugh ...
> – Mike Leigh (1999: ix)

The magic will of course not necessarily be apparent to all viewers. Many will come to *Topsy-Turvy* with scarcely a clue to what *The Mikado* might once have meant, and for them it may well resemble some strange species of vanished pop art. It's hard for me to imagine coming to Gilbert and Sullivan cold, in the middle of life, having been born into the latter phases of a world where they were part of the décor.
> – Geoffrey O'Brien (2000: 16)

... of course we all went ... to see Gilbert and Sullivan. To this day I remain a closet Savoyard; I play G&S records when I'm on the rowing machine at home.
> – Mike Leigh (in Movshovitz 2000: 39)

Though I am only a year younger than he is, unlike Leigh, who would seem (like O'Brien) to have also grown up in a world in which Gilbert and Sullivan 'were part of the décor', I managed to grow up hardly aware of their existence. Far from having, like Leigh (in the words of a 1997 interviewer), 'nursed a deep affection [for them] since compulsory childhood visits to the D'Oyly Carte' (Movshovitz 2000: 127), I had somehow decided by the time I reached adulthood that life was too short to spend any part of it listening to light operas or musicals. I was therefore definitely one of those who came to see *Topsy-Turvy* 'cold'. If not for the fact that I had loved *Naked* and *Secrets and Lies*, I would never have gone to see such a movie. I went without enthusiasm, full of apprehension. And was I immediately bowled over? No, I was not. On first viewing, I thought it was interesting and much better than I had thought it could possibly be. But I was not bowled over.

I am now, however. It has grown on me. After a number of viewings, I have come to think of it as one of Leigh's masterpieces. Though Peter Wollen was the only one of the critics who responded to the recent *Sight and Sound* poll on 'The Ten Greatest Films of all Time' to put it on his list, I do not think his choice of *Topsy-Turvy* (as his number eight) was by any means a ridiculous one.

Topsy-Turvy is of course in many ways radically unlike the rest of Leigh's oeuvre and so, though I will be arguing that it can usefully be seen as the third film in two separate trilogies (the one including *Secrets and Lies* and *Career Girls*, the other *Naked* and *Secrets and Lies*), I will begin by acknowledging how different it is. But in order to do this more effectively, let us recall the opening twelve minutes or so of this astonishing film.

The opening sequence

Over a blank screen we first hear a man's voice ('One, two – two, two'), then the sound of a piano and then, as the credits start to appear, we hear (but do not see) three young women singing from *The Mikado*:

Women:	So please you, Sir, we much regret
	If we have failed in etiquette
	Towards a man of rank so high…
Woman 1:	But youth, of course, must have its fling,
	So pardon us… (Leigh 1999: 3)

When they stop singing and the piano solo fades, we get the film's title and then '*dissolve to a sea of empty blue theatre seats*' (1999: 4). A caption tells us that this is 'London, January 5th 1884' and, as the camera cranes down to the first row and then tilts up to the balcony, we see three men in black suits who are at work slowly checking each seat, row by row.

From this the film cuts to Sir Arthur Sullivan (Allan Corduner) who quickly sits up in bed '*in shock as though suddenly having woken from a bad dream*' (ibid.). It is eight o'clock and, though his manservant, Louis, tries to dissuade him, he is determined to go to the theatre. With the assistance of Louis (who gives him his morphine shot, shaves him and helps him dress) and the maidservant, Clothilde (who makes him hot coffee), he is quickly got ready, escorted (by Louis) to the cab and driven to the theatre. Once there, Louis helps him off with his hat and coat, and his musical director first gives him a flask of brandy to drink, then puts a cigarette in Sullivan's mouth and lights it. Thus fortified, Sullivan himself puts on the white kid gloves (that Louis hands him) and we next see him (as if we are on stage, facing out into the blue seats which are now all occupied) emerging from the podium and facing the audience who greet his appearance with loud applause. Obviously delighted by this reception, he then turns to face the stage (and us) and it is at this point – as he begins to conduct the orchestra through the overture to *Princess Ida* – that the last credit (Written and Directed by Mike Leigh) comes on the screen.

The opening night performance of *Princess Ida* has now begun and we get a couple of excerpts from it: first the chorus singing about how they are 'string[ing up]/The faithless King/In the old familiar way!'; then – after we have seen a call-boy asking and receiving Mr Cook's permission to knock on Mr Grossmith's dressing-room door and inform him he is to be on stage in five minutes – we see Mr Grossmith (Martin Savage) acting the part of 'a genuine philanthropist' who cannot understand why everyone finds him 'a disagreeable man'. In another brief back-stage scene, the Armourer tells W. S. Gilbert, who looks quite miserable, that the show is '*un succès certain*'. This is then followed by an equally brief scene in which (the show now over) we see Sullivan collapsing – and then recovering with the help of Louis and others – on his way out of the theatre.

We cut from this to Gilbert (Jim Broadbent), who is '*clutching a newspaper*' and striding '*purposefully through the hall of his house*'. It is the following morning. '*He steams into the breakfast room*' where three '*servants, a middle-aged butler, a housekeeper and a maidservant*' are waiting '*in a line by the door*' and his '*wife is sitting at the table in her black riding apparel*'. Standing '*in front of a nautical portrait of himself*' (1999: 10), Gilbert then reads out the *Times'* review of the previous night's performance of *Princess Ida*. Though much of it is complimentary, he dismisses those sections as 'sugared words' and focuses on the criticism it offers instead. He is particularly irritated by the reviewer's claim that 'W.S. Gilbert abundantly proves he is still the legitimate monarch of the Realm of Topsy-Turvydom'. The scene ends with Gilbert striding out of the room while his wife (Lesley Manville) '*scuttles down the hall after [him]*' and the '*servants, still in a line, crane forward to watch their master and mistress disappear into a room at the far end of the hall*' (1999: 11).

We are now almost at the ten-minute mark and we pass over it early in the next scene, which takes place in Sullivan's bedroom. Sullivan, who is sitting up in bed, has visitors: Richard D'Oyly Carte (Ron Cook) and Carte's assistant, Helen Lenoir (Wendy Nottingham). They tell him that *Princess Ida* is doing well and he tells them he has made some resolutions, the first of which is 'to travel to the Continent … as soon as [his] health permits' and the last to 'write no more operas for the Savoy.' He feels that he must 'write a grand opera', that he 'cannot waste any more time on these trivial soufflés', that this 'work with Gilbert is quite simply killing [him]'.

The last scene in this opening section takes place in the bedroom of Gilbert's wife, Kitty. She is sitting up in bed, holding an open book. He is in evening wear and sitting in an armchair. He has evidently just dropped by to say goodnight. He looks unhappy and we understand why when, as if talking to himself (around twelve minutes into the film), he cites and comments on *The Times'* verdict: '"The King of Topsy-Turvydom". Humiliating.'

What makes this film stand out from Leigh's other films?

The most obvious, then, of the various ways in which *Topsy-Turvy* marks a new departure for Leigh is that it is set in the late-nineteenth century and is based on the lives of some actual real-life figures, Gilbert and Sullivan and the people around them. It is the only one of his films so far that is not set in the present and whose characters are not fictional. Though Leigh has suggested that all of his films 'aspire to the condition of documentary' (Movshovitz 2000: 32), there is a sense in which (because of its working to recreate a moment in history) this one might reasonably be said to be more documentary-like (without of course *being* one) than any of the others. But, at the same time, because it has so much music – on the soundtrack, in rehearsal, in performance – this (Leigh's only) historical film can also be thought of as a musical, and there is certainly no other Leigh film of which *that* might be said.

But the feature of *Topsy-Turvy* that distinguishes it most dramatically from the rest of the films is made up of a combination of the extraordinarily creative nature of – and the extraordinary position occupied by – its two central characters. If we hear on the stage the chorus celebrating the stringing up of a 'faithless King/In the old familiar way,' what we hear and see off-stage is Gilbert and Sullivan being treated as if *they* are the new royalty, indeed the monarchs that the *Times'* review called them (or called Gilbert). If the film opens with our hearing the three little maids of *The Mikado* offering a cheeky apology ('But youth, of course, must have its fling') for their having 'failed in etiquette', Gilbert and Sullivan always receive the 'deference due/To [men] of pedigree'. At the same time, though Gilbert and Sullivan are treated like kings, they are not idle. Far from it. They actually work extremely hard and they are very productive.

Considering that Leigh is best-known for his commitment to ordinary life, this is a radical departure, as Leigh would seem to be reminding us near the end when Kitty asks her husband if he does not think it would 'be wondrous if perfectly commonplace people gave each other a round of applause at the end of the day?' Though it is true that many of the 'perfectly commonplace' (if also strikingly idiosyncratic) characters in Leigh's films have their extraordinary moments, *Naked*'s Johnny is the only one of Leigh's characters before *Topsy-Turvy*'s Gilbert and Sullivan who can be said to be extraordinarily creative (even if, in his case, the creativity often manifests itself negatively). Unlike the lower-class and unemployed Johnny, they, however, are extremely popular artists who have been handsomely rewarded for their work. They have servants, as we have seen, who cater to their every need. So while they are not the first of Leigh's characters to enjoy an upper-class lifestyle – think of some of the characters in *Who's Who*, of the Earl in *A Sense of History* and of Laetitia and Rupert in *High Hopes* – they are the only ones who are extraordinary by virtue of their being both creative and wealthy. This combination explains some of the other things that make *Topsy-Turvy* so different.

On the one hand, the fact that Gilbert and Sullivan are so well-off means that they live and move in houses and buildings whose rooms are much more spacious than the rooms in which much of the action in Leigh's other films take place. Take, for example, the long hall in Gilbert's house, through which we see him striding after he has read *The Times* review to his wife and assembled servants. In fact, there is an air of spaciousness *throughout* the mostly indoor world of *Topsy-Turvy*, whether we are in houses or restaurants or the Savoy theatre.

At the same time, the nature of Gilbert and Sullivan's creativity means that, as we enter their world, we enter a sophisticated world of culture, one that prides itself on (among other things) its cosmopolitanism. Thus, the lengthy corridor in Sullivan's apartment – through which Louis rushes when he is getting his master ready for the opening performance of *Princess Ida* – is decorated in a maroon-coloured, Moroccan style and his servants speak with foreign accents, German in Louis' case, Belgian in Clothilde's. This is a film in which almost all of the characters take pleasure in the act of stringing words together and quite a few of them derive further enjoyment from their ability to speak sentences in foreign languages, usually French but we hear the occasional German and Italian phrase too.

So the film *sounds* very different to any of Leigh's other films, both because of the music and lyrics of Gilbert and Sullivan and because almost all of the characters are so much more articulate than Leigh's characters usually are.

And, in addition to sounding very different, *Topsy-Turvy* also *looks* very different, mainly because it is so much more colourful than any of Leigh's other films. The colours in question are not, however, those of the English countryside that feature so prominently in most of the Heritage films. They are the colours of clothes, of painted walls or wallpaper and of brightly-lit interiors, the most striking of which is the stage in the Savoy theatre. In his piece on the film, Malcom Sweet explains that 'cinematographer Dick Pope commissioned the General Electric Company to hand-blow several thousand period light bulbs':

> We did everything we could to exactly reproduce how it was in 1885. Deep, saturated colours on the stage, bathed in this new electric light. The Savoy was the first public building in the world to be lit by electricity. We wanted it to be like actually being in the Victorian period. (Pope quoted in Sweet 2000: 1)

The result is that many of the scenes are quite gorgeous to look at – and again, 'gorgeous' is not a word that seems appropriate to use in response to any aspect of Leigh's other films.

But over and above all of this, possibly the most important difference can be seen in the sheer size of the cast – the collaborative nature of Gilbert and Sullivan's art is such that it requires the talents of a large number of variously talented individuals to bring it to performance. In short, it requires a theatre *company* and we will see that there is a real sense in which it can be said that this company is *Topsy-Turvy*'s true protagonist.

There are of course other differences too, including some on the level of film technique. But these tend to be fairly minor. Since, for example, Leigh noted in interview that he never uses dissolves (Fuller 1995: xxix), it is interesting to see that he uses one this time near the beginning of *Topsy-Turvy*. But the point to make about this – and also about the few occasions in the film when the camera tracks in quickly on something – is that these camera movements still manage to be what Leigh has said he always wants them to be: 'unobtrusive' (Fuller 1995: xxvii).

So much, then, for the major (and some of the minor) differences. Now to the matter of the two trilogies *Topsy-Turvy* can be said to be completing.

Art and work: the two trilogies

In one of them, it is preceded by *Secrets and Lies* and *Career Girls*. If, in the studio-portraits sequence of *Secrets and Lies*, we see Leigh becoming more self-reflexive, and if *Career Girls* provides a kind of meta-commentary on his art, *Topsy-Turvy* offers a documentary-like account of the collaborative creation of an actual piece of popular art, Gilbert and Sullivan's *The Mikado*. In this trilogy, then, we are frequently being made aware of the fact that we are watching films, which is to say that these three films frequently interrupt the illusion of reality that they otherwise work so hard so create. Of countless possible examples in *Topsy-Turvy*, here are just two: first, the opening shot, in which we find ourselves looking directly at the theatre's empty seats; and second, one of the dressing-room scenes in which Durward Lely (Kevin McKidd) complains about the authentic costume he has to wear in *The Mikado* – he points out that he is 'not actually a Japanese peasant' and Gilbert agrees, reminding Lely that he is 'a Scotch actor who's taking the part of a Japanese prince who is posing as an itinerant minstrel'. Although it seems accurate to say that such scenes interrupt the illusion of reality on one level, they do so while simultaneously enhancing our sense that this is an extremely realistic portrayal of actors working together to put on a show.

If, in this trilogy, the focus is on *Topsy-Turvy*'s being about a work of *art*, in the other trilogy – in which this film is preceded by *Naked* and *Secrets and Lies* – the focus is on *Topsy-Turvy*'s being about the *work* of art. As discussed earlier, *Naked* and *Secrets and Lies* can be seen to adopt totally opposed attitudes towards work – with the latter arguing (implicitly) that we should admire anyone who rolls up his or her sleeves and 'gets on with the job at hand', and the former maintaining (in effect) that many jobs are pointless so that 'getting on with them' may be not at all admirable but rather a waste of time. For its part, *Topsy-Turvy* celebrates work but of a very special kind, the kind that goes into the creation of a collective art-work.

By bringing together as it does the two main concerns – work and art – of the three films (*Naked, Secrets and Lies* and *Career Girls*) that preceded it, *Topsy-Turvy* affords us a glimpse of a utopian possibility.

Kitty:	Highly amusing, Willie.
Gilbert:	Fatuous.
Kitty:	Oh. Surely Arthur likes it [*The Mikado*, which Gilbert has just been reading out to his wife]?
Gilbert:	He hasn't said otherwise.
Kitty:	(*subtly; dry irony*) It certainly is rich in human emotion and probability. (Leigh 1999: 68)

As we have seen, the film's opening sequence ends with Gilbert expressing dissatis-faction. He finds it humiliating to be known as the 'King of Topsy-Turvydom'. But we have also seen that Sullivan is even more dissatisfied. So much so that he maintains that 'work with Gilbert is … killing [him]'. When he tries later on to explain, it turns out that what he objects to is nothing less than Gilbert's 'world of topsy-turvydom' and its reliance on 'magic potion[s]'. Later still, he tells Gilbert that in his latest work-in-progress, he seems 'merely to have grafted on to the first act the tantalising suggestion that we are to be in the realms of human emotion and probability, only to disappoint us by reverting to [his] familiar world of topsy-turvydom'. And since, as Gilbert points out in response, Sullivan's taking 'exception to topsy-turvydom' means that he is taking exception to much of the work they have done together, the prospects for their continuing partnership do not look good. But then Kitty insists on taking her reluctant husband to a Japanese exhibition in Knightsbridge and he begins to get the idea for *The Mikado*. And when he starts to introduce it to Sullivan, the latter's interest is immediately aroused. Which – as we see Kitty noting above – seems a bit ironical in the light of his earlier objections.

After all, whatever else is to be said about the world of *The Mikado*, it is definitely a world of at least one kind of topsy-turvydom. Here, to make the point, is a summary.

The action begins with the arrival of Nanki-Poo in the courtyard of Ko-Ko's official residence, Ko-Ko being the Lord High Executioner of the town of Titipu. Nanki-Poo is the son of the Mikado of Japan but he is disguised as a wandering minstrel. A year earlier he had fallen in love with Yum-Yum but she was 'betrothed to her guardian Ko-Ko, a cheap tailor' at the time. So Nanki-Poo had left the town in despair. Having 'heard, a month ago, that Ko-Ko had been condemned to death for flirting' (Gilbert and Sullivan n.d.: 299), Nanki-Poo has now returned, only to discover, however, that the townspeople have not only released Ko-Ko from jail, they have made the former 'cheap tailor' both their 'Headsman' and the Lord High Executioner of Titipu, 'the highest rank a citizen can attain' (300).

In the words of a Chorus of Nobles, Ko-Ko is now a 'personage of noble rank and title' to whom everyone is expected to defer ('Defer, defer,/To the Lord High Executioner'); he is usually accompanied by Pooh-Bah, 'a particularly haughty and exclusive person, of pre-Adamite ancestral descent' (301), who is described in the Dramatis Personae as 'Lord High Everything Else'. And, as it happens, Nanki-Poo has turned up on the very day Ko-Ko and Yum-Yum are to be married.

Still, all is not lost. Yum-Yum's school-mate tells Nanki-Poo that Yum-Yum much prefers him to Ko-Ko. And if Yum-Yum herself is at first unromantically resigned to her fate ('a wandering minstrel … is hardly a fitting husband for [her]' [309]), she becomes more interested when Nanki-Poo explains that he is really the son of the Mikado and that he was forced to flee in disguise to avoid being married against his will to 'Katisha, an elderly lady of [his] father's Court' (310). For his part, Ko-Ko does not seem particularly upset by the fact that Yum-Yum – who he refers to as 'that little parcel' – is now more interested in Nanki-Poo than in him. But at this point he receives a letter from the Mikado, who is disappointed by the lack of executions in Titipu. Sadly, Ko-Ko announces the news: 'unless somebody is beheaded within one month the post of Lord High Executioner shall be abolished, and the city reduced to the rank of a village!' (311). In the event, Nanki-Poo agrees to be executed in one month on condition that he be allowed to marry Yum-Yum. And to this proposal Ko-Ko agrees:

> He yields his life if I'll Yum-Yum surrender.
> Now I adore that girl with passion tender,
> And could not yield her with a ready will,
> Or her allot
> If I did not
> Adore myself with passion tenderer still! (315)

But just when one obstacle to Yum-Yum and Nanki-Poo's getting together has been removed, Katisha turns up and the first Act ends with her threatening vengeance for the wrongs she has suffered.

The second Act begins with Yum-Yum 'seated at her bridal toilet, surrounded by maidens, who are dressing her hair and painting her face and lips, as she judges of the effect in a mirror' (320). Declaring herself 'the very happiest girl in Japan' (321), she has clearly forgotten that Nanki-Poo is to die in a month. And not too long after she is reminded of this, Ko-Ko turns up to let her and Nanki-Poo know that he has 'just ascertained that, by the Mikado's law, when a married man is beheaded his wife is buried alive'. At which point, while protesting that she does not 'want to appear selfish' (324), Yum-Yum starts to back out of her arrangement with Nanki-Poo. As Ko-Ko sings, 'To her life she clings!/Matrimonial devotion/ Doesn't seem to suit her notion' (325).

But now there is another development. Ko-Ko learns that the Mikado is about to arrive and since he will presumably expect an execution to have occurred, and Ko-Ko is unable to actually kill anyone or even anything, this puts Ko-Ko in a dilemma. His solution is to get Yum-Yum and Nanki-Poo to hide and he then lies to the Mikado, maintaining that he *has* executed someone. But his plan quickly backfires when the Mikado discovers that the man supposedly executed was the heir to the throne, his son Nanki-Poo. So now Ko-Ko (once again) faces the threat of execution. But he manages to survive by forcing himself (since he has no other option) to seduce and propose marriage to the powerful Katisha, which leaves Nanki-Poo free to marry Yum-Yum. And so *The Mikado* ends on a celebratory

note of 'laughing song/And merry dance,/With joyous shout and ringing cheer...'
(343).

In the light of this summary, it should not be too difficult to understand the following response from Geoffrey O'Brien:

> One phase of childhood ended with an awakening to the authentic grotes-querie and misanthropic animus in Gilbert's libretti. Now one could begin to savour the mordant variations on themes of vanity and avarice, self-serving unctuousness and moral cowardice ... The parade of cynics, toadies, grasping senescent father figures, gleefully duplicitous bureaucrats, and self-infatuated romantic leads continuously undercut any tendency toward mawkishness in what had once seemed [to 'a childish listener'] tender love stories.
>
> The possibility of anything like charitable impulse was remote in Gilbert's world ... At the bottom of everything was cold calculation, no matter how sweet Sullivan's music, as in the glee from Mikado: If I were Fortune – which I'm not –/B should enjoy A's happy lot,/And A should die in misery –/That is, assuming I am B. (O'Brien 2000: 16)

Of course, there is more to it than this, as O'Brien himself obviously knows very well. 'This', says O'Brien, 'was where Sullivan came in, to suggest with his music a world of emotional realities beyond Gilbert's reach' (ibid.). And it is the tension between Sullivan's music and Gilbert's words that makes this work *The Mikado live*.

But before turning back to the film, one further point about Gilbert's libretto. At the risk of belabouring the obvious, what *primarily* characterises it is of course its irreverent playfulness. The prevailing attitude is summed up in the 'Three little maids from school' song:

Yum-Yum:	Everything is a source of fun. (*Chuckle*.)
Peep-Bo:	Nobody's safe, for we care for none! (*Chuckle*.)
Pitti-Sing:	Life is a joke that's just begun! (*Chuckle*.) (Leigh 1999: 306)

And if we ask what this play impulse is predominantly being exercised *on*, what Gilbert is playing *with*, the answer has to be class (rank).[1] While it is true that 'nobody's safe', those in high positions are particularly vulnerable. Like the corrupt (bribe-taking) and ridiculously snobbish Pooh-Bah, for example, who reacts to the cheek of the little maids as follows:

> I think you ought to recollect
> You cannot show too much respect
> Towards the highly titled few;
> But nobody does, and why should you? (ibid.)

Or like the Mikado himself who has no sooner informed us that he expects obedience 'from every kind of man', than he is undercut by the voice of the much more intimidating Katisha, 'his daughter-in-law elect' (328). But the 'merriment' which the Mikado calls 'harmless' and 'innocent' (329) – but which is also (in the words of Katisha's self-description) 'just a little teeny weeny wee bit bloodthirsty' (340) – is to be found at work everywhere, starting with the ludicrous-sounding names. In a number of ways *The Mikado* anticipates the later anarchic comedy of the Marx brothers. This brings us back to Leigh's film.

'Topsy-Turvy': a special kind of work

> I have always been fascinated ... by the way in which [Gilbert and Sullivan] and their collaborators fought and struggled to produce such harmonious, delightful and profoundly trivial material.
> – Mike Leigh (1999: xii)

The press-kit that was prepared when *Topsy-Turvy* was first distributed in North America opens with a 'Synopsis' in which we are told that it is only after Sullivan has given the go-ahead to Gilbert's conception of *The Mikado* and the production has come together that 'the *truly* hard work begins':

> The actors ... must be rehearsed, coddled, and rehearsed again. While striving to cohere as a company, the players' private lives color their work – but none more so than Gilbert and Sullivan's own, as *The Mikado* makes the difficult, but ultimately rewarding, transition from page to stage.

It is tempting to say that while *The Mikado* celebrates *play*, *Topsy-Turvy* celebrates *work*. But as already noted, the work in question is of a very special kind, the kind that goes into the creation and production of a collective art-work. This means that the work is creative. Or, as I would prefer to put it, it is work that has a large element of play in it.

This is preferable because it helps explain why I think *Topsy-Turvy* gives us a glimpse of a utopian possibility. I am thinking of Friedrich Schiller's celebration of what he called the 'joyous realm of play' (1965: 137) in his letters *On the Aesthetic Education of Man* and of Herbert Marcuse's commentary on this in his book on *Eros and Civilization*.[2]

According to Schiller, man 'is only wholly Man when he is playing' (1965: 80); our humanity is to be found in the delight we take 'in *appearance*' (by which he does not mean the kind of keeping up appearances discussed in chapter four), in our 'disposition towards *ornament* and *play*' (1965: 125). Schiller maintains that the 'animal *works* when deprivation is the mainspring of its activity, and it *plays* when the fullness of its strength is this mainspring, when superabundant life is its own stimulus to activity' (1965: 133). As Marcuse points out, then, what Schiller was trying to imagine was 'a non-repressive order' that would be 'essentially an order of *abundance*' ('the necessary constraint [being] brought about by "superfluity" rather than need') and it would involve, among other things, the 'transformation of toil (labour) into play, and of repressive productivity into "display"' (1962: 176).

Marcuse first argued in the 1950s that the dominant ideology relegates 'real possibilities to the no-man's land of utopia' (1962: 136) but perhaps it has to be admitted that today it is even more difficult than it was fifty years or so ago to believe that the 'transformation of toil (labour) into play' is a real possibility. Yet it would be difficult to deny that the mainspring of the work that *Topsy-Turvy* shows us going into the production of *The Mikado* has its source in 'superabundant life', or a kind of 'superfluity'. And it is also true that what is being *produced*, *The Mikado* itself, is also (in a certain sense) superfluous. It certainly is not necessary or useful, not from the point of view of the still dominant ideology, which I take to be still a form of utilitarianism. Indeed, strictly speaking, from the point of view of the latter, the production of such 'profoundly *trivial* material' is clearly wasteful.

But if it is exhilarating to watch 'the *truly* hard work' that we see getting done in *Topsy-Turvy*, this is not just because of the play impulse that animates it. It is also because of its collective nature and because of the spirit that informs it. The Savoy theatre is organised in terms of a hierarchy with the three young men whom we see checking the theatre seats in the film's opening shot at or near the bottom of it and Sir Arthur Sullivan, whom we see next, waking up from a nightmare, at the top (along with W. S. Gilbert). But, as the formal dress (the black suits and white gloves) of the young men clearly indicates, everyone is expected to take pride in their work. And as we witness the early exchange between a call-boy (Shrimp) and a gentleman dresser, we realise that everyone is to be treated with respect:

Shrimp: (*Saluting*) Permission, Mr Cook?
Cook: (*Saluting*) Permission, Shrimp.
          (*Shrimp knocks on a dressing-room door.*) (Leigh 1999: 7)

This is not to say that there are no lapses. Later on, for example, we see the actress Jessie Bond (Dorothy Atkinson) being rude to Madame Leon (Alison Steadman) (the ladies' costumier) and the actor Durward Lely (Kevin McKidd) being rude to Wilhem (the gentlemen's costume designer). But these *are*, precisely, lapses. And for the rest of the time – within the theatre, at least – almost everyone's manners are just about perfect. One thinks especially of the lengths to which D'Oyly Carte is prepared to go to accomodate Gilbert and Sullivan but also of the way in which he manages to be just as courteous and considerate to George Grossmith and Leonora Braham (Shirley Henderson), both of whom need to be treated with some delicacy. Of course, this is his job: he is the one most responsible for seeing (along with assistant Helen) that the company holds together. But the spirit in which he does his share of the work – setting the tone, perhaps, for the entire company – is more than just diplomatic: it is generous and sensitive. And, in fact, whether or not they are taking their cue from D'Oyly Carte, the tone is impressive throughout the company. Take, for example, the way Temple (Timothy Spall) addresses Lely and Lely's dresser, Mr Butt, in one of the dressing-room scenes. Thus, after he has just broken down and complained that Gilbert 'poaches [him] like a fucking haddock':

Temple: Forgive my Anglo-Saxon, Mr Butt – do have a biscuit.

Butt: Oh, thank you, sir. I'll take one 'ome with me for me supper.
(Leigh 1999: 20)

And moments later, while disagreeing with Lely about Gilbert's work: 'With all due respect, my dear Durward ... Do forgive me, dear boy'. Or consider the way in which Sullivan corrects the bassoonist, Mr Hurley, during rehearsal:

Sullivan: Good morning, Mr Hurley.
Hurley: Good morning, Dr Sullivan.
Sullivan: (*cockney accent*) You was late, Mr 'Urley.
             (*Everybody laughs – except Mr Hurley.*)
Hurley: My profuse apologies to you, sir.
Sullivan: Thank you. (1999: 103)

If, as Edmund Burke once maintained, 'manners are what vex and soothe, corrupt or purify, exalt or debase, barbarise or refine us' (quoted in Tanner 1996: 27), the manners on display in this film leave us feeling soothed, purified, exalted and refined. So that when, at one point, we hear, in one of the excerpts from *The Mikado*, some Japanese nobles explaining that if we think they 'are worked by strings,/Like a Japanese marionette,' we 'don't understand these things:/It is simply Court etiquette' – we realise that this applies to D'Oyly Carte's company: *its* etiquette is courtly too. Which is why it is so disturbing when Gilbert is called an 'arsehole' by '*a filthy dishevelled hag*' (1999: 124) who accosts him after he has left the theatre during *The Mikado*'s first performance.

But if this particular obscenity is shocking because of the way it rips right through the atmosphere that has been created by the courtly etiquette inside the theatre, it may be that it has another function as well: to prevent us from taking too sentimental a view of the act of solidarity that occurs near the end of the film. After the last rehearsal before the opening of *The Mikado*, when he is addressing the entire cast, Gilbert announces that he has decided to make one cut, the Mikado's song. Since this was to have been Temple's chance to shine, he is crestfallen. But it is immediately clear that most of the others feel that this is a mistake. Afterwards, in the dressing-rooms of the Ladies' and Gentlemen's Choruses, it is the main topic of discussion. Flagstone thinks Gilbert has made 'a misjudgement' and, after Bentley has expressed agreement with this, Flagstone says that 'someone should tell him'. Then, after Conyngham has admitted that Gilbert 'scares the living daylight out of [him]', Pryce (Mark Benton) asks, 'What about us?' Pryce wonders why they cannot 'speak to Mr Gilbert': 'Well', he adds (and as he does so the camera quietly tracks in on him), 'we could all go together'. And, despite the fact that Kent now warns against it ('You must consider yourself, and your position. This is tantamount to professional suicide'), this is what – the next day – they do. But before they do it, there is another brief scene in which we see Carte, Sullivan and Helen all expressing their sympathy to Temple. The fact that they too obviously consider the decision to cut Temple's song a mistake makes it clear that, at this point in the proceedings, Gilbert is the one who has the last word. So it does take some courage to challenge him. Nevertheless, the following day, *'on the landing, by a door signposted "To the Stage", Pryce is waiting [for Gilbert] with a dozen or so fellow choristers – ladies and gentlemen'* (1999: 115). Gilbert is visibly impressed by this initiative and he agrees to reinstate Temple's song.

It is a wonderful scene. All the more so, incidentally, if one has seen *Career Girls* and remembers that Mark Benton, the actor now playing the brave Mr Pryce, played Ricky, the 'idiot savant' (Leigh 1997a: 75) in the earlier film. Not that this is the only such pleasure *Topsy-Turvy* provides: to take just one more example, Ron Cook, who plays Richard D'Oyly Carte, played the down-and-out Stuart in *Secrets and Lies*. Such metamorphoses are in themselves deeply moving and remind us of something that Leigh seems much more aware of than most, of the fact that there is something magical about the acting profession. And of course there is also a kind of magic in the fact that Leigh's actors do their own singing and their own dancing. I think especially of the marvelous Timothy Spall here, who one may be tempted to nominate as Leigh's *alter ego*, just as Marcello Mastroianni was Fellini's in *8½* (1963).

But, at the same time, it may be that, even *within* the worlds of the theatre and cinema, there is a limit to what such metamorphoses can achieve. So that while *The Mikado* is definitely a work of collaboration, the fact remains that, in the last analysis, no matter how impressive we (like Gilbert) find Pryce's intervention and the support Pryce receives from the rest of the company, it is Gilbert who makes the decision to reinstate Temple's piece. And, in a similar way, if, on the one hand, Leigh can often be found insisting to interviewers that all 'film-making has to be in some way collaborative, and [that his] film-making is more collaborative than any' (Movshovitz 2000: 70), on the other hand, he also insists that in the last analysis he himself is 'very much in control of it' (Movshovitz 2000: 77).

And *Topsy-Turvy* would not be nearly as powerful as it is if it was not itself working to remind us of some of the problems of life lived *outside* the theatre or *off* the stage. For example: Sullivan has diabetes; the actress Leonora, who plays Yum-Yum, has a young son, whom she refers to as her little 'secret' because she is hoping to marry a nice gentleman and, whenever she mentions her son's existence to a possible candidate, 'then he's off, quick smart'; Leonora shares her dressing-room with another actress, Jessie, who is also hoping to meet an eligible partner and Jessie is suffering from '*a severe varicose vein*' (Leigh 1999: 46) that needs to be regularly treated and bandaged when she is on her feet too long (which – on stage – she often is); we at one point see a third actor, Grossmith, putting away a hypodermic syringe, having just injected himself with the drug that he takes to help him cope with *his* difficulties (which seem to include stage-fright); and outside of the theatre, we are a number of times alerted to the fact that Gilbert's marriage is a sexless union and that his wife, Kitty, is not happy.

Now of course Leigh has often dealt with Kitty's kind of problem in earlier films so this might seem to strike a familiar (some will no doubt feel overly-familiar) note but it has to said that Leigh's treatment of it here is masterly. The problem is one women have to face when they are either denied sexual love or a partner who will help them bring up a child or help with an unexpected pregnancy. In an absolutely brilliant stroke, Leigh ends the film by focusing – in what might seem an ironic comment on the programmatic glee of *The Mikado*'s three little maids sequence – on Kitty, Fanny (Sullivan's mistress) and Leonora.

The sequence begins in Kitty's bedroom with Gilbert confessing that he does not 'quite know how to take praise' and Kitty saying that 'it must be rather pleasant to receive it, nonetheless'. Gilbert appears not to notice her irony although he does applaud her when, after confessing that she 'should rather like to be an actor upon the stage', she says it would 'be wondrous if perfectly commonplace people gave each other a round of applause at the end of the day'. He then prepares to leave, however, suggesting, as he invariably does, that she 'must be tired'. But this time she gets him to remain a while longer. Having ascertained that there is no chance of their making love ('Any thoughts racing round in that old brain of yours?'/ 'Thoughts of what nature?'), Kitty says that perhaps his next piece should involve 'something completely and utterly different and unusual.' She then proceeds to imagine something. It 'should have a young and beautiful heroine' and, as she grows older, the ladies' chorus gets younger. (At this point '*music cue 19*' gets taken up and while Kitty imagines her idea we hear the music of ''Tis said that Joy in Full Perfection' from the Finale, Act II, of *The Yeomen of the Guard*.) She first suggests that the men's chorus would be 'fat leeches' but she then changes her mind: 'No, they'd be gentlemen ... and the ladies would be chasing after them, endeavouring to talk to them, but they wouldn't be listening – they'd all be far too busy.' It is a bit like the world of Alice in Wonderland. The heroine's husband had 'made a vow to give her the key, but he never does'. The heroine 'decides to try the door, and it opens':

Gilbert: Ah, so it wasn't locked after all.
Kitty: And she climbs up the stairs, and there, on the sands, are
              hundreds of nannies, all pushing empty perambulators about!
              (*Pause. Gilbert is affected by this. Tears have appeared in
              Kitty's eyes. Music cue 19 ends.*)
              And every time she tries to be born ... he strangles her with
              her umbilical cord.
Gilbert: Mm ... I shouldn't imagine Sullivan'd much care for that.
              (Leigh 1999: 133)

Here, then, quite devastatingly, we see Kitty expressing the same desire a number of Leigh's earlier heroines expressed: the desire to be a mother, to have a child. But at the same time she also expresses the desire to be born herself.

From this we cut to Sullivan's bedroom, where his mistress Fanny (Eleanor David) informs him that she is again pregnant. He offers 'to make the arrangements' but she says it 'won't be necessary', she has made her 'own arrangements'. She does not seem at all angry. 'You light up the world', she tells him. 'You can't help it.' And then, after kissing him on the cheek, she tells him she 'must fly' and she's off.

As Maurice observes in *Secrets and Lies*, life is not fair. And from Kitty, who wants a child, and Fanny, who does not, we turn to Leonora, the working mother.

Two more brief scenes remain, the first in Leonara's dressing-room, where she is *'fully made up and dressed as Yum-Yum'*, the second on stage as Leonora (the single mother) sings Yum-Yum's sun and moon song. In the first of these two scenes Leonora has been drinking and, as she gazes at her reflection in the mirror, she recites Yum-Yum's soliloquy from Act II: 'Yes, I am indeed beautiful … Can this be vanity? … No!' This is then followed by Leonora's (somewhat shrill but still affecting) rendering of the song in which Yum-Yum proudly declares that she 'mean[s] to rule the earth,/As he [the sun] the sky' – also, that she and the moon 'are not shy;/We're very wide awake,/The moon and I!'

The truth, then, is that both Sullivan *and* Gilbert do 'light up the world'. Among other things, they do help Leonora, for example, to realise an important part of her potential and, in that sense, to give birth to at least part of herself. If, in another part of herself, she remains lonely and unfulfilled, that is not their fault. On the other hand, Gilbert is largely responsible for Kitty's plight and *The Mikado* has a strong trace of misogyny running through it, especially, for example, in the role it gives to Katisha. There is no denying, furthermore, that the light Gilbert and Sullivan manage to provide is of course limited in its reach. Yet the point of the film's ending is by no means a debunking one. It is Leigh's signature point: to ensure that the celebration is grounded in a sense of the real.

CHAPTER TWELVE

'In the messianic light'

Perspectives must be fashioned that displace and estrange the world, reveal it to be, with its rifts and crevices, as indigent and distorted as it will appear one day in the messianic light.

> – Theodor Adorno (1984: 247)

I feel that this film [*All or Nothing*] is entirely about redemption.

> – Mike Leigh (Malcom 2002b)

In my judgment, *All or Nothing* is a work of comparable stature to *Naked*, *Secrets and Lies* and *Topsy-Turvy*, which is to say that it too is a major work of the cinema. But if *All or Nothing* is indeed a masterpiece, I think it has to be admitted that it is – for many – an initially much more difficult to appreciate masterpiece than the three other films just mentioned. Like *Career Girls*, which seems to be also very fine but (at least in comparison to the other four) a bit slight and so relatively minor, *Secrets and Lies* and *Topsy-Turvy* are of course easy to like and full of obvious pleasures. And while *Naked* may be just as disturbing (even shocking) as *All or Nothing*, those who dislike it would be hard-pressed to deny the powerful impact made by the extraordinary verbal inventiveness of its central character. But there is nothing comparable to that in *All or Nothing*. In fact, it is easy to see why one reviewer, disheartened by the 'poverty of [its] language', came away with the impression 'that the three most common utterances in the film are "Wot?", "Shut up" and "Fuck off"' (Quinn 2002).

It may be that Leigh underestimates the difficulty of this film. 'I have no wish', he told Coveney in the mid-1990s, 'to be seen only by a few people in art houses. I want my work to be popular, mainstream, and enjoyed by the greatest possible audience. I try for that all the time' (1997: 110). Shortly after *All or Nothing* opened in England, Leigh restated this position in a public discussion with Derek Malcom and members of the audience at the National Film Theatre, London. Asked if he ever gets frustrated when his films 'are only shown at selected cinemas', Leigh responded as follows:

> I am totally frustrated by that. That's never the intention. The idea that a film like this, or any film I have ever made, should be dumped in what are regarded as art house cinemas isn't on. I am not concerned with making esoteric, obscure kinds of films. These are films that can share and talk to anybody about real things. The good news with *All or Nothing* is that it is being released in the UK by UGC and they are going to put it in multiplexes.

But that was in early October and it became clear, within the next couple of months, that, despite its not being an 'esoteric, obscure' kind of film, *All or Nothing* was also not going to be the kind of 'popular, mainstream' film that Leigh had hoped it would be.

Perhaps the remarks just cited should be understood as Leigh expressing the sort of optimism without which any artist would be unable to do his or her work. It is true, in any case, that another of the remarks he made during the NFT discussion implicitly identifies the problem. Commenting on Maureen's (Ruth Sheen) delightful singing during the karaoke evening, Leigh explains that – considering 'the journey [he is] asking [us] to go on' in a film like this one – he feels 'the audience should have treats. They should be things that work with what's going on and are completely believable but are nevertheless in themselves some sort of treat. I think it's a treat when she gets up there.' But what is this if not an admission that, for most of us, the experience of watching this film is likely to be something of an ordeal? Why else would we need 'treats' during it?

It seems possible to recognise that much of *All or Nothing* is undeniably difficult to watch while simultaneously agreeing with 'The Wolf', who reviewed it on the web and ended up by reporting that – somehow, however paradoxically – the film's 'two hours pass in a flash'. But what of the use of the word 'ordeal'? Ryan Gilbey remarked that 'there are shots here, even entire scenes, when you pull back from the screen as if from a furnace, usually because the camera itself has forsworn any such retreat' (2002: 14). This can usefully remind us of some of Simone Weil's reflections on affliction – in particular of her claim that 'it is as easy to direct one's thought voluntarily towards affliction as it would be to persuade an untrained dog to walk into a fire and let itself be burnt' (1977a: 87–8). Weil reflected long and hard on this subject and her conclusion – that 'thought flees from affliction as promptly and irresistibly as an animal flies from death' (1977d: 440) – can help to better understand the unlikelihood of a film like *All or Nothing* ever becoming popular.

This is not to say that this film is about affliction, a term Weil reserved for a form of suffering much more extreme than any we see in *All or Nothing*.[1] But, on the other hand, if there is one thing that most of the reviews agree on, it is that this is a film about human misery. Thus, for example, on BBC-Derby's homepage, Jamie Russell calls Leigh 'Britain's leading poet of cinematic miserabilism'; in the *Washington Post* Desson Howe refers to 'a miserable, heaving sea of gloom'; in Philip French's *Observer* review we are told that 'there's misery aplenty on this council estate'; Samuel Blumenfeld in *Le Monde* speaks of '*la misère sociale*'; J. Hoberman in the *Village Voice* complains about having been put through 'two hours of low-grade misery'; in *Cinemascope* Liam Lacey refers to 'kitchen-sink miserabilism'. It is true that most of these reviews emphasise that there is another, positive, side to the film. But, even so, there would seem to be fairly widespread agreement that, as Xan Brooks put it in *Sight and Sound*, this is 'surely the director's bleakest film since *Naked*'. And considering what Rick Groen in the *Globe and Mail* calls 'the sheer grimness of it all', J. Hoberman would seem to be speaking for everyone when he observes that '*All or Nothing* can be rough going – even a bit gruelling'. Yet, in another way, Hoberman's review is unrepresentative since it and Liam Lacey's are the only two in my admittedly selective sample that are predominantly negative, all the rest being at least respectful and ranging from the wholly enthusiastic to praise with reservations.

In the circumstances, then, it perhaps should not be a surprise to discover that, faced with such painful material – it is tempting to call it the supreme example of Leigh's traumatic realism – a number of the reviewers had recourse to the kind of distancing humour that may best be seen as defensive, as, for example, in such titles as 'Mike Leigh's Gloom with a View' (Howe) and 'Doom with a View' (Quinn), and of the repetition of the word 'miserable' in the opening of Chris Chang's *Film Comment* review:

> There's a moment in Mike Leigh's miserable new movie when one of the miserable characters has her whole miserable life summed up by the placement of simple, ironic art direction. A sign on the wall in the nursing home where Rachel (Alison Garland) toils away at her miserable job proclaims: TELL ME AGAIN HOW LUCKY I AM TO WORK HERE. It might as well say: KILL YOURSELF NOW. But it doesn't, and she doesn't, and we then endure two hours of painstaking Leigh-style realism. (Chang 2002: 71)

Actually, this is one of the mixed reviews, with Chang showing real appreciation for Leigh's understanding of 'the dimensions of human misery in every form' ('Suffering has been elevated into an art form') but not liking the film's upbeat ending. But it seems to me that there is a certain glibness in Chang's opening, which reminds me of a moment in Nathanael West's *Miss Lonelyhearts* when we are told that the cynical Shrike has encouraged the central character to handle suffering with 'a thick glove of words' (1969: 33).

For Anthony Quinn, a large part of the problem is to be found in the film's setting. Here are the opening lines his 2002 review:

> 'Life is divided up into the horrible and the miserable,' says Woody Allen in *Annie Hall*. The horrible would involve being blind, he explains, or crippled, or terminally ill. And the miserable would be 'everyone else'. Such is the prevailing sensibility of Mike Leigh's *All or Nothing* ... [the film] is set in a mean south-London housing estate, and follows a number of its inhabitants over a long weekend: in short, the horrible, as experienced by the miserable.

Though it may be an exaggeration to call the housing estate in question 'horrible', Quinn's comments are illuminating. Indeed it may help explain an otherwise puzzling comment made by Akin Ojumo in an *Observer* column written during the Cannes Festival for 2002. Ojumo linked Leigh's film (which he was to refer to the following week, without enthusiasm, as 'Leigh's social realist *All or Nothing*' [Ojumo 2002b: 9]) to Ken Loach's *Sweet Sixteen* and remarked that 'their council-estate realism will be very familiar to Cannes regulars' (Ojumo 2002a: 9). Really? How many of the films regularly seen at Cannes (how many of Leigh's for that matter?) are set on council estates? It seems to me that what Ojumo is really saying here is that for him this is a case of a little goes a long way. And something similar would seem to motivate the observation made – sometimes in the form of an apology, sometimes as a complaint – by a number of the reviewers of *All or Nothing* to the effect that Leigh is revisiting old, familiar territory rather than 'reaching for new horizons' (Brooks 2002: 38).

Still, whatever individual viewers think about the council-estate, what just about everyone agrees with is the fact, as Quinn aptly puts it, that watching *All or Nothing* feels like being on 'a carousel of woe' and this is painful. Indeed, to use the word that Phil, one of the film's central characters, uses at one point to describe his own situation, at times it feels almost 'unbearable'. And, as I understand it, Leigh's achievement is to take this and make it – potentially, at least – not just a bearable experience but, by the time we get to the end of the film, an exhilarating one.

At the centre of the film are Phil Bassett (Timothy Spall), his common-law wife (Penny [Lesley Manville]), and their two children (Rachel [Alison Garland] and Rory [James Corden]). Phil is a taxi-driver, Penny works at a check-out counter in Safeway, Rachel cleans in a home for the elderly and Rory is unemployed. Next come the single mother (Maureen [Ruth Sheen]), who works alongside Penny at Safeway, and her daughter (Donna [Helen Coker]), who works as a waitress in a local café. In the third family we have Ron (Paul Jesson), another taxi-driver; Carol (Marion Bailey), his alcoholic wife; and their unemployed daughter, Samantha (Sally Hawkins). These three families all live on the council-estate, as does Craig (Ben Crompton), another unemployed youngster who dotes on Samantha. Other important characters are Jason (Daniel Mays) (Donna's boyfriend), Sid (Sam Kelly) (an older man who works with Rachel), Cécile (Kathryn Hunter) (one of Phil's customers), and Neville (Gary McDonald) (who runs Gladiator Cars, the firm for which Phil and Ron work).

After claiming (in his review in the London *Observer*) that 'the delightful *Topsy-Turvy* ... differs from [Leigh's] previous works by virtue of its colourful milieu and focus on professional success,' Philip French added this:

> Everyone would like to have met Gilbert and Sullivan and the next best thing is encountering them in *Topsy-Turvy*. Few people would care to spend time with the characters in Leigh's other movies, and certainly not the three working-class London families in his excellent new picture, *All or Nothing*. (French 2002)

This seems to go straight to the heart of the matter. If few people would care to spend much time with these characters it is because they have so many problems, are so deeply unhappy and (with the sole exception of Cécile) are barely managing to get by. Phil has difficulty getting out of bed in the morning and so misses the best fares. Like himself, his two children are overweight and Rory also sleeps late in the morning. Rory is aggressive and regularly curses his mother, just as Samantha and Donna regularly curse their parents, and Jason curses (even more violently than the others) everyone he comes into contact with. Apart from anything else, spending time with – entering into the lives of – these characters means being exposed to a good deal of often extremely violent verbal abuse, with the ever-present threat, when Jason is around, of its becoming physical too.

We follow their lives over a five-day period, from a Thursday through the weekend to a Monday, with the longest amount of time being spent on the Sunday. The film opens with the camera positioned at one end of a *'long, empty, institutional corridor'* (Leigh 2002: 3) and it does not move for around two minutes as we see, from some distance, two figures come into view; first Rachel, who is mopping the floor, and then an elderly lady, who is *'supporting herself on a handrail and with a stick'*. The sadness of the scene is emphasised by the mournful music Andrew Dickson has composed for the soundtrack. And as Rachel stops rinsing her mop to allow the old lady to pass, she speaks the film's opening words. First: 'Be careful – the floor's wet.' And then, since the old lady ignores her: 'D'you wanna 'and?'

It seems highly significant that the film should open (in *'a care home for elderly people'*) with this offer of a helping hand and this expression of concern. The fact that the offer is rejected (*'Rachel goes to help her, but the old lady shrugs her off, and moves away'*) only makes it seem all the more poignant. I take it that Rachel's gesture and words are also meant to function both as an implicit promise made by Leigh that this will be a film in which the utmost care has been taken in the selection of the smallest details and as a signal to us, the viewers, as a way of advising us, at the outset of our journey, that we too need to be careful, careful to keep both our minds and our hearts open and responsive to whatever we may be about to encounter. In keeping with this, it is beautifully appropriate that 'You wanna be careful, you' – the loving words Penny speaks to her son Rory – should be almost the film's *last* words (at least its last clearly audible ones). So that, in effect, the film is framed by these expressions of care, which are made all the more touching by the ways in which the film has deepened our awareness of essential human vulnerability and loneliness.

If the opening shot seems to last longer than it does (as, for example, Anthony Quinn would seem to be testifying when he says that it 'lasts for some minutes'), this is because of what we are watching: first a young woman mopping the floor and then the slow progress of (in Quinn's words) 'an elderly patient [who] *inches* on a walker past [her]' [Quinn 2002, my emphasis]). It is difficult to think of any other director today who would both think this *worth* watching and be willing to risk alienating the audience by showing it. It is easy to understand, therefore, when Ryan Gilbey tells us that, 'half way through that opening shot ... its stubbornness, its austerity and its almost self-parodic bleakness' produced in him 'the urge to cheer' (Gilbey 2002).

From this opening shot of Rachel at work, we cut, rather abruptly, to a brief scene of her father at work. Like his daughter, Phil also reaches out to establish friendly contact and he too is rebuffed. He asks '*a grubby young man in biker's gear*' who is drinking a can of beer in the back seat of his taxi if he has had an accident. This perfectly reasonable question enrages the young man who angrily tells Phil 'No ... some fuckin' monkey cunt nicked my bike, man!' and then starts to violently punch the back of the front seat to the accompaniment of 'Fuckin' cunt! Fuckin' cunt! Fuckin' cunt!' Not surprisingly, Phil looks alarmed. And we are surely made to feel a bit anxious on his behalf: he seems so nice and so vulnerable.

We then move, again abruptly, inside the supermarket where Penny is working at her till alongside Maureen. But in this scene, it is not Penny who reaches out (as we have just seen her daughter and husband do) but Maureen, who asks her friend if she fancies going out on Saturday evening. Penny says yes ('alright, then') but she '*has a tired, pinched, weary look*' and is clearly preoccupied. Undaunted, Maureen adopts a jokey manner: 'Oh, don't be so enthusiastic!'

We are still only three minutes or so into the film: we have already been introduced to four of the main characters and three of them look exceptionally sad. The speed with which this has occurred, the brevity of the scenes (that follow the opening one) and the rapid cutting between them, does indeed make it feel as if we are caught up on a carousel – and there is a strong hint of danger in the air.

From the supermarket, we cut first for a second or two back to Phil's taxi and then for a bit longer to Ron's. We see Ron carelessly reverse into a concrete bollard and then claim, over the walkie-talkie that 'some bitch in a Volvo's smacked [him] up the arse' ('She's buggered me tail-lights') and so he has to get his car fixed. This is followed by a quiet, haunting scene, in which Phil drops an elderly gentleman with a bunch of flowers off at a cemetery and then pauses to watch him, thoughtfully, as the man walks between the gravestones. After which, having (along with his elderly passenger) heard the end of Ron's exchange over the walkie-talkie, Phil stops by the crash-repair garage and offers Ron a lift home.

So now, at the five-minute mark, we are at the end of the work-day and the next thing we see is Maureen and then Penny emerging from Safeway, about to go home, Maureen by bus, Penny on her bike. Penny looks so small and vulnerable and determined that the sight of her – her shopping in the front basket and wearing a rucksack and a crash helmet – cycling at some speed through heavy traffic, is very moving. It is also troubling because, in the midst of so many cars and lorries, she looks in real danger of an accident. After all, we have just seen one car crash (even if it was more comic than tragic) and we have just been reflecting on death (in the cemetery scene, but also in the film's opening shot).

We continue to be worried on Penny's behalf when she arrives back at the council-estate and almost immediately has to stop a seemingly unprovoked fight that her son, Rory, gets into with another youngster, Craig. As a hand-held camera heightens a sense of tension by closely following behind the mother who is in turn following her son along their sixth-floor walkway, Rory is seething with anger and frustration. When she points out to him that Craig is smaller than he is, we are bound to reflect that so, of course, is she – much smaller. Rory angrily accuses her of taking Craig's side. She denies she is doing this. 'Yes, you fuckin' are', says Rory. And when she asks him not to swear, he responds by pounding aggressively on the front door. It almost seems for a second as if he has the strength and is enraged enough to break it down.

In the event, however, though Rory's abuse of his mother escalates, it does not become physical but takes the form of his uttering more obscenities. Thus, for example, when Phil arrives home and asks Rory (who is lying on the sofa watching television) what he has been up to during the day, Penny answers on Rory's behalf ('E's been fightin' today') and she asks Phil when he is going to take his son to the Job Centre. This produces the following exchange:

Rory:	Fuck's sake, I'll get a job when I want, it ain't got nothin' to do wi' you – just stop goin' on about it!
Penny:	Rory, calm down – nobody's 'avin' a go at yer, I'm just tryin' to 'elp yer.
	(*Gunshots on the TV.*)
Rory:	Fuck off!
	Penny looks expectantly at Phil, but he says nothing, and moves away to hang up his coat in the hall. (Leigh 2002: 21)

But if this is not physical violence, it is violence nevertheless and it is disturbing. Let us therfore consider questions concerning the film's obscenity.

Violent language[2]

A number of the reviewers were understandably struck by this aspect of *All or Nothing*. J. Hoberman makes light of it by telling us that the film's characters 'ward off clinical depression by challenging the Guinness world record for use of the term "fuck off"'; Samuel Blumenfeld reports that '"fuck off" *ponctue presque chaque assertion*'; Philip French notes that 'one of the things that unites these families is the children's shared response to any rebuke or advice from their parents – "Fuck off!"'. In fact, however, the question 'Alright?' (usually asked as an expression of caring and concern) is heard more often than 'fuck off'. But still, there is undeniably a lot of obscenity in the film and the question is, what are we to make of it?

Two days on from Phil's failure to rise to his wife's defense, during the family's Sunday lunch, Rory again tells his mother to fuck off and on the second occasion he manages to be even more abusive than on the first. Earlier, on Thursday evening, we see the Bassetts having their evening meal and, after Rory has upset his mother by leaving the table to flop onto the sofa before they have finished, the film cuts away to show us how the other two families are doing. This technique of creating parallel (though not identical) situations is of course one of Leigh's favourites, though perhaps never used more effectively than here. Ron and Carol are both drinking and seem uninterested in eating – Carol especially, since she is much further gone than her husband. So when Samantha announces she is starving, we get the following exchange:

Ron:	You ain't done nothin' since you got up!
Samantha:	Well, what about 'er? Lazy cow.
	(*She refers to Carol, who sips her beer, and takes no notice.*)
Ron:	When are you goin' to get a job?
Samantha:	Fuck off. (Leigh 2002: 27)

From this we cut to Maureen and Donna, the mother trying to interest her daughter in something to eat. When Maureen tells her she looks 'like a skeleton', Donna tells her to 'Shu' up!' And when Donna agrees that she will ''ave a few chips', Maureen tries to brighten things up by asking ''Ow many's a few?' 'Shu' up!' says her daughter again but, far from being offended, Maureen is clearly amused. She is even amused when, still later on the same evening, returning from having delivered some ironing (her part-time work) and running into Donna who is going out with her boyfriend, Jason, Donna responds to her mother's friendly 'Be good. If you can't be good, be careful' with 'Fuck off!' Maureen reacts to this by laughing good naturedly.

But it is difficult to imagine even Maureen laughing at the next outburst, though Samantha (who watches it from above) finds it funny. From the moment we first see him, Jason gives the impression that he is physically bursting at the seams, having difficulty restraining himself from hitting something. And as he and Donna leave the estate, he sees Craig looking in his direction (probably at Donna who has greeted him with 'Alright, Craig?'). At this point, '*Jason suddenly lurches towards Craig*', dragging Donna, who is holding his hand, with him. 'Why', he asks, 'd'you keep fuckin' lookin' at me for? Don't fuckin' look at me – I'll fuckin' slice you, you cunt!' When Donna tries to restrain him, he calls Craig a 'Fuckin' mug! Fuckin' wanker!' and then '*barks at Donna*': 'Get your fuckin' 'ands off me!'

Thursday evening ends up with the sequence in which (since he has not had a good week) Phil is reduced to asking his children and wife for spare money to make up the amount that he needs to pay his boss Neville every Friday. Not much happens on the Friday but on the Saturday there are two events that especially stand out and Leigh interweaves them. The first is that Donna tells Jason she is pregnant with his child and the second is Maureen, Carol and Penny's night-out at karaoke. Jason reacts to Donna's news with the most vicious and brutal display of sheer ugly nastiness in the movie. Fortunately, his violence remains purely verbal but it is still frightening and made even more so by the fact that he seems on the edge of physically assaulting Donna throughout the entire scene. As he storms off, violently slamming the door against the wall and vowing that he will 'bury' her ('you cunt! Fucking mug!'), we cut to the karaoke evening where we hear a young woman singing 'Stand By Your Man' ('But if you love him,/You'll forgive him,/Even though he's hard to understand'). The juxtaposition is obviously ironical and the ironic effect is strengthened by the fact that 'Stand By Your Man' was preceded a bit earlier by the MC singing 'Delilah' ('That girl was no good for me./But I was lost like a slave that no man could free./At break of day,/When that man drove away,/I was waiting … I felt the knife in my hand and she laughed no more') and it is soon followed by Maureen's splendid rendition of 'Don't It Make My Brown Eyes Blue' ('You've found someone new'). But if listening to Maureen sing is a treat, it is soon terminated by Carol's drunkenness.

This brings us to Sunday morning, when Maureen learns that Donna (who now has a black eye) is pregnant and reacts with love and understanding. Jason turns up once more, just as thuggish, psychopathic and menacing as before, but this time Maureen is there beside her daughter, who is finally brought to realise that she is better off without him. But *before* Jason turns up, we cut to the Bassetts's Sunday lunch and Rory's second outburst:

> (*Rory has finished his food. He puts his knife and fork on the plate.*)
>
> Rory: That was shit. (*He gets up and lies on the sofa.*)
> Penny: Rory!
> Rory: What?!
> Penny: There's no need to talk like that.
> Rory: Fuck off!
> Penny: Rory, will you stop being rude to me, please?
> Rory: For fuck's sake! What is your problem?! (*He gets up.*) I only said I didn't like my dinner! I can't do nothin' round 'ere without you 'avin a go at me! You're doin' my fuckin' 'ead in – Why don't you fuck off?! (*He storms out of the room.*)
> (*Pause.*)
> Phil: Take no notice.
> (*Penny is shaken.*) (Leigh 2002: 87)

At this point, it is tempting to turn again (as we did in the discussion of *Topsy-Turvy*) to Edmund Burke: if, as Burke maintained, manners 'give their whole form and colour to our lives', if they 'are what vex and soothe, corrupt or purify, exalt or debase, barbarise or refine us', then Rory's manners are just barbaric. But if we want to do justice to what the film shows us, we need to go more deeply into the matter. For one thing, we need to note how Maureen deals with her daughter's use of basically the same language. At one point in the scene just prior to this one, soon after Maureen has learned that her daughter is pregnant, we get this exchange:

Maureen: I thought you 'ad more sense, Donna.

Donna:	Fuck off!!
Maureen:	Oh, don't get the 'ump, you silly cow! Does yer face 'urt?
	(Leigh 2002: 86)

The film obviously wants this to remind us of two earlier moments, one during the karaoke evening when Carol gets aggressive ('You gi's a fuckin' look') and Maureen calms her down by asking (with a slight laugh) 'You gettin' the 'ump again?'; the other much earlier when Samantha is wanting her evening meal and she refers to her mother as a 'lazy cow'. Not only is Maureen not upset herself when Donna tells her to 'Fuck off', she clearly recognises that this particular 'Fuck off' is an indication of how upset *Donna* is. And Maureen's only concern is to try to comfort her daughter. Her 'don't get the 'ump' is an apology and, in context, Maureen's 'you silly cow' (unlike Samantha's 'lazy cow') is an affectionate term of endearment. That Donna understands it as such is made clear by her acceptance of her mother's subsequent offer to make her a cup of tea.

The point here is that we need to discriminate among the various uses of obscenity. I am not suggesting that Rory's lunchtime 'fuck off' to his mother is just as harmless as Donna's, after Donna's mother has said she thought her daughter had more sense. And while it is true that, by immediately following Rory's outburst with the scene in which Jason forces his way inside Maureen's door (and she has to use force to get him out again), Leigh inevitably makes us reflect that Rory is *nowhere near* as violent as Jason (just as, in *Naked*, Johnny is nowhere near as violent as Jeremy), it surely does not follow that we are wrong if we still find *Rory's* violence shocking. As, I confess, I still do. Mainly, for the simple reason that it is so hurtful to his mother. And yet Chris Chang may well be exaggerating unjustly when he tells us that Rachel's 'brother (James Corden) is a nihilistic, dangerously overweight, unemployable slob whose only mode of communication is to figuratively spew acid' (2002: 71). What this film challenges us to do is to *adjust* our feelings, in the light of the new understanding it offers us near the end.

The scene in which Maureen pushes Jason out the door ends up with mother and daughter coming much closer together, so that, even if the situation is tinged with sadness (one single mother supporting another single-mother-to-be), things nevertheless seem to be taking a definite turn for the better in their lives. Then there are two major developments. The first is that Phil has a life-changing conversation with one of his passengers, the Frenchwoman, Cécile. The second, which occurs at the same time, just over an hour into the film, is that Rory has a heart-attack. Again, the film cuts back and forth between these two scenes to maximum ironical and emotional effect. So that, for example, when Phil's taxi emerges from Blackwall Tunnel into the sunshine, we cut back to the estate where we see that *three youths are winding up Rory. They pass his ball between them, taunting him with provocative jibes*:

First youth:	Come on, fat boy!
Second youth:	Go on, fat boy – come and get your ball back, mate!
	(2002: 100)

This is presumably the kind of thing Rory has had to put up with on a daily basis and it goes a long way towards explaining his behaviour. But on this occasion he is so wound up that he has a heart attack and, if not for the fact that Maureen and Samantha were able to come to the rescue and quickly get an ambulance, it might have been fatal. And while this is happening we cut back to the taxi where Phil is now proudly telling Cécile about Rachel and Rory. But Phil's conversation with Cécile only becomes life-changing when – sandwiched in between Samantha's possibly life-saving efforts on Rory's behalf – we get this:

Cécile: You are caring for your wife?
Phil: Pardon?
Cécile: Do you love your wife?
Phil: Yeah. Oh yeah... (Leigh 2002: 107)

Cécile's sometimes awkward English makes a crucial point: love *is* to a large extent a matter of caring. And there is suddenly no doubt about the depth of Phil's caring for Penny. This is the first moment in the film when, as he reflects on the love he has for his wife, he looks happy. But the look of happiness does not last long, presumably because this is when he begins to realise what has been making him miserable for so long: the fact that his wife no longer loves him.

Soon after Phil has dropped Cécile off, he turns off both his mini-cab walkie-talkie and his mobile and – just as Rory is being rushed to the hospital and Penny is rushing to be with him – Phil then (unaware of these developments) drives off to the coast to reflect. In the circumstances, it is not surprising, therefore, that, when he eventually turns up in Rory's hospital room later that evening, Penny should be angry with him. Nor that she be first incredulous when he asks Rory 'D'you wanna go on 'oliday?' and then – when they (Penny, Phil and Rachel) are back home and he announces his determination to change his ways (to work longer hours so he can keep his 'promise' to his son about 'goin' on 'oliday') – again angry:

Penny: Phil, it ain't about goin' on 'oliday. It's about gettin' by,
            week in, week out. It ain't a game. (*Pause*). Just 'cos you've
            suddenly got some bee in your bonnet about gettin' up in
            the mornings and goin' to work – when you've been lying
            in bed for years, 'til God knows what time. And we're all
            supposed to be grateful 'cos you've decided to do what
            normal people do – I get up in the mornings. Rachel gets up
            in the mornings. You make me sick... (Leigh 2002: 137–8)

Penny is discharging here what she obviously feels is a justifiable sense of long-pent-up resentment. She is aggrieved and (speaking as a mature, responsible adult) she lets Phil (the immature, irresponsible Phil) have it. She is in no doubt that this is the talking-to he needs and deserves, a strong dose of reality, a long overdue wake-up call.

I imagine that, on a first viewing at least, most viewers are likely to find Penny's words perfectly reasonable and justified. But what is now about to happen is that we are suddenly going to find ourselves presented with an entirely different perspective, according to which, even if there is a sense in which Penny's words *are* reasonable and justifiable, at the same time, they also turn out to be mistaken.

A new perspective

Pressed by Penny to explain why he switched off his mobile and walkie-talkie, Phil at first says that he had ''ad enough'. This provokes another outburst of righteous indignation from Penny:

> You'd 'ad enough? 'Ad enough o' what? 'Ad enough of workin' for five minutes, so you switched it off? What can I switch off when I've 'ad enough? 'Ad enough of gettin' up every mornin', goin' to work, doin' the shoppin', comin' 'ome, cookin' the tea, cleanin' the 'ouse, doin' the ironin', makin' sure everyone's got clean clothes on their back...

At this point, there is a slight pause as Rachel leaves the room and, when Penny repeats her question (''Ad enough of what, anyway?'), Phil's response is, simply, 'Everything'. Moment's later, as if by way of explanation, he says that she does not love him. What, she wants to know, has 'that got to do with anything'. Looking straight at her, with tears in his eyes, he tells her that 'it's got to do with everything'. And he refuses to be deflected by her reminding him (as if he were a child who had forgotten) that 'Rory ... 'as 'ad a 'eart attack.' Still looking straight at her, he replies as follows:

> You ain't loved me for years. You don't like me; you don't respect me; you talk to me like I'm a piece of shit.

Interestingly enough, it is the last accusation that she denies: 'I, I don't Phil – I don't talk to you like you're a piece of shit.' But he insists that she does, even though she does not know she is doing it, and claims that the situation he is in – her talking to him in that way and his not knowing whether or not she loves him ('Do you love me? I gotta know') – is 'unbearable'.

Phil then speaks in the hyperbolic language of the film's title, which turns out to be also that of St Paul's First Letter to the Corinthians (13: 1–13):

> When we first met, I couldn't believe it. A pretty girl like you, goin' with a fat bloke like me. People lookin' at us. I felt, I felt like the bee's knees. We ain't got much ... but we got each other ... and that's enough. But if you don't want me, we ain't got nothing. We ain't a family. And that's it.

Or, as St Paul put it: 'Though I speak with the tongue of angels, if I have not love, I am become as hollow brass.' A family without love is like an empty shell: it 'ain't a family'. Either/Or: either we have love, in which case (even if, in material terms, we 'ain't got much') we have Everything; Or, if we do not have love, we have Nothing (in St Paul's words: 'if I have not love, I am nothing').[3]

In effect, if it is a life or death situation that has prompted Phil to bring this up, he in turn is implicitly claiming that the question of love between him and his wife is also a life or death issue for him – in a way he is insisting that it is *equal* in importance to Rory's heart attack. He (Phil) may die (emotionally, spiritually) if Penny does not love him – and the family may die too. Hyperbolic this may be, but we are clearly meant to feel that it is actually grounded in the real and also that we should be prepared to reconsider just about everything that precedes it in its light.

We can start with Penny's insistence that life 'ain't a game' or 'about goin' on 'oliday', that it is 'about gettin' by, week in, week out'. It is easy to see why she thinks this, since she has been carrying much more than her fair share of the responsibility for looking after the family – both economically and in terms of preparing meals and being concerned about Rory. We hardly ever see her relaxing: she is constantly moving, on call, literally running to her son's bedside when Ron's taxi collides with another vehicle. When does she get a chance to announce *her* needs? She has had a hell of a day but it is Phil – who's taken a few hours off in silence (after sleeping in late for years and refusing to pay serious attention to his son's misery and needs and assault on Penny's dignity and respect) – who gets to announce *his* needs. Where's the justice in that?

But still, the fact remains that, once Phil has raised the question of love, we have to face the possibility that, without love, their life together may not contain any real 'life' at all. And perhaps it cannot really be 'love' if there is not an element of playfulness, or of the holiday spirit, in it. What, in other words, this crucial moment in *All or Nothing* helps us to see is that the humour and the desire for festivity that (as noted in chapter two) Leigh's films have in common with the Hollywood comedies of remarriage is not an optional extra but close to being their life-blood.

From this point of view, it is no peripheral detail but absolutely central that, after Phil and Penny have embraced and exchanged loving kisses a bit further on in the same scene, Penny reminds him that he 'used to make [her] laugh'. At which point, '*They smile. Then Phil puffs up his cheeks, and Penny "bursts" them. They laugh. They caress each other*' and they decide to 'go to bed', which we understand, in this context, as also meaning that they are going (for what seems to be the first time in ages) to make love.

But if this is Penny's first laugh in the film, it is not Phil's – as we can see in the following excerpt from his conversation with Cécile:

Cécile:	And your son? 'E work with you in the taxi?
Phil:	No, 'e don't do nothing.
Cécile:	Comment celà?
Phil:	I beg your pardon?
Cécile:	'Ow 'e don't do nothing?
Phil:	He does a lot of nothing.
Cécile:	Eh?
Phil:	Mind you … if eatin' was an Olympic event, 'e'd be the world champion by now.

| Cécile: | (*mirthlessly*) Ah, it is a joke ... It is very funny. 'E is fat, like you? |
| Phil: | Yeah ...'e's a big boy, yeah... (*He chortles*) (Leigh 2002: 103–4) |

What this shows is that, if Phil has not made Penny laugh earlier in the film, it may be because she has not let him. In fact, it is easy enough to see, in retrospect, that there has been a consistent pattern, in scene after scene, of her closing him down, shutting him out. When, for example, after Penny has uncharacteristically expressed the desire to go for a walk (and Rachel has turned down her suggestion that they should go together), Phil's offer to take her out for a drink is greeted with a curt 'No'. When Phil offers to help her with her crossword puzzle, she at first agrees but then quickly puts it aside and says she needs to go to sleep. When they leave Rory's hospital room to go home and Phil puts his arm around Penny's shoulder, she soon removes it. When he borrows money from her on the Thursday night, she reproaches him ('Why don't you get up earlier in the mornings? Drive people to work, take 'em to the airport?') and, when he repays her on Saturday night, she responds with an impatient 'Not now, Phil'. It is true of course that, when he repays what he owes her it is just after three a.m. and she is exhausted, having fallen asleep on the sofa waiting up for Rory to come home, so it may be easy to understand and sympathize with Penny's behaviour. Indeed one can see how a questioner at the NFT session could think that the film 'seems to take quite a negative view of the white British male', while emphasising 'the strengths of white British women.' Or as Derek Malcom put it, 'the women in the film are stronger than the men [with] more inner resources'. Yet, while conceding that 'that's true of Maureen,' Leigh insists that it is 'not about stronger women and weaker men ... you can only talk about the central relationship between Penny and Phil in terms of a symbiotic relationship'. If I seem to be taking Phil's side in this, I do not mean to be. What I am tying to draw attention to is the way the film itself is working in the end to correct an imbalance by allowing Phil back into the picture, as it were.

When (again, for understandable reasons) Penny closes herself off from Phil she is effectively denying the symbiotic nature of their relationship as she shuts out something absolutely essential to life. It expresses itself in the combination of humour, tolerance and fatherly pride – all philosophically-inflected by the aptly named Phil – that is evident in the above exchange with Cécile. This was referred to in chapter two as the quality of 'too muchness', of that which *adds* something over and above what is strictly-speaking necessary (what Penny calls 'getting by'), like, for example, the wonderful formulation 'He does a lot of nothing.' A particularly illuminating example occurs during the Bassetts' first meal together. It begins as follows:

Phil:	Filled the car up with petrol this morning. Thirty-eight quid.
	(*Pause.*)
	Been busy?
Penny:	Yeah. Rory, can you put your plate on the table, please?
Rory:	Yeah, alright!
	(*He puts his plate down aggressively.*) (Leigh 2002: 21–2)

What is more important? Sharing a conversation together or good table manners? Of course, it may be that one depends on the other and the ideal would no doubt be to have both together but the problem here is that Penny is so bothered by Rory's behaviour that she is unwilling or unable to rise to her husband's invitation to tell them about *her* day. From one point of view, this is where the father should step in to back the mother up. But instead of doing this, Phil tries again to start a conversation:

Phil: Picked up a doctor's surgery, dinner time. Old bloke ...'e 'ad one o'them, er ... wossername, frames...
Rachel: Zimmer.
Phil: Yeah. 'E only wanted to go to the next street. I says ... 'Sorry, mate, I gotta charge you the minimum fare, three pound fifty.'
Penny: You shouldn'ter charged 'im nothin'!
Phil: No ... I know. I said, 'Oh ... call it a coupla quid.'
Penny: You shouldn'ter called it nothin'!
Phil: Well ... e' wasn't 'avin it – 'e insisted on givin' me the full fare.
Penny: But you didn't 'ave to take it, though, did yer?
Phil: No ... but ... it's wossername, innit, 'is...
Rachel: Dignity.
Phil: Yeah. No price on that when you're old. (Leigh 2002: 22)

What father and daughter grasp here, and what the mother fails or refuses to see, is that, where generosity is concerned, it is (paradoxically) sometimes not enough just to give, that sometimes one must be willing to take what the other has to offer. What is at stake is precisely a sense of dignity (or 'respect', which is what both Phil and Neville ask for at different times), which is another manifestation of that surplus or extra quality of too muchness without which life is fatally impoverished. And it would seem to depend on a different kind of economy to the one Penny observes.

But what about *Penny's* dignity? Is that not exactly what is at stake when Rory tells her to fuck off and Phil stands by and does nothing? Certainly it is a vitally important part of what is at stake but this raises again the question of language, which we can now approach differently, in the light of Phil's claim that Penny has been talking to him as if he is 'a piece of shit'. Nor, it turns out, is he alone in thinking this. 'You do talk to 'im like that', Rachel tells her a bit later. 'Do I?' says Penny. 'Sometimes', says her daughter. But, if so, she has been doing it without using any obscenities (or, as she would say, swear words) at all, almost, one might say, while speaking with (what St Paul might have called) the tongue of an angel. One thinks, to take just one example, of the moment soon after Phil's late arrival at Rory's hospital bedside when Penny chastises him for his having turned his radio and mobile off. 'It's pathetic', she tells him. And at this point Rory startles her by quietly telling her to 'Leave it out, Mum ... Stop 'aving a go at 'im'.

Now 'pathetic' does not seem like a particularly strong word at all but, in this context, it makes Phil lower his eyes in shame. So what about the words Rory speaks to his mother during their earlier Sunday lunch? The screenplay confirms, what seems evident enough on screen, that '*Penny is shaken*'. But what she actually *says*, when he exclaims that what he has just eaten 'was shit', is quite mild: 'There's no need to talk like that.' And then, after he has told her to 'Fuck off!', she asks him to please 'stop bein' rude to [her]'. That's all. Though obviously upset by her son's remark, Penny understands it as rudeness. As for Rory, what does *he* think? He thinks he has 'only said [he] didn't like [his] dinner'. So why is his mother making such a fuss? And when, as he storms out, he asks her why she does not 'fuck off?!', he presumably means no more than 'why don't you leave me alone?'

Is it not because he understands Rory's words in some such way that Phil tells Penny to 'take no notice'? Or does Phil say this because – unlike Penny, who senses the real danger level of Rory's anger – Phil is oblivious to his son's misery, too depressed and tired and lacking in energy to notice much outside his own needs? There is no doubt, in any case, that, in general, he understands his son's behaviour in a much more lenient way than Penny does. So that, for example, when she tells Phil – after he has greeted Rory on his return from work ('Alright, boy? What you been up to today, then?') – that Rory's 'been fighting today', he asks his son, 'You been clumpin' people again?' His use of the word 'clumpin'' is surely an attempt to defuse the situation by introducing some light humour into it. It is interesting, furthermore, that at one point Leigh himself uses the word in the screenplay while describing the moment when Rory impatiently and very aggressively hits the front door to try to get Rachel to hurry up and open it: '*Rory pounds on a front door*' and '*Rory gives the door another clump*' (2002: 14). On its own, 'pounds' does not seem quite strong enough and 'another clump' makes it sound almost playful. Though this impression remains over repeated viewings, the same cannot be said for the significant differences in the use of obscenity that are easier to detect on repeated viewings.

Take, for example, three of Rory's fuck off's. First, his telling his father to fuck off when Phil is searching for spare coins that might have got lodged between the cushions on the sofa that Rory is lying on. This particular usage has no hostile or aggressive intent whatsoever and Phil hardly seems to notice it. Second, his telling his sister to fuck off (quietly, '*under his breath*') after the doctor has asked if Rory smokes: his mother has said 'No' and Rachel has said 'Yeah, 'e does a bit'. Not only is this too completely inoffensive in its context, it is also – in its unexpectedness – one of the funniest moments in the film. Third, either of the two occasions when he tell his mother to fuck off. Unlike the other two, these are indeed instances in which the words are charged with the mixture of frustration and anger that Rory is feeling at the time. But, in retrospect, I wonder if even these two usages are *more* offensive and hurtful to the recipient than some of the apparently much milder things that Penny says to Phil. It is no longer obvious that they are. The only thing that *is* is that, once Penny feels that her son's life is in danger, her behaviour towards him – like his towards her – changes dramatically. Suddenly the only *real* thing is their obvious love for one another.

The last scene

The success of *All or Nothing* depends on the ending, which takes place some days after Rory has had a heart attack and his parents have rediscovered their love for one another. The scene that ends up with Phil and Penny declaring their intention to go to bed takes place in a dark room and it closes with the screen fading to a blackout and then remaining blank for a few seconds. As we then cut to Phil, Penny and Rachel approaching the hospital ward to which Rory has been moved, the thing we are initially most struck by is how light everything is. This is mainly due to the fact that Rory is now in a bed that is next to a big window and it is a sunny day. But at virtually the same moment as we are struck by the light, we also notice that Phil and Penny have been dramatically transformed. Phil has been unshaven throughout the film and he has now had a clean shave. Penny has some lipstick on. After having looked perfectly miserable throughout almost the entire film, they now look – and clearly are – happy. It is an astonishing metamorphosis.

Nor is this all. Whereas the night before Phil and Penny had sat on opposite sides of Rory's bed, they now sit together, while Rachel sits on the other side. And we see that their parents's newfound happiness is not lost on the two children. So that for the first time in the film we see them forming a real family. Rory is clearly loving being the centre of a different kind of attention than he has received throughout the film and, when he tells them about the fish dinner he has eaten, they are properly impressed. It seems that he has always been unwilling to eat fish unless it is in batter and this fish was prepared differently. 'What', his father asks 'they tie you down, did they?' And we see Rachel smiling. On the other hand, when Phil goes on to amuse them with an anecdote about a Greek Cypriot family he took to the airport early that morning (one of two little boys had complained to his father that their grandmother had just farted and the father had turned around and started 'clumpin' 'em', Rachel is obviously sad and the only one not either smiling or laughing. Yet whatever the nature of Rachel's problems, it seems natural to assume that she too can only benefit from the fact that her parents have effectively remarried, which is of course what the couples in Cavell's Hollywood comedies do.

After Phil has told his joke, and Penny has told Rory 'You wanna be careful, you', presumably a warning against having another heart attack, we cut away 'to a long shot, from the other end of the ward' and we only half-hear what they are saying, with the last remark being a reference to the greetings card that Rory has received from his nan. The effect is to make us feel that they are now just like any other family. Or, to be more precise, like any other momentarily *happy* family, one that is fortunate enough to be bathed in the light of a newly rediscovered love for one another. This, I take it, is nothing less than the light to which Adorno refers in the following passage:

> The only philosophy which can be responsibly practised in face of despair is the attempt to contemplate all things as they would present themselves from the standpoint of redemption. Knowledge has no light but that shed on the world by redemption: all else is reconstruction, mere technique. Perspectives must be fashioned that displace and estrange the world, reveal it to be, with its rifts and crevices, as indigent and distorted as it will appear one day in the messianic light. *To gain such perspectives* without velleity or violence, *entirely from felt contact with its objects* – this alone is the task of thought. (Adorno 1984: 247)

Here it is clear in context that by 'messianic' Adorno does not mean something specifically or mainly Christian – any more than Walter Benjamin and, more recently, Jacques Derrida intend a Christian meaning when they use the term.[4] Given this, then, the light at the end of *All or Nothing* is 'the messianic light' that is 'shed on the world by redemption'.

So that, from this point of view, Leigh's achievement in *All or Nothing* is to have carried out what is, in the 'face of despair' the essential 'task of thought', to have fashioned just such perspectives as Adorno claims are necessary and to have done so 'without velleity or violence, *entirely from felt contact with its [thought's] objects*'.

Concluding remarks

I am painfully aware of so much that has either been left out completely or not given anywhere near enough attention to in the above account of this extraordinary film. So I wish to end by at least mentioning some of these things.

(i) *Rachel*

Even if the light that we see at the end of the film is in some sense 'messianic', this does not of course mean that all the problems have been solved, or that there is no more suffering.

Each of the first four days begins with Rachel at work in the care home for the elderly. And on the Friday, Saturday and Sunday mornings we see one of her co-workers – a much older man named Sid (Sam Kelly) – making awkward advances on her. Soon after telling her, for example, on Sunday morning that he was so hot the night before that he could not wear his pyjamas ('Lay there, stark naked'), he invites her out for 'a stroll in the park', after which they might go back to his flat where they could sit 'on the bed. Watch a video.' Rachel has mentioned none of this to her parents or brother but she is obviously upset by it. And when she is sitting opposite her parents alongside Rory's hospital bed near the end of the film, Rory asks her if she is alright. She says that she is but her mother explains to Rory that Rachel has not 'been back to work yet'. This prompts Rory to ask first why she has not 'been in' and then, when Rachel says she has not 'been sleepin'', to ask 'why not?' Since Rachel does not reply, Penny says that it is because she has 'been worried'. 'What about?' Rory wants to know. 'About you', his mother tells him. 'We all 'ave.' Though Rachel is clearly loved by her parents, she has been getting far less attention than her brother. And Penny has been simply too preoccupied with Rory to notice that Rachel has her own problems.

(ii) *Loneliness*

While it seems likely that Rachel stands a better chance of having her problems recognised and receiving support and understanding at the end of the film, now that her parents are back in love with one another, the film also makes us keenly aware of the limits of human sympathy by bringing home to us how *alone* almost everyone seems to feel at times. One thinks, for example, of a moment shortly before Rory has his heart attack when he is kicking a ball on his own and is approached by Carol who (partly no doubt because she herself is drunk as usual) comes up close to him and says 'You're on your own, in't yer?' while stroking his hair and face. Rory's response is a puzzled 'So?' At one point in his conversation with Cécile, Phil reflects that 'if you're not together, you're alone. You're born alone, you die alone. Nothing you can do about it.' 'You are right', says Cécile, 'it is fuckin' lonely.' In a similar vein, when she and Phil are making up, Penny confesses that she feels 'cut off all the time. Lonely.' One might also think here of Craig, with his probably hopeless love for Samantha, and of Samantha herself, especially, for example, after Craig has shown her the letter S he has carved onto his chest as proof of his love for her and we see Samantha alone in her bed sobbing '*her heart out*'.

(iii) *Silence*

Most of the film's suffering is endured in silence. Rachel, for example, never does get to articulate her problems so that, as the screenplay puts it, after Penny has told Rory 'You wanna be careful, you', she and Phil '*share a moment*' and she then looks at Rachel who '*has all sorts of thoughts and feelings and emotions. And [Rachel] reflects on her lot*' (2002: 152). Silently. But then, so many of this film's key moments are silent or close to being silent. Indeed part of the film's greatness is to be found in some of the ways in which it approaches the kind of power that we associate with silent movies at their best, in particular the ways in which silent films were obliged by necessity to express so much through the faces and bodies of the actors. I know of nothing outside of the silent cinema quite like the haunted expression that Phil has on his face throughout most of *All or Nothing*. Furthermore, it is perfectly obvious that much of the film's power derives from the simple visual and silent contrast between Penny's relatively tiny body and the large, over-sized bodies of her husband and two children. In addition to this, it seems that almost all the main characters in this film have such distinctive and memorable ways of inhabiting their bodies that they would succeed in communicating a good deal even if they were forced to be silent.

(iv) *Something biblical*

If *All or Nothing* can sometimes remind us of the kind of stripped-down, pure cinema of the silents, there are also moments when, as already noted, we find ourselves reflecting that there is something Biblical about it. Another example of this would be when Penny is doing her crossword puzzle and the clue she gives Phil, when he asks her for one, is: 'Biblical son of Isaac; five letters, starting with a J'. Phil first suggests Jonah and then changes it to Jacob. Though he is then not sure, Jacob is the correct answer. And since Jacob was the father of the people of Israel, the invoking of his name at this point in the film is highly suggestive. It conjures up a sense of Israel's suffering and despair, especially (though not only, obviously) in 'The Lamentations of Jeremiah', an example that seems appropriate simply because of the claim we have seen Leigh make that his works typically involve both lamentation and celebration. Of course, as soon as one starts thinking along these lines, one starts wondering about the name Rachel too. And about the possibility that Phil's struggle with Penny might be seen as in some way resembling Jacob's wrestling with the Angel of God.

(v) Leigh

Finally, in his brief but appreciative review of the film, Geoff Andrew refers to 'the Ozu-like opening shot' and 'the dark, almost Bergmanesque intensity of the climactic confrontation [between Phil and Penny]' (2002: 14). Both these comparisons seem justified and there are indeed similarities with some moments in Bergman's *Persona* when, in the midst of that last confrontation, the faces of Penny and her daughter Rachel practically fill the screen. But Leigh is very much his own master here, more audacious and daring than he has ever been before.

CONCLUSION

A Sense of the Real

The aim of a robust art still remains: that it be hearty, that it be savage, that it serve to feed audiences with the marrow of its honest presence … [I]n return for roiling the delicacies of more than one fine and valuable nervous system, it gives in return light and definition and blasts of fresh air to the corners of the world, it is a firm presence in the world, and so helps to protect the world from its dissolution in compromise, lack of focus, and entropy…

– Norman Mailer (1972: 122)

This is not the first book on Leigh, nor, I am sure, will it be the last; my hope is that subsequent works will do some of the things I either ignore or – in my concern to demonstrate that Leigh's *range* is much broader than it is often thought to be – do not go into enough. I am, for example, aware of the fact that I have not spent enough time on the actual *look* of the films. Though I have tried to address this more in Part Three, I give very little attention to it in Part Two. And while it would seem perverse to insist on the continuous insertion of commentary on camera angles and set-ups when Leigh has made it plain that his instinct is 'for the camera to be unobtrusive' (Fuller 1995: xxvii), there is certainly more to be said about them than I say here. There is also much more that needs to said about the other elements of the *mise-*

en-scène. And finally, though it is, I take it, blatantly obvious that hardly any film director deserves the title of *auteur* more than Leigh, it is also true that probably no other film director's oeuvre is as much the product of so much collaborative input from the actors as Leigh's. There is of course a great deal that could and should be said about the contributions made by Leigh's actors, one of the finest of whom (Katrin Cartlidge) died prematurely in 2003.

Though I realise that the reader must certainly be ready to judge (either positively or negatively) an author's sense of priorities, in the end, like all authors I hope this book will be judged more on the basis of what it does than on what it fails to do.

My first priority has been to emphasise the sense of the real that we get from Leigh's films and I would like here to say a little more about this; more specifically, about its two main distinguishing features, which I take to be (i) the way in which it is grounded or precisely located in terms of social class; and (ii) the way it is embodied.

In 'the minefields of English class-consciousness'[1]

> This is a deeply class-ridden society like nowhere else, and everything resonates around that. Since I make films which are about England, because I'm specifically concerned with creating a real world, implicitly and inevitably, problems of class are part of the texture.
>
> – Mike Leigh (Movshovitz 2000: 91)

> I do not see class as a 'structure', nor even as a 'category', but as something which in fact happens ... in human relationships.
>
> – E. P. Thompson (1968: 9)

> As the English historian E. P. Thompson has said, class is ... something that happens between people. Leigh's films define and negotiate this in-between realm.
>
> – John Lahr (1996: 53)

Commenting on the film *Paris is Burning*, Zizek claims that class is 'the ultimate "trauma"' – not 'race nor gender identity, but *class*'. He argues that the 'point of the film is that, in the three divides subverted by it (class, race and gender), the class divide ... is the most difficult to cross' (Zizek 2000: 328–9). I do not intend to argue (any more than Zizek does) that class is always and everywhere the *ultimate* trauma because I do not believe it is. But I do think that its impact on the social body – which is to say, on our collective self – takes the form of 'a series of traumatic cuts or separations'.[2] And from this point of view, the key word here is 'divide' ('the class *divide*').

It could easily be maintained that all of Leigh's films are pretty centrally about class. Except that, as Ian Buruma has pointed out, 'to say that Leigh's films are *about* class is like saying that Bunuel's films are about the Catholic church' (1994: 9). It is so pervasive, in other words, that it is like the air people breathe, the element in which they exist.

Still, at the risk of stating the obvious, it nevertheless has to be said that one main reason why Leigh's characters seem so exceptionally real is that they are so exactly situated within the English class system.[3]

The 'material bodily principle'

> It's about the joy of putting real life and the texture of real life on the screen.
> It's people on the screen. Warts and all. Drips on the ends of old men's noses.
>   – Mike Leigh (Movshovitz 2000: 83)

Up to a point, in its attitude towards the body, Leigh's work might be said to resemble that of Rabelais', in which, as Bakhtin once noted, 'the material bodily principle, that is, images of the human body with its food, drink, defecation and sexual life, plays a predominant role' (1984: 18). If, moreover, as Bahktin maintains, in Rabelais' 'grotesque realism ... the bodily element is deeply positive' (1984: 19) – and nowhere more so, it seems, than in 'that which *protrudes* from the body, all that seeks to go beyond the body's confines' (1984: 316, my italics) – then we have to recognise that there is a strand of such realism at play in Leigh's imagination too.

Let us look at two of Leigh's responses to his interviewers (each of them supplemented by further clarifications). The first is part of his reaction in 1996 to the question 'Why did you want to become a film-maker?':

> Well, when I was twelve, on a very, very snowy and cold day in the middle of winter in Manchester, I stood in the front hall of my grandparents' house. My grandfather was carried downstairs in a coffin by four old men with drips at the ends of their noses. And my response to this tragic-comic occasion was the thought that it would be great to make a film about this ... I'm just reporting on an impulse that came out of a particular moment and a specific memory that may in some way answer that question. You know, you're an artist if you can draw or make music or whatever it is you can do, because you find that you can do it. And then you do it by compulsion, by need ... it's a matter of compulsion, need and urgency. You know, it's a disease. (Movshovitz 2000: 82–3)

In another interview given in the same year, Leigh offers a slightly different version of this memory of 'grandpa's funeral'. In it he calls the four old men 'ancient pallbearers ... schlepping his coffin down the stairs' and in this version only one 'of them had a long drip hanging from his nose' (Movshovitz 2000: 89).

Considering the discussion in chapter two about the importance of ordinary, everyday, ritualistic occasions in Leigh's work, it seems to me worth noting that this is a memory of a funeral, more precisely of a Jewish funeral, the Yiddish word 'schlepping' – together with the reference to those 'ancient pallbearers' – giving the incident much of its colour. But it is of course those running noses that most strikingly capture our attention.

The second response comes from an earlier interview given in 1991. Noting how, while watching Leigh's films 'you have to keep reminding yourself that these are actors', the interviewer claims that 'there's sort of a paradox in that kind of intense creation of reality: in the end, in a certain way they're not real, they're super-real characters'. In his reaction to this Leigh mentions that obviously 'there are considerations involved which have to do with heightening things – which actually are *not* heightening beyond what's real, but because you look at it, you actually start to perceive'. Here is the example Leigh then provides:

> As when you're in a subway, right up against someone, you have to look at them, though you try not to, you have to see them, hear them, smell them. That's what it's about, really. (Movshovitz 2000: 20)

Here too, it is at least partly a matter of compulsion (of 'hav[ing] to'). And when we are pressed up against someone in this way and obliged to see them close-up, what do we see? Sometimes, at least, we see what one of the 1996 interviewers wondered about in *Career Girls:* 'In *Career Girls* we see a lot of signs of physical distress, like rashes and tics, that literally 'flesh out' your characters. What about that?' This time Leigh begins his answer by saying he thinks 'it's no big deal ... we're all susceptible to tics and twitches of one kind or the other. That's idiosyncratic, and that's how people are.' The problem is that most movies do not show us people as they are:

> On the whole, characters in movies behave like actors behave when they're playing characters in movies. Which is to say, with all the twitches, tics and behavioral and physical characteristics and defects removed and sort of blanded and bleached out of existence. (Movshovitz 2000: 82)

The problem, in other words, is that a need is felt to ensure that the characters in most movies are effectively *cleansed* – with the dictionary definitions of 'bland' (meaning 'smooth and soothing in manner or quality', 'exhibiting no personal concern or embarrassment') and 'bleach' (meaning 'to remove colour or stains from' and 'to make whiter or lighter' [*Webster's New Collegiate*]) effectively summarising the main ways in which the mainstream media tries to erase the real.

I now want to try to go a bit more deeply into these matters by noting first a certain similarity – and then a more important difference – between what Leigh has to say about running noses and subways and something Zizek has had to say about the Lacanian Real in the films of David Lynch and Krzysztof Kieslowski. Here to begin with is an excerpt from Marek Wieczorek's introduction to Zizek's little booklet on Lynch's *Lost Highway*:

> Illustrating his point about the Lynchean Real, Zizek has ... invoked the famous opening scene from *Blue Velvet*: the broad shots of idyllic small-town Middle America with a father watering the lawn; suddenly, the father suffers a stroke or heart-attack while the camera dramatically zooms in on the grass with its bustling microscopic world of insects. 'Lynch's entire

ontology,' Zizek writes, 'is based upon the discordance between reality, observed from a safe distance, and the absolute proximity of the Real. His elementary procedure involves moving forward from the establishing shot of reality to a disturbing proximity that renders visible the disgusting substance of enjoyment, the crawling and glistening of indestructible life.' Zizek notes how in Lynch's universe the Real eerily invades daily existence, with the camera's point of view often too close for comfort, with uncanny details sticking out, or close-ups of insects or decomposing bodies. One is reminded here of Dali's fascination with insects… (Wieczorek in Zizek 2002: ix)

Up to a point, this is undeniably reminiscent of Leigh's explanation as to how he tries to position his viewers, as if we were 'in a subway, right up against someone' – forced into 'a disturbing proximity', 'too close for comfort, with uncanny details sticking out'. But on the other hand, Leigh's camera is almost always unobtrusive: it never 'dramatically zooms in'. And while it seems quite right for Wieczorek to be reminded here of Dali, it would be entirely inappropriate in Leigh's case. When faced, for example, with the suggestion that the 'scenes with Aubrey and Paula in *Life is Sweet* border on the surreal,' Leigh is (in my view, quite rightly) adamant: 'No, it's not surrealism at all' (Fuller 1995: xxxiii). I take this to be a clear and bracing (if also, for the would-be critic, a somewhat intimidating) sign of the importance Leigh attaches to getting things exactly right, of his distaste for casually suggestive but actually imprecise analogies.

According to Zizek, 'the experience of nausea with regard to life as such is a primordial ontological experience' (2001: 204) but I have to admit that I am far from being persuaded by this. Especially since, in this particular case, the claim is linked (in a footnote) to what seems to me a definite misreading of what Zizek considers to be a 'key detail' in Kieslowski's *Three Colours: Blue*, Julie's discovery of the mouse 'who gives birth to a large litter … in a back room of her new apartment in the rue Mouffetard':

> The view of this thriving life disgusts her, since it stands for the Real of life in its thriving, humid vitality. Her stance of disgust is the one that, more than fifty years ago, was perfectly rendered by Sartre's early novel *Nausea* – a disgust at the inert presence of life … life becomes disgusting when the fantasy that mediates our access to it disintegrates, so that we are directly confronted with the Real… (Zizek 2001: 169)

While I can see how the disintegration of the mediating fantasy-frame can *sometimes* make life seem disgusting, I do not see that happening here.[4] Nor do I think this is Julie's experience. She speaks, after all, of fear, not of disgust – and I see no reason to suppose she is mistaken. But, in any case, this highlights what seems easily *the* most importance difference involved here, the fact that Leigh seems to feel none of the disgust Zizek considers necessary. And if we recall the two examples – the running noses and 'the rashes and tics […] that literally "flesh out"' some of Leigh's characters – that point us in the direction of the Leighean real, the fact (if I am right) that the latter is not intended to arouse our disgust is surely worthy of comment. After all, these two examples can certainly remind us of 'the old definition of dirt' that the anthropologist Mary Douglas gives us in her book *Purity and Danger* – 'dirt' or 'uncleanness', 'as matter out of place' (1969: 35, 40) – and dirt is usually found to be more or less disgusting.

Yet as Leigh invites us to see it, the first especially of these examples of what '*protrudes* from the body', of 'matter out of place', functions in pretty much the (non-disgusting) way the *punctum* (as opposed to the *studium*) functioned for Roland Barthes. Barthes uses the second of these two terms to describe the kind of (only moderate) interest he has in most photographs ('The *studium*', he tells us, 'is that very wide field of unconcerned desire … [It] is of the order of *liking*, not of *loving*'). But if most photographs 'provoke only a general and, so to speak, *polite* interest,' this, he maintains, is because 'they have no *punctum* in them' (1981: 27). The *punctum* is the kind of detail that – showing 'no preference for morality or good taste' (it 'can be ill-bred' [1981: 43]) – 'rises from the scene, shoots out of it like an arrow, and pierces me' (1981: 26). Here is what Santner has to say about Barthes' *punctum*:

> The *punctum* is not an intervention of another order of reality, but a rising to consciousness of a non-symbolisable surplus within an otherwise intelligible reality, a sort of stain on the horizon of cultural intelligibility. (Santner 2001: 74)

Furthermore, this 'stain' is what Santner has in mind when he refers (as we noted at the end of chapter three) to a '*surplus of the real within reality*' (ibid.).

Thus, it is not disgust but rather joy that Leigh feels at the thought of putting this (and various other) 'sort[s] of stain' ('the texture of real life') on the screen.

The question of a title

> The British don't like to see themselves portrayed warts and all … He gets under people's skins over here; he shows what's inside the dustbin.
> – Dick Pope (quoted in Movshovitz 2000: 91)

The first title I considered for this book was *Looking the Negative in the Face*. The phrase is used by Hegel in the 'Preface' to his *Phenomenology*:

> The life of Spirit is not the life that shrinks from death and keeps itself untouched by devastation, but rather the life that endures it and maintains itself in it. It wins its truth only when, in utter dismemberment, it finds itself … Spirit is this power only by looking the negative in the face, and tarrying with it. This tarrying with the negative is the magical power that converts it into being. (Hegel 1997, par. 32)

Looking the negative in the face, tarrying with it – this still strikes me as giving an excellent description of what Leigh is doing throughout such films as *Bleak*

Moments, *Hard Labour*, *Meantime* and *Naked* and at key moments in most of his other films too. But if I finally rejected this first idea, it was because such a title could easily have been misleading, as if it were denying another equally important side of Leigh's work, the side I thought for a while of foregrounding in another possible title: *The Collaborative Creativity of Mike Leigh*.

Here I would have been drawing on what F. R. Leavis has to say about collaborative creativity in his *Little Dorrit* essay.[5] And there are two main ways in which I think the idea fairly begs to be applied to Leigh's work: first on the level of the extra-curricular contributions Leigh's actors make to his films; but also on the level of so much of the content of these films – as, for example, in the kinds of collaborative creativity we see in the endings of *Meantime* and *Life is Sweet* when (in each case) one sibling supports another; in the friendship we see growing in *Career Girls*; in such husband and wife partnerships as the one between Eugene and Collette in *Four Days in July*; and of course in all sorts of ways throughout *Topsy-Turvy*.

I would like *A Sense of the Real*, the title I finally settled on, to be understood as pointing to *both* sides of Leigh's imaginative world: to the sense of the real we get when we look the negative (or devastation) in the face – as we do most dramatically in the case of Johnny's 'unemployed negativity' in *Naked*; on the other hand, to the sense of the real we get when we witness the transforming power of love (especially between the husband and wife in *All or Nothing*).[6]

Finally, then, I would suggest that we think of Leigh's art as the kind of 'robust art' Mailer once described – sometimes 'hearty', sometimes 'savage' and always serving 'to feed audiences with the marrow of its honest presence' (1972: 122), which is to say, with the kind of food that strengthens 'our sense of the real'. This, I take it, is the point Maurice is making in *Secrets and Lies* when he insists to Roxanne – who has just learned that she has a sister and is waiting at a bus stop, ready to flee her own birthday party as a result – that she has 'gotta face up to it!' In my view, facing up to the real is what Leigh is trying to get us (his audience) to do – 'the pressure toward self-transformation' (Santner 2001: 8) he is exerting on us – in all of his films.

NOTES

PREFACE

1   More precisely, these are five little films of five minutes each. They were commissioned by the BBC in 1975 but not broadcast until 1982 (see Coveney 1997: 98–9).

2   There are no longer any existing copies of this item.

CHAPTER ONE

1   Perhaps I should add that my video store has a large foreign-language section too, with sub-sections devoted to the films of each country. This makes the 'Outlaw Film-makers' stand out even more.

2   Colin MacCabe's critique (in his 'Realism and the Cinema' article) of what he termed the 'classic realist text' was particularly influential here. And, as Jacob Leigh notes in his recent book on Ken Loach, 'despite criticism of the classic realist text model, in writing about Loach, arguments about realism continue, and the formula of the classic realist text demonstrates a surprising longevity: Colin McArthur, John Caughie, Derek Paget and John Hill all use it as a theoretical model' (Leigh 2002: 15).

3   Saul Steinberg's recently published account of his discovery of 'how hard it is to do a drawing from life' (2002: 32) seems to me worth pondering in this connection.

4   In this connection it may be worth noting what Coveney calls the 'interesting contempt for British cinema' that Peter Greenaway expressed back in 1993: 'The main centre line is *Saturday Night and Sunday Morning*, on to *My Beautiful Laundrette*, on to something by Mike Leigh. It's British cinema taking over Italian neo-realism and following it through. Making no doubt acerbic and acute Real Life movies whose political circumstance is particularly germane to England, especially south-east England. I can respect that kind of cinema, I can see its heart is in the right place, but frankly I find it very

boring' (quoted in Coveney 1997: 12). If it was only Greenaway who thought like this, the comment could be ignored. But the truth is that when things become over-familiar, we all get bored. Indeed, the over-familiar is boring by definition. Often, however, as I believe is the case here with Leigh's films, the problem is not with the things as such but rather with the tired categories or groupings that prevent us from seeing the things as they really are. This enables us to do what Lawrence said could not be done: to dodge the new experience by pigeon-holing it.

CHAPTER TWO

1   There are of course many other works devoted to a study of the everyday, most famously no doubt, Henri Lefebvre's *Everyday Life in the Modern World* and Michel de Certeau's *The Practice of Everyday Life*. Both of these are discussed (along with others) by Ivone Margulies' *Nothing Happens: Chantal Akerman's Hyperrealist Everyday*. I regret the fact that I was unable, while writing this book, to see *Jeanne Dielman*, the main film on which Margulies makes her case for Akerman. My main reason for choosing to focus on the books by Klevan and Santner is that I find they give me the most help with Leigh's work, especially when it comes to thinking about his pursuit of the real.

CHAPTER FOUR

1   It seems to me worth noting, therefore, that in his Introduction to Rosenzweig, Nahum Glatzer speaks of an 'ability to wait' (1999: 31) and Rosenzweig himself claims that to '*refuse* stubbornly to wait with patience is to surrender life' (1999: 41, my italics).

CHAPTER FIVE

1   Since I have pointed out some of Leigh's affinities with D. H. Lawrence, it might, by way of contrast, be worth noting that in the latter's novella, *St Mawr*, it is a horse that temporarily becomes (in Lou Witt's mind) 'the only thing that was real' (1997: 16). Here we come upon an instructive difference between Lawrence's sensibility and Leigh's. One imagines that Leigh would find the idea that a *horse* could body forth the real in this way – even (as in the case of St Mawr) temporarily – hopelessly romantic. One of the definitions of the real provided by Sarah Kay might be helpful here: 'The real is the disgusting, hidden underside of reality which we cannot fail but step on, however much we imagine that our minds are set on higher things. Indeed, the more we keep our heads in the air, the more it clings to our feet' (Kay 2003: 4). But this kind of real is surprisingly rare in Leigh's work and the main reason we might possibly be reminded of it at this point is no doubt the fact that – quite unusually – this film's central characters have their minds 'set on higher things'.

2   In his review of Ray Carney's book on Leigh, John Hill refers to this episode and summarises the film as follows: '*Nuts in May* … is a slightly silly comedy of manners set in the country which comes complete with jokes about farting in tents and crapping in the bushes' (Hill 2001: 58). Actually, there is only one joke about farting (Finger farts in Ray's tent) and one about crapping in *Nuts in May* and, in a film that has some brilliant comic one-liners in it, it seems odd to remember only the ones about farting and crapping. What Hill's comment fails entirely to register is the fact that, in addition to being sometimes farcical, *Nuts in May* is predominantly satirical. Convinced (mostly, it seems, by those two jokes) that it is only 'a slightly silly comedy', Hill feels no need to engage with it on the level of ideas or intellectual content – if indeed he even notices that it *has* any.

3   I am reminded here of a passage in Rosenzweig's 'On Being a Jewish Person': 'What is intended to be of limited scope can be carried out according to a limited, clearly outlined plan – it can be 'organised'. The unlimited cannot be attained by organisation … The highest things cannot be planned: for them readiness is everything' (Rosenzweig 1967: 222).

4   It seems to me that the psychoanalyst Jonathan Lear is getting at something similar in a recent

essay entitled 'Knowingness and Abandonment: An Oedipus for Our Time'. Lear suggests that in *Oedipus Tyrannus* 'Sophocles is offering a diagnosis of "knowingness" … a critique of *its thinness as a way of being in the world* …'. He claims that 'insofar as this "knowingness" presents itself as reason, Oedipus the tyrant becomes … Oedipus tyrannised – tyrannised by what *he* takes to be the reasonable movement of his own mind (1988: 48, my italics). In other words, like Oedipus, Keith has 'confidence in his powers of practical reason' – and also, in Keith's case, in guide books, systems, rules, codes, the law – a confidence which 'shields him from recognition of another realm [of] meaning … the realm of unconscious meaning' (Keith 1988: 51, 54).

5   Since Lear sounds like Santner here, I had perhaps better explain that they are colleagues at the University of Chicago and that each acknowledges the other's influence in their books. In a similar way, Santner and Zizek also acknowledge one another's work. I would say that what we have here are a number of distinct but related and overlapping intellectual projects.

6   Yet Carney also maintains that all of *The Kiss of Death* is 'devoted to pointing out the limitations of [Linda and Sandra's] designs for living'; 'They are know-it-alls'; 'Leigh's narrative project throughout this film is to assault Linda's systems of knowing' (2000: 70, 71, 73).

CHAPTER SIX

1   Letter to Ernest Chevalier, 31 December 1830. Reprinted in *Madame Bovary*, Bersani (ed.), 1972: 311.

2   'Pound on Joyce'. 4. Kenner is quoting from Flaubert's *Dictionary of Received Ideas*. He is introducing Pound's article on 'James Joyce and Pécuchet', which was first published in 1922. Pound argues that in the chapter of René Descharmes' book *Autour de Bouvard et Pécuchet* that is devoted to 'received ideas', 'a relation between Flaubert and Joyce is apparent' (1952: 14).

3   Thelma Whiteley appeared as Susan when *Abigail's Party* was first performed at the Hampstead Theatre, London, on 18 April 1977. Harriet Reynolds appeared as Susan in the Hampstead Theatre production (from 18 July 1977) and also in the television version transmitted as a *Play for Today* on BBC1 on 1 November 1977.

4   Though the play version differs in a few places from the BBC production, I am only quoting passages that are the same in both versions.

5   It is tempting to read this insistence in the light of Santner's description of the Superego as the agency that paradoxically demands not only our obedience but also our transgression, the Superego 'as the voice whose monotonous command is "Enjoy!"' (Santner 2001: 102).

6   Carney apparently thinks that if Leigh's attitude to Rupert and Laetitia in *High Hopes* was one of anger, this would have to mean that he was 'in an unresolved emotional state' and that he must be 'threatened by them' (Carney 2000: 271–2).

7   Unlike Flaubert, Leigh shows no signs of becoming obsessed with stupidity. On Flaubert's obsession, see (in the Bantam edition of *Madame Bovary*), among others, Nietzsche, Henry James and Jean-Paul Sartre.

8   See F. R. Leavis on this, in 'Dickens and Blake: *Little Dorrit*' (1972: 349–50).

9   See Ginette Vincendeau's introduction to her book *Film/Literature/Heritage*.

10   'It ought, thus', Santner adds, 'to be very clear why Rosenzweig could never become a Zionist in any recognisable sense of that term' (2001: 117–18).

11   Frances Barber was later to play another social worker as Rosie in Stephen Frears' *Sammy and Rosie Get Laid* (1988).

CHAPTER SEVEN

1   I claim in the last chapter, however, that a kind of remarriage occurs at the end of *All or Nothing*.

2   It is interesting in this connection to note Naomi Scheman's explanation that the clue to her 'unease

with Cavell's readings [of the Hollywood comedies], with the films themselves, and with the feminism they embody is found in the double state of motherlessness (neither having nor being one) that is requisite for the heroines' (1988: 66).

3   But perhaps this is a slightly misleading way of putting it. Nicola's lover says he wants a 'conversation' as a way of avoiding (delaying? postponing?) having sex with her. We have seen from their earlier encounter that this means acting out her fantasy scenario of being tied up and having her breasts covered in chocolate spread, which he is expected to lick off. Her lover had been clearly reluctant to do it the first time ('Not again – it's borin'' [1995c: 144]) and now, on the later occasion, he says he wants to treat her 'like a real person instead of some fuckin' shagbag' (1995c: 169). On the face of it, then, he is obviously the reasonable one. But Michael Haneke's *The Piano Teacher* (2001) suggests another possible way of viewing the situation. In Haneke's film a young male pianist falls in love with his older teacher (played by Isabel Huppert). Here is Zizek's useful summary of the relevant part: 'Things take a fateful turn and start to slide towards the inexorable tragic ending (the teacher's suicide) at a precise moment: when, in answer to the boy's passionate sexual advances, the "repressed" teacher violently opens herself up to him, writing him a letter with a detailed list of her demands (basically, a scenario for masochistic performances...). It is crucial that these demands are *written* – what is put on paper is too traumatic to be pronounced in direct speech: her innermost fantasy itself. When they are thus confronted – he with his passionate outbursts of affection and she with her cold, impassionate distance – this setting should not deceive us: it is she who in fact opens herself up, laying her fantasy bare to him, while he is simply playing a more superficial game of seduction' (Zizek 2002a: 20–1). As Zizek invites us to see it, the proper response is clear-cut: while we can understand the young man's failure to respond ('No wonder he withdraws in panic' [2002a: 21]), we should unreservedly admire the teacher for her courage in laying bare her 'innermost fantasy'. My point is that this can (if we let it) disturbingly complicate our feelings about the situation Leigh gives us. (For a more detailed and moving commentary on Haneke's film, I recommend Robin Wood 2002.)

CHAPTER EIGHT

1   As Geoffrey O'Brien (the editor of the Library of America) put it in his review of *Topsy-Turvy*, 'Thewlis' nomadic, ceaselessly verbalising Johnny in *Naked* may turn out to be one of the more enduring British literary creations of this period' (2000: 18).

2   I am not suggesting that Leigh was consciously influenced by, or even particularly aware of, this source. Bernstein notes that, 'although specialists agree that [Dostoevsky] knew Diderot's work well, the genealogy [he is] tracing is independent of such direct transmissions. Instead, what matters is the "genre memory", the ways in which Diderot and Dostoevsky each appropriated a classical topos and then uncovered, through the act of "making it new" for their own eras and idioms, fresh formal and thematic possibilities in its structure' (1992: 94).

3   We might think here of the following reflection from Adorno's *Minima Moralia*: 'As people have altogether too few inhibitions and not too many, without being a whit the healthier for it, a cathartic method with a standard other than successful adaptation and economic success would have to aim at bringing people to a consciousness of unhappiness both general and – inseparable from it – personal, and at depriving them of the illusory gratifications by which the abominable order keeps a second hold on life inside them, as if it did not already have them firmly enough in its power from outside (1984: 38). Elitist intolerance, or the kind of bracing challenge from which we could *all* benefit from time to time? It seems to me a bit of both.

4   In effect, he does what Bataille says the man of unemployed negativity does and 'confronts his own negativity as if it's a wall' (1988: 125).

5   Of course, other thinkers besides Winnicott might come to mind in this context. I think, for example, of a passage in Henry Staten's *Nietzsche's Voice*. Having just asked the question as to whether 'we know what we have said when we use the terms "erotic" or "sexual" to describe the character of

the fundamental drive energy in Freud?' Staten adds this: 'Very attentive reading of Freud's later works shows how confused are his attempts to keep eros separate from aggressiveness and the death drive, so much so that Laplanche is driven to conclude that 'the death drive is the very soul, the constitutive principle, of libidinal circulation'. And Leo Bersani argues that 'we don't move *from* love *to* aggressiveness in *Civilization and Its Discontents*; rather, love is redefined, re-presented, *as* aggressiveness' (Bersani 1993: 99).

CHAPTER NINE

1   Thomas Vinterberg's *The Celebration* (1998) is closer to being such a tale and since its subject matter is in some ways similar to that of Leigh's film (even if its upper-class setting is obviously very different), it may be helpful if we pause for a moment to consider Zizek's reading of it. According to Zizek the problem Vinterberg's film poses is 'how *really* to get rid of the apparently "superficial" mask of civilised symbolic rituals': 'the message is … not the one about disclosing the traumatic family secret that lurks beneath the civilised surface, threatening to explode at any moment, but, rather, the opposite one: even if the allegedly traumatic message *is* publicly disclosed, the "superficial" ritual of dinner is not disrupted, it drags on and on…' (2002c: lxvii). It seems to me that this is the kind of misreading that helps us to see more clearly. Even though the dinner does drag on and on, it *is* eventually disrupted and the family (minus the grossly abusive father) is therefore able to come together in a true spirit of celebration at breakfast the following morning. It would seem that for Vinterberg, as (is definitely the case) for Leigh, the task is to do the work that will make it possible to cut through the superficial mask and revivify precisely such 'civilised symbolic rituals' as family dinner.

2   Like most viewers, I imagine, there are moments when I find Brenda Blethyn's Cynthia extremely hard to take. What a relief it would be if we could just dismiss her as a whiner, which she certainly is at times! Or even perhaps hate her, as we surely hate the demonised character Blethyn plays in Mark Herman's *Little Voice* (1998). But Leigh does not allow us to do either of those things: his and Blethyn's Cynthia is much too troublingly complex for that.

CHAPTER TEN

1   This last phrase is missing from the published screenplay.

2   In a way it might be said Leigh inverts the symbolic geography of *Wuthering Heights*, with Annie from the north, living near the Brontes' house, visiting the south and discovering in Hannah's company something of the rough manners that, in the novel, Lockwood, the Londoner, finds in the north.

3   About Annie's facial rash, I completely agree with Leigh, who says, when asked about it in an interview, that 'It's no big deal' (Movshovitz 2000: 82). But I have to admit that I did not feel that way when I first saw it. My own experience is of finding it diminish in significance the more one resees the film.

CHAPTER ELEVEN

1   The words 'topsy-turvy' might well remind some of us of the title of one of Christopher Hill's books on the English Revolution: *The World Turned Upside Down*. And to say that much of the fun of *The Mikado* is had at the expense of the class system is to say, from a certain point of view, that what we find ourselves laughing at is the stuff of which History is made (Hegel's Master-Slave dialectic, Marx's class struggle). So that, with these connections in mind, it might almost seem as if *The Mikado* were affording us a glimpse of the end of History. And this can seem oddly, even bizarrely appropriate, to those familiar with the famous – perhaps notorious – footnote to his *Introduction to the Reading of Hegel* (see 1980: 161–2) in which Alexander Kojève maintained (in 1959) that we are already at the end of History. Because according to Kojève, if we want to know what life at the end of history (in post-historical society) is like, we should look at Japan. As Jacques Derrida has noted, this is

so because of what Kojève 'names, in that profoundly offhand, nutty, and pataphysician manner which is, to be sure, his genius but which is also his entire responsibility, "the Snobism in the pure state" of the cultural formalism of Japanese society' (1994: 71). There is, as Derrida points out, 'a French tradition, a kind of "French speciality" of peremptory diagnoses upon returning from a quick trip to a faraway land whose language one does not even speak and about which one knows next to nothing' (1994: 70–1). And there is no doubt but that, as Derrida clearly implies, Kojève's remarks on Japan – made, as Kojève confesses, after 'a recent voyage to Japan (1959)' (1980: 161) – do indeed belong to this tradition. Yet however 'nutty' Kojève's manner may be at this point, and however unrealistic and perhaps potentially offensive his comments might seem if they were to be taken as offering accurate commentary on actually-existing Japanese society, his praise of what he calls 'specifically Japanese snobbery' (161–2) remain interesting to anyone trying to imagine what the Marxist-Hegelian end of History – in which we move from the realm of necessity (History) into a realm of freedom – might look like. For those readers who are wondering how this could possibly have anything to do with film, I will recall the provocative last words of Jean-Luc Godard's 1967 film *Weekend*. Not just *Fin* but *Fin de Cinéma*. My point is not that this gesture was made with Kojève in mind. It is that it was made under the at-that-time still powerful influence of the discourse produced by 'those whom we could', as Derrida says, 'nickname the *classics of the end*' (Derrida 1994: 15) – and Kojève made a major contribution to this discourse. I take it that the seriousness of Godard's gesture is proved by the radically different kind of film-making he went on to produce after that date. As for Leigh's film, if it is true that an important part of the achievement of *Topsy-Turvy* lies in the way in which it revivifies our sense of history, I think that while doing this it simultaneously manages to remind us of (what was once – not so very long ago – considered to be) a utopian possibility. Or to put it another way, while solidly grounded in the realm of necessity, it does not forget (or allow us to forget) about the realm of freedom.

2   Since Marcuse seems to be little read today, I will mention, for those unfamiliar with the connection, that he was affiliated with the Frankfurt School, so that his work is related to that of Walter Benjamin and Adorno.

CHAPTER TWELVE

1   Here are two more passages in which Weil tries to distinguish affliction from other forms of suffering: 'There is not real affliction unless the event which has gripped and uprooted a life attacks it, directly or indirectly, in all its parts, social, psychological and physical. The social factor is essential. There is not really affliction where there is not social degradation or the fear of it in some form or another' (1977d: 440–1); 'When affliction is seen vaguely from a distance, either physical or mental, so that it can be confused with simple suffering, it inspires in generous souls a tender feeling of pity. But if by chance it is suddenly revealed to them in all its nakedness as a corrosive force, a mutilation or leprosy of the soul, then people shiver and recoil' (1977c: 332). The following passage, related by the narrator of Herman Melville's great short story 'Bartleby', seems to me also worth having in mind when pondering the difficulty the reviewers of *All or Nothing* found themselves presented with: '... a prudential feeling began to steal over me. My first emotions had been those of pure melancholy and sincerest pity; but just in proportion as the forlornness of Bartleby grew and grew to my imagination, did that same melancholy merge into fear, that pity into repulsion. So true it is, and so terrible, too, that up to a certain point the thought or sight of misery enlists our best affections; but, in certain special cases, beyond that point it does not' (Melville 1970: 79).

2   I am reminded here of the last three pages of Norman Mailer's essay 'Some Dirt in the Talk'. In particular, of this: 'Today obscene language bears about the same relation to good society that the realistic portraits of the naturalistic novel of Zola's time brought to the hypocrisies and niceties of the social world of France ... Zola was tasteless, Zola outraged, Zola's work was raw as bile, but in its time it was essential, it gave sanity to the society of its time' (1972: 121). I have put this in a footnote

because I want to minimise the possibility that those who read a text too quickly will come away with the impression that I think *All or Nothing* is a work of naturalism. I do not think that. But I do think it has some of the power that Mailer so eloquently attributes to Zola.

3   I am quoting from the (very slightly) adapted version used in Kieslowski's *Three Colours: Blue* (1993).

4   At one point in his *Specters of Marx* Derrida explains that he uses the term 'messianic' instead of '*messianism*, so as to designate a structure of experience rather than a religion' (1994: 167–8). For Derrida, 'the messianic … would be the opening to the future or to the coming of the other as the advent of justice, but without horizon of expectation and without prophetic figuration' (1998: 17).

CONCLUSION

1   See my comments on Dennis Potter's review of *Abigail's Party* in chapter one.

2   I have appropriated this phrase from Eric Santner, who uses it in a very different context (see Santner 2001: 105).

3   I find it inconceivable, therefore, that Leigh could have done (some English equivalent of) what Robert Altman did when – while using some of Raymond Carver's stories as the basis of his film *Short Cuts* (1993) – he upgraded several of Carver's couples in class terms (the doctor and the successful artist played by Matthew Modine and Julianne Moore, for example) and changed the setting to Los Angeles. So much for Altman's respect for the care Carver had taken to establish *his* sense of the real. On the other hand, Leigh cites *Short Cuts* as 'another example of a film that looks at people the way people are, without prejudice' (Fuller 1995: xxiv). If (as I suspect he has not) he had read and come to care for Carver's stories, he might feel a bit differently.

4   The classic novella, Conrad's *Heart of Darkness*, may make it easier to understand why, as Zizek seems sometimes to be suggesting, we might need 'some fantasy-frame' to protect us from full exposure to 'some traumatic Real'; and what, according to Zizek, 'Lacan has in mind when he says that fantasy is the ultimate support of reality: [that] "reality" stabilises itself when some fantasy-frame of a "symbolic bliss" closes off the view into the abyss of the Real' (1993: 118). Think, for example, of Marlow's decision at the end of *Heart of Darkness* to lie to Kurtz's Intended. Does he not tell this lie in order to enable her to hold on to her sense of 'reality'? Does the lie he tells her about Kurtz's last words not constitute precisely such a 'fantasy-frame of a "symbolic bliss"' (the strongly idealised, white-washed, version of Kurtz that the Intended receives in a state of exaltation) that 'closes off [her] view into the abyss of the Real' (which is to say, into the horrors Kurtz has perpetrated)? In short, what is this if not an anticipation of what Zizek calls 'the fundamental thesis of the Lacanian psychoanalysis … that what we call "reality" constitutes itself against the background of such a "bliss", i.e., of such an exclusion of some traumatic Real' (ibid.). But if, on the one hand, Marlow's lie to Kurtz's Intended – by staging 'the gradual reconstitution of the [Intended's] fantasy that gives [her] access to reality' (2001: 176) – does something similar to what Zizek finds happening in Kieslowski's *Blue*; and if, as Zizek says, this trajectory is 'the obverse of the psychoanalytic treatment' (ibid.), the aim of which is not to reconstitute the fantasy but rather to *traverse* or go through it, thus 'obtaining distance from it, … experiencing how the fantasy-formation just masks, fills out a certain void, lack, empty place in the Other' (1989: 74); well, at the same time, Conrad also makes sure that Marlow's wider audience, us, the readers of *Heart of Darkness*, have the experience of '"going through the fantasy"' that defines 'the final moment of the analysis' (1989: 133). In other words, *Heart of Darkness* performs something like 'the Lacanian notion of the psychoanalytical *act*', with the latter understood 'as a gesture which … touches the dimension of some impossible Real' (Zizek 2000: 121). Whether we traverse or reconstitute the fantasy, either way we pay a price. At least, that is the impression we get from Zizek. On the one hand, if, by reconstituting the fantasy, 'we … gain access to "reality"', 'something – the real of the trauma – must be "repressed"' (1993: 119). On the other hand, with Kieslowski's *Blue* in mind, Zizek maintains that 'life becomes disgusting when the fantasy that mediates our access to it distintegrates, so that we are directly confronted with the Real' (2001: 169). And though I am not

persuaded by Zizek's example, his main point would seem to receive at least some support from Marlow's state of mind towards the end of *Heart of Darkness*, when he returns to the European city that he has told us earlier always makes him 'think of a whited sepulchre' (Conrad 1950: 73): 'I found myself back in the sepulchral city resenting the sight of people hurrying through the streets to filch a little money from each other ... They were intruders whose knowledge of life was to me an irritating pretense, because I felt so sure they could not possibly know the things I knew' (1950: 149). What does this mean if not that, by virtue of his coming into contact with 'some impossible Real', Marlow has been turned into a somewhat embittered outsider, who is filled with disgust at the thought of even the slightest contact with ordinary people. But the moral is not, as I understand it, that one should abandon the pursuit of the real. It is that there is of course more than one real and that, while it seems important to point out that anyone pursuing it – in any of its guises – ought to proceed with caution, disgust and embitterment are not the inevitable outcome. What (to anticipate the next footnote) the character of (Dickens') Little Dorrit and the Kurtzian abyss have in common is that both represent two faces of the real, which are traumatic in the precise sense that the kinds of 'reality' that Mr Dorrit and Mrs General (in Dickens' novel) and Kurtz's Intended (in Conrad's novella) inhabit cannot survive prolonged contact with them. So we can say that these kinds of 'reality' are based on the suppression or exclusion of these faces of the traumatic real. But whereas Marlow's decision to traverse the fantasy and touch (or allow in) the (Kurtzian) real leaves him feeling embittered, another character's (Clennam's) decision to traverse the fantasy and to touch – or befriend – a very different but equally traumatic face of the real (Little Dorrit's) leaves him enriched and strengthened.

5   In this essay Leavis argued that the 'inquest into contemporary civilisation that [Dickens] undertook in *Little Dorrit*' committed him to 'an enterprise of thought', the kind that it is of the greatest importance to get recognised *as* 'thought – an affair (that is) of the thinking intelligence directed to a grasp of the real' (1972: 286). When Leavis tells us that, when they are reinstated 'in wealth and position, the Dorrit family in Italy ... can afford – as they desire – never to be reminded of the real', and that Mrs General and Mr Gradgrind 'represent complementary "social" ways of emptying the reality out of life', he is saying something about Dickens' novels that is (in one respect at least) similar to what Zizek is saying when, in the course of expounding Lacanian thought, he claims that 'the Social itself is *constituted* by the exclusion of some traumatic Real' (Zizek 2000: 311). And indeed, if, as Zizek maintains, 'the Lacanian Real is that traumatic "bone in the throat" that *contaminates* every ideality of the symbolic' (2000: 310), then, insofar as she is to her father a constant unwanted reminder of the Marshalsea, Little Dorrit might even be said to function a bit like 'the Lacanian Real'. Zizek also, incidentally, repeatedly describes the latter as being like 'the kernel which resists social integration' (2000: 323) and this too can remind us of the plight of Little Dorrit. (Just as by the same token it might also remind us of a character who otherwise seems to have nothing in common with Little Dorrit: Leigh's Johnny in *Naked*.)

6   It is worth noting here that in her book on Zizek, Sarah Kay, maintains that 'his recent writings on Christianity ... lead to a new and original purchase on the real as the domain of grace, by contrast with that of law' (2003: 5). She also claims that, in Zizek's *The Ticklish Subject* (1999), 'love is ... the force of the real that resists the law' (2003: 121). I like what Kay is saying and think she may be right. But if so, I wish that Zizek had managed to be as explicit about this as she is.

BIBLIOGRAPHY

This bibliography is split into two sections: the first focusing on works by or on Mike Leigh – screenplays, books, articles, reviews and collections of interviews; the second including more general works on cinema and the wider cultural and intellectual context within which Leigh's films can be helpfully evaluated. Full filmographies can also be found in Coveney (1997), Carney (2000) and Movshovitz (2000).

Focus on Mike Leigh

Andrew, Goeff (2002) 'Review of *All or Nothing*', *Sight and Sound*, 12, 7, 14.

Andrews, Nigel (1993) 'Misogynist on the Rampage', *Financial Times*, 4 November, 17.

Blumenfeld, Samuel (2002) '*All or Nothing: la misère sociale noircie jusqu'a la farce*', *Le Monde*, 4 December.

Bradshaw, Peter (2002) 'Review of *All or Nothing*', *Guardian*, 18 October.

Brooks, Xan (2002) 'Review of *All or Nothing*', *Sight and Sound*, 12, 11, 38.

Brown, Georgia (1993) 'Review of *Life is Sweet*', *Village Voice*, 21 December, 70.

Bruzzi, Stella (1997) 'Review of *Career Girls*', *Sight and Sound*, 7, 9, 38.

Buruma, Ian (1994) 'The Way They Live Now' [review of *Naked*], *New York Review of Books*, 13 January 7–10.

Burchill, Julie (1993) 'Crass Struggle', *The Sunday Times*, 7 November, 9, 5.

Carney, Ray (2000) *The Films of Mike Leigh: Embracing the World*. Cambridge: Cambridge University Press.

Chang, Chris (2002) 'Review of *All or Nothing*', *Film Comment*. 38, 5, 71.

Christie, Ian (2002) 'The Rules of the Game', *Sight and Sound*, 12, 9, 24–7.

Combs, Richard (1994) 'Down and Out almost Everywhere' [review of *Naked*], *Guardian*, 6 January.

Coveney, Michael (1997) *The World According to Mike Leigh*. London: HarperCollins.

French, Philip (2002) 'The Bleakest Link' [review of *All or Nothing*], *The Observer*, 20 October.

Fuller, Graham (1995) 'Mike Leigh's Original Features, an interview by Graham Fuller', in *Naked and Other Screenplays*, vii–xli.

Gilbey, Ryan (2002) 'Reasons to be Cheerful: With new films from Leigh and Loach, UK cinema is remembering its bad manners', *Sight and Sound*, 12, 10, 14–17.

Groen, Rick (2002) 'Doing what he does best' [review of *All or Nothing*], *Globe and Mail*, 1 November.

Hoberman, J. (2002) 'Deconstructing Hairy' [review of *All or Nothing*], *Village Voice*, 23–29 October.

Howe, Desson (2002) 'Mike Leigh's Gloom with a View' [review of *All or Nothing*], *Washington Post*, 4 November.

James, Nick (2002) 'Cannes 2002' [review of *All or Nothing*], *Sight and Sound*, 12, 7, 14.

Kael, Pauline (1991) Review of *High Hopes* in *Movie Love: Complete Reviews 1988–1991*. New York: Plume, 87–9.

Lacey, Liam (2002) 'Nothing at All' [review of *All or Nothing*], *Cinemascope*, 11, 53–4.

Lahr, John (1996) 'This Other England', *The New Yorker*, 23 September, 50–4.

Laprevotte, Gilles (1993) *Mike Leigh*, Amiens: Trois Cailloux.

Leigh, Mike (1983) *Abigail's Party; and Goose Pimples*. Harmondsworth: Penguin.

____ (1995a) On *L'Albero degli Zoccoli* (*The Tree of the Wooden Clogs*), in John Boorman and Walter Donogue (eds) *Projections 4¹/₂: Film-makers on Film-Making*. London: Faber and Faber, 113–17.

____ (1995b) *Naked and Other Screenplays*. London: Faber and Faber.

____ (1995c) *Life is Sweet*, in *Naked and Other Screenplays*. London: Faber and Faber, 97–183.

____ (1995d) *High Hopes*, in *Naked and Other Screenplays*. London: Faber and Faber, 185–262.

____ (1997a) *Career Girls*. London: Faber and Faber.

____ (1997b) *Secrets and Lies*. London: Faber and Faber.

____ (1999) *Topsy-Turvy*. London: Faber and Faber.

____ (2002) *All or Nothing*. London: Faber and Faber.

Lepage, Aleski K. (2002) 'Le vrai monde, la vraie vie' [review of *All or Nothing*], *La Presse*, 16 November.

Malcom, Derek (2002a) 'Derek Malcom at Cannes' [review of *All or Nothing*], *Guardian*, 17 May; http://film.guardian.co.uk/cannes2002/story/0,11895,717365,00.html.

____ (2002b) 'Mike Leigh at the NFT', *Guardian*, 7 October; http://film.guardian.co.uk/interviewpages/0.6737,809562,00.html.

Medhurst, Andy (1993) 'Beyond Embarrassment', *Sight and Sound*, 11, 3, 7–10.

____ (2000) 'The Mike-ado' [review of *Topsy-Turvy*], *Sight and Sound*, 10, 3, 36–7.

Monk, Claire (1993) 'Review of *Naked*', *Sight and Sound*, 11, 3, 48.

Movshovitz, Howie (ed.) (2000) *Mike Leigh: Interviews*. Jackson: University Press of Mississippi.

O'Brien, Geoffrey (2000) 'Stompin' at the Savoy', *New York Review of Books*, 24 February, 16–19.

Peranson, Mark (2002) 'Cannes 2002: Minority Reports', *Cinemascope*, 11, 39–42.

Potter, Dennis (1977) 'Trampling the mud from wall to wall', *The Sunday Times*. 6 November.

Pride, Ray (2000) 'Stark Naked: *Naked*', *Cinemascope* 2, 61–2.

Quart, Leonard (2002a) 'Going Beyond Despair: An Interview with Mike Leigh', *Cineaste*, 28, 1, 39.

____ (2002b) Untitled review. *Cineaste*, 28, 1, 40.

Quinn, Anthony (2002) 'Doom with a view' [review of *All or Nothing*], *Independent*, 18 October.

Rafferty, Terrence (1991) 'Under One Roof' [review of *Life is Sweet*], *New Yorker*, 4 November, 101–4.

Romney, Jonathan (1993) 'Scumbag Saviour' [review of *Naked*], *New Statesman*, 5 November, 34.

Russell, Jamie (2002) 'Review of *All or Nothing*', *BBC-Derby*, 21 November.

Spencer, Charles (2002) 'A Great but Guilty Pleasure', *Daily Telegraph*, December.

Sweet, Matthew (2000) 'The Very Model' [review of *Topsy-Turvy*], *The Independent on Sunday* (culture supplement) 30 January.

Taubin, Amy (1993) 'Heir to the Anger', *Village Voice*, 14 December, 70.

Wapshott, Nicholas (1982) 'The man stirring up the British class system' [review of *Home Sweet Home*], *The Times*, 16 March, 10.

Watson, Garry (2002) 'Are You With Me? Unemployed Negativity in Mike Leigh's *Naked*', *Cineaction*, 58, 32–45.

Watts, Carol (1996) 'Mike Leigh's *Naked* and the Gestic Economy of Cinema', *Women: A Cultural Review*, 7, 3, 271–8.

Wider film critical, cultural and intellectual context

Adorno, Theodor (1984) *Minima Moralia: Reflections from Damaged Life* [1951]. Trans. E. F. N. Jephcott. London: Verso.

Bakhtin, Mikhail (1984) *Rabelais and His World*. Trans. Helene Iswolsky. Bloomington: Indiana University Press.

Barthes, Roland (1981) *Camera Lucida: Reflections on Photography*. Trans. Richard Howard. New York: Noonday Press.

Bataille, Georges (1988) 'Letter to Blank, Instructor of a Class on Hegel...', in *Guilty*. Trans. Bruce Boone. Venice, CA: The Lapis Press, 123–5.

Benjamin, Walter (1973) *Charles Baudelaire: A Lyric Poet in the Era of High Capitalism*. Trans. Harry Zohn. London: NLB.

Bernstein, Michael André (1992) *Bitter Carnival: Ressentiment and the Abject-Hero*. Princeton: Princeton University Press.

Booth, Wayne C. (1988) 'Rabelais and the Challenge of Feminist Criticism', in *The Company We Keep: An Ethics of Fiction*. Berkeley: University of California Press, 383–418.

Caughie, John with Kevin Rockett (1996) *The Companion to British and Irish Cinema*. London: BFI/Cassell.

Cavell, Stanley (1976) *Must We Mean What We Say?* [1969]. Cambridge: Cambridge University Press.

_____ (1981) *The Pursuits of Happiness: The Hollywood Comedy of Remarriage*. Cambridge, MA: Harvard University Press.

_____ (1984) 'The Ordinary as the Uneventful (A Note on the *Annales* Historians', in *Themes Out of School*. San Francisco: North Point Press, 184–94.

_____ (1990) 'Ugly Duckling, Funny Butterfly: Bette Davis and *Now, Voyager*', *Critical Inquiry*, 16, 2, 213–47.

Cinemascope (2000) 'The Best of the Nineties: Poll of 150+ critics, directors, film-makers', *Cinemascope*, (Winter), 2, 51–8.

Conrad, Joseph (1950) *Heart of Darkness* [1899]. New York: Signet.

Crouse, Jeffrey (2002) 'Cinema's Recounting of the Ordinary', *Cineaction*, 57, 69–71.

Derrida, Jacques (1998) 'Faith and Knowledge: The Two Sources of "Religion" at the Limits of Reason Alone', trans. Samuel Weber, in Jacques Derrida and Gianni Vattimo (eds) *Religion*. Stanford: Stanford University Press, 1–78.

_____ (1994) *Specters of Marx*. Trans. Peggy Kamuf. New York and London: Routledge.

Dickens, Charles (1967) *Little Dorrit* [1857]. London: Penguin.

_____ (1969) *Hard Times* [1854]. London: Penguin.

_____ (1979) *Great Expectations* [1861]. London: Penguin.

Douglas, Mary (1969) *Purity and Danger: An Analysis of Concepts of Pollution and Taboo*. London: Routledge.

Edgar, David (1988) *The Second Time as Farce: Reflections on the Drama of Mean Times*. London: Lawrence & Wishart.

Eliot, George (1961) *Middlemarch: A Study of Provincial Life* [1871–72]. London: Oxford University Press.

Eliot, T. S. (1970) 'Burnt Norton', in *Four Quartets* [1944]. London: Faber, 14.

Elsaesser, Thomas (2002) 'Tales of Sound and Fury: Observations on the Family Melodrama', in

Christine Gledhill (ed.) *Home is Where the Heart is: Studies in Melodrama and the Woman's Film.* London: BFI, 43–69.

Felman, Shoshana (1993) *What Does a Woman Want? Reading and Sexual Difference.* Baltimore: Johns Hopkins University Press.

Fielding, Henry (1973) 'Preface', *Joseph Andrews* [1742]. London: J.M. Dent & Sons, i–vi.

Flaubert, Gustave (1972) *Madame Bovary* [1857]. Trans. Lowell Blair, Leo Bersani (ed.). New York: Bantam.

Forster, E. M. (1973) *Howard's End* [1910]. Harmondsworth: Penguin].

Foster, Hal (1996) *The Return of the Real: The Avant-Garde at the End of the Century.* Cambridge, MA: MIT Press.

Freud, Sigmund (1963) *Beyond the Pleasure Principle.* Trans. James Strachey. New York: Bantam.

Gilbert [W. S.] and Sullivan [Arthur] (n.d.) 'The Mikado; Or, The Town of Titipu' [1885], in *The Complete Plays of Gilbert and Sullivan.* New York: International Collector's Library, 295–343.

Glatzer, Nahum (ed.) (1999) 'Introduction', in *Understanding the Sick and the Healthy* [Franz Rosensweig, 1921]. Cambridge, MA: Harvard University Press, 21–33.

Gledhill, Christine (ed.) (2002) *Home is Where the Heart is: Studies in Melodrama and the Woman's Film.* London: BFI.

Hadot, Pierre (1995a) 'Spiritual Exercises', in Arnold I. Davidson (ed.) *Philosophy as a Way of Life: Spiritual Exercises from Socrates to Foucault.* Trans. Michael Chase. New York: Blackwell, 81–125.

_____ (1995b) 'The Figure of Socrates', in Arnold I. Davidson (ed.) *Philosophy as a Way of Life: Spiritual Exercises from Socrates to Foucault.* Trans. Michael Chase. New York: Blackwell, 147–78.

Harding, D. W. (1940) 'Regulated Hatred: An Aspect of the Work of Jane Austen', *Scrutiny*, 8, 4, 346–62.

Hegel, G. W. F. (1977) *Phenomenology of Spirit* [1807]. Trans. A. V. Miller. Oxford: Clarendon Press.

Hill, Christopher (1975) *The World Turned Upside Down: Radical Ideas During the English Revolution.* London: Penguin.

Hill, John (1999) *British Cinema in the 1980s.* Oxford: Clarendon Press.

_____ (2001) Untitled review of Ray Carney's *The Films of Mike Leigh: Embracing the World, Cineaste*, 26, 2, 57–8.

James, Henry (1968) 'Gustave Flaubert, 1902', in Morris Shapira (ed.) *Henry James: Selected Literary Criticism.* London: Peregrine, 252–81.

James, Nick (2002a) 'Nul Britannica', *Sight and Sound*, 12, 9, 38.

_____ (2002b) 'Modern Times', *Sight and Sound*, 12, 12, 20–1.

Jonson, Ben (1975) 'Timber: or Discoveries', in George Partfitt (ed.) *The Complete Poems.* London: Penguin, 373–458.

Kay, Sarah (2003) *Zizek: A Critical Introduction.* Cambridge: Polity Press.

Keats, John (1969) *Selected Poetry and Letters*, Richard Harter Fogle (ed.). San Francisco: Rinehart Press.

Kenner, Hugh (1952) 'Pound on Joyce', *Shenandoah*, 111, 3, 3–8.

Klevan, Andrew (2000) *Disclosure of the Everyday: Undramatic Achievement in Narrative Film.* Trowbridge: Flicks Books.

Kojève, Alexandre (1980) *Introduction to the Reading of Hegel* [1947]. Trans. James H. Nichols, Jr. Ithaca: Cornell University Press.

Krips, Henry (1999) *Fetish: An Erotics of Culture.* Ithaca: Cornell University Press.

Larkin, Philip (1974) 'Annus Mirabilis', in *High Windows.* London: Faber, 34.

Lawrence, D. H. (1933) *Studies in Classic American Literature* [1924]. London: Martin Secker.

_____ (1970) 'Autobiographical Sketch', in Warren Roberts and Harry T. Moore (eds) *Phoenix II: Uncollected, Unpublished and Other Prose Works by D. H. Lawrence.* New York: Viking, 592–6.

_____ (1972) 'Review of *Bottom Dogs* by Edward Dahlberg' in in Edward McDonald (ed.) *Phoenix: The Posthumous Papers* [1936]. New York: Viking, 267–73.

_____ (1997) *St Mawr* [1925], in *St Mawr and Other Stories*. Harmondsworth: Penguin, 19–155.

_____ (1999) *Sketches of Etruscan Places and Other Italian Essays*. Simonetta De Filippis (ed.), Harmondsworth: Penguin.

Lear, Jonathan (2000) *Happiness, Death and the Remainder of Life*. Cambridge, MA: Harvard University Press.

_____ (1988) 'Knowingness and Abandonment: An Oedipus for Our Time', in *Open Minded: Working Out the Logic of the Soul*. Cambridge, MA: Harvard University Press, 33–55.

Leavis, F. R. (1967a) '*Anna Karenina*', in *Anna Karenina and other Essays*. London: Chatto & Windus, 9–32.

_____ (1967b) '*The Pilgrim's Progress*', in *Anna Karenina and other Essays*. London: Chatto & Windus, 33–48.

_____ (1972) 'Dickens and Blake: *Little Dorrit*', in F. R. and Q. D. Leavis, *Dickens the Novelist*. London: Pelican, 282–359.

Leigh, Jacob (2002) *The Cinema of Ken Loach: Art in the Service of the People*. London: Wallflower Press.

MacCabe, Colin (1974) 'Realism and the Cinema: Notes on some Brechtian Theses', *Screen*, 15, 2, 7–27.

_____ (2001) 'Preface', in Slavoj Zizek, *The Fright of Real Tears: Krzysztof Kieslowski Between Theory and Post-Theory*. London: BFI, vii–ix.

Mailer, Norman (1966) *Advertisements for Myself* [1959]. New York: Berkley Medallion.

_____ (1972) 'Some Dirt in the Talk', in *Existential Errands*. New York: Little Brown, 89–123.

Marcuse, Herbert (1962) *Eros and Civilization: A Philosophical Inquiry into Freud* [1955]. New York: Vintage.

Margulies, Ivone (1996) *Nothing Happens: Chantal Ackerman's Hyperrealist Everyday*. Durham and London: Duke University Press.

Melville, Herman (1970) 'Bartleby' [1856], in Harold Beaver (ed.) *Billy Budd, Sailor and Other Stories*. Harmondsworth: Penguin, 57–99.

Mottram, James (2000) *The Coen Brothers: The Life of the Mind*. Dulles, Virginia: Brassey's.

Nowell-Smith, Geoffrey (2002) 'Minnelli and Melodrama', in Christine Gledhill (ed.) *Home is Where the Heart is: Studies in Melodrama and the Woman's Film*. London: BFI, 70–4.

Ojumo, Akin (2002a) 'Can Cannes still cut it?' *Observer*, 12 May, 9.

_____ (2002b) 'Stars and gripes', *Observer*, 19 May, 9.

Orwell, George (1982) *The Lion and the Unicorn: Socialism and the English Genius* [1941]. London: Penguin.

Pascal, Blaise (1977) *Pensées*. Trans. A. J. Krailsheimer. Harmondsworth: Penguin.

Peranson, Mark (ed.) (2000) *Cinemascope*. Special issue on 'The Best of the Nineties', 2.

Phillips, Adam (1988) *Winnicott*. Cambridge, MA: Harvard University Press.

Pinter, Harold (1970) *The Homecoming* [1965]. London: Methuen.

Pound, Ezra (1952) 'James Joyce and Pécuchet', *Shenandoah*. 111, 3, 1–20.

Putnam, Hilary (1999) 'Introduction, 1999', in Nahum Glatzer (ed.), *Understanding the Sick and the Healthy* [Franz Rosensweig, 1921]. Cambridge, MA: Harvard University Press, 1–20.

Rosenzweig, Franz (1967) 'On Being a Jewish Person', in *Franz Rosenzweig: His Life and Thought*. Presented by Nahum N. Glatzer. New York: Schocken, 214–27.

_____ (1985) *The Star of Redemption* [1930]. Trans. William W. Hallo. Notre Dame: University of Notre Dame Press.

_____ (1999) *Understanding the Sick and the Healthy* [1921], N. N. Glatzer (ed.). Cambridge, MA: Harvard University Press, 1999.

Santner, Eric L. (2001) *On the Psychtheology of Everyday Life: Reflections on Freud and Rosenzweig*. Chicago: University of Chicago Press.

Scheman, Naomi (1988) 'Missing Mothers/Desiring Daughters', *Critical Inquiry*, 15, 1, 62–89.

Schiller, Friedrich (1965) *On the Aesthetic Education of Man* [1795]. Trans. Reginald Snell. New York: Frederick Ungar.

Staten, Henry (1993) *Nietzsche's Voice* [1990]. Ithaca: Cornell University Press.

Steinberg, Saul (2002) 'Reflections on Art and Life', *New York Review of Books*, 15 April, 32–3.

Tanner, Tony (1986) *Jane Austen*. Cambridge, MA: Harvard University Press.

Thompson, E. P. (1968) *The Making of the English Working Class*. London: Penguin.

Thomson, David (2002) *The New Biographical Dictionary of Film*. New York: Alfred A. Knopf.

Thoreau, Henry David (1966) *Walden and Civil Disobedience*. New York: Norton.

Vincendeau, Ginette (ed.) (2001) *Film/Literature/Heritage: A Sight and Sound Reader*. London: BFI.

Watson, Garry (1980) 'Doing as one likes', *The Compass*, 8, 79–103.

Weil, Simone (1977a) 'Letter to Joe Bousquet', in George A. Panichas (ed.), *The Simone Weil Reader*. New York: David McKay, 86–93.

_____ (1977b) 'Morality and Literature', in George A. Panichas (ed.), *The Simone Weil Reader*. New York: David McKay, 290–5.

_____ (1977c) 'Human Personality', in George A. Panichas (ed.), *The Simone Weil Reader*. New York: David McKay, 313–9.

_____ (1977d) 'The Love of God and Affliction', in George A. Panichas (ed.), *The Simone Weil Reader*. New York: David McKay, 439–68.

West, Nathanael (1969) *Miss Lonelyhearts* [1933] (with *The Day of the Locusts* [1939]*)*. New York: New Directions, 1–58.

Wieczorek, Marek (2002) 'The Ridiculous, Sublime Art of Slavoj Zizek', in Slavoj Zizek, *The Art of the Ridiculous Sublime: On David Lynch's 'Lost Highway'*. Seattle: University of Washington, viii–xiii.

Williams, Linda (2002) '"Something Else Besides a Mother": *Stella Dallas* and the Maternal Melodrama', in Christine Gledhill (ed.) *Home is Where the Heart is: Studies in Melodrama and the Woman's Film*. London: BFI, 299–325.

Williams, Raymond (1971) *Orwell*. London: Fontana.

Wood, Robin (1990) 'Authorship Revisited', *Cineaction*, 21/22, 46–56.

_____ (2002) '"Do I disgust you?" Or, Tirez sur *La Pianiste*', *Cineaction*, 59, 54–61.

Woolf, Virginia (1979) 'Professions for Women' [1931], in *Women and Writing*. London: The Women's Press, 57–63.

Zizek, Slavoj (1989) *The Sublime Object of Ideology*. London: Verso.

_____ (1993) *Tarrying with the Negative: Kant, Hegel and the Critique of Ideology*. Durham: Duke University Press.

_____ (1997) 'The Abyss of Freedom', in Slavoj Zizek and F. W. J. Von Schelling, *The Abyss of Freedom/Ages of the World*. Ann Arbor: University of Michigan Press, 1–104.

_____ (2000) *Contingency, Hegemony, Universality: Contemporary Dialogues on the Left*. With Judith Butler and Ernesto Laclan. London: Verso.

_____ (2001) *The Fright of Real Tears: Krzysztof Kieslowski Between Theory and Post-Theory*. London: BFI.

_____ (2002a) *Welcome to the Desert of the Real*. London: Verso.

_____ (2002b) *The Art of the Ridiculous Sublime: On David Lynch's "Lost Highway"*. Seattle: University of Washington.

_____ (2002c) 'Foreword to the Second Edition', *For They Know Not What They Do: Enjoyment as a Political Factor*. London: Verso, xi–cvii.

INDEX

The Directors' Cuts Series

The titles in this ambitious series focus on the work of the most significant contemporary international film-makers, illuminating the creative dynamics of world cinema.

Forthcoming titles in the Director's Cuts series include volumes on John Carpenter, Theo Angelopoulos, Lars von Trier, John Sayles, Wes Craven and Steven Spielberg.

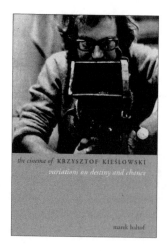

The Cinema of Krzysztof Kieslowski
Variations on Destiny and Chance

Edited by Marek Haltof

In this timely study, Marek Haltof provides a comprehensive review of Kieslowski's cinema, from his early documentaries and student films to television projects and award-winning features. The book discusses industrial practices and the context of Polish cinema from the late 1960s as well as wider European film-making, and stresses that the director is more than merely a 'great East-Central European auteur', his films being as unique to Poland as elsewhere.

'The most comprehensive review of Kieslowski's career that will no doubt become the primary book for anyone interested in his films. Thouroughly researched, meticulously documented and fluently written ... Through extensive coverage of his body of work, Haltof is able to trace Kieslowski's artistic evolution in new ways and with compelling arguments.'
— Tomasz Warchol,
Georgia Southern University

2004
£14.99 pbk   1-903364-91-4
£42.50 hbk   1-903364-92-2
208 pages

The Cinema of David Lynch
American Dreams, Nightmare Visions

Edited by Erica Sheen
& Annette Davison

David Lynch is an anomaly. A pioneer of the American 'indie' aesthetic, he also works in Hollywood and for network television. He has created some of the most disturbing images in contemporary cinema, and produced startlingly innovative work in sound. This collection offers a range of theoretically divergent readings that demonstrate not only the difficulty of locating interpretative positions for Lynch's work, but also the pleasure of finding new ways of thinking about it. Films discussed include *Blue Velvet*, *Wild at Heart*, *The Straight Story* and *Mulholland Drive*.

"A ground-breaking collection of new essays presenting a range of challenging theoretical perspectives on, and insightful readings of, Lynch's work."
— Frank Krutnik, Sheffield Hallam University

2004
£14.99 pbk   1-903364-85-X
£42.50 hbk   1-903364-86-8
208 pages

The Cinema of Nanni Moretti
Dreams and Diaries

Ewa Mazierska & Laura Rascaroli

The Cinema of Nanni Moretti provides an analysis of the work of the most important Italian film-maker of the past thirty years and an outstanding figure in contemporary European cinema. Interdisciplinary and wide-ranging, the authors use Moretti's films as a lens to view and discuss contemporary phenomena such as the crisis of masculinity and authority, the decline of the political Left, and the transformation of the citizen's relationship to the State. Films discussed include *Aprile*, *Dear Diary* and *The Son's Room*, winner of the Palme d'Or at Cannes 2001.

"A long-overdue, illuminating introduction to Italy's most innovative contemporary film director. This book offers an excellent discussion of some recurrent features in Moretti's films and helps us fully understand the depth and breadth of his cinematic achievements."
— Guido Bonsaver, Royal Holloway, London

2004
£14.99 pbk   1-903364-77-9
£42.50 hbk   1-903364-78-7
208 pages

2003

£14.99 pbk   1-903364-89-2
£42.50 hbk   1-903364-57-4
208 pages

The Cinema of Andrzej Wajda
The Art of Irony and Defiance

Edited by John Orr
& Elzbieta Ostrowska

This book is a major re-assessment of the great Polish director Andrzej Wajda, who received a Lifetime Achievement Academy Award in 2000. It covers all aspects of his work from his early trilogy of the 1950s – *A Generation*, *Kanal*, *Ashes and Diamonds* – to his 1999 epic *Pan Tadeusz*, and looks at his daring innovations in style, his concern with Polish history and nationhood, and his artistic defiance of authoritarian rule during the Cold War. A timely look at a prolific film-maker whose work over four decades reflects the changing nature of cinema itself.

"The most comprehensive and multifaceted compilation on Wajda's film-making published in English ... A desideratum for anyone drawn to Wajda's films or Polish cinema in general"
– Renata Murawska, Macquarie University

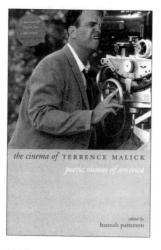

2003

£14.99 pbk   1-903364-75-2
£42.50 hbk   1-903364-76-0
208 pages

The Cinema of Terrence Malick
Poetic Visions of America

Edited by Hannah Patterson

Terrence Malick is one of Hollywood's most enigmatic and legendary film-makers. Despite his limited output, and a famous twenty-year absence from cinema, *Badlands*, *Days of Heaven* and *The Thin Red Line* have challenged genre expectation and redefined notions of contemporary film language. This collection explores his work from a series of vantage points, encompassing issues of identity, the poetics of cinema, representation of the road, youth culture and the American West, depiction of landscape and nature, use of sound and music, and the influence of philosopher Martin Heidegger. Particular emphasis is placed on *The Thin Red Line*, Malick's haunting evocation of human suffering during World War II, an important classic of modern cinema.

"Terrence Malick is a screen poet, an incomparable film-maker ... This comprehensive study explores his unique vision and illuminates every facet of his work"
– Martin Sheen

The Cinema of Gerorge A. Romero
Knight of the Living Dead

Tony Williams

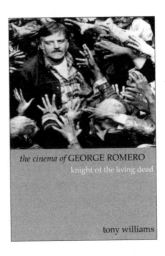

The Cinema of George A. Romero: Knight of the Living Dead is the first in-depth study in English of the career of this foremost auteur working at the margins of the Hollywood mainstream. In placing Romero's oeuvre in the context of literary naturalism, the book explores the relevance of the director's films within American cultural traditions and thus explains the potency of such work beyond 'splatter movie' models. The author explores the roots of naturalism in the work of Emile Zola and traces this through to the EC Comics of the 1950s and on to the work of Stephen King.

'This thorough, searching and always intelligent overview does full justice to Romero's '*Living Dead*' trilogy and also at last rectifies the critical neglect of Romero's other work, fully establishing its comnplexity and cohesion.'
— Robin Wood

2003

£14.99 pbk   1-903364-73-6

£42.50 hbk   1-903364-62-0

208 pages

The Cinema of Robert Lepage
The Poetics of Memory

Aleksandar Dundjerovic

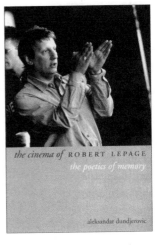

The Cinema of Robert Lepage is the first critical study of one of the most striking artists of Québecois and Canadian independent film-making. The book examines Lepage's creative methods of film-making in their cultural and social context, providing historical and industrial background to his many projects, and argues that his film work cannot be seen separately from his opus as a multi-disciplinary artist. In focusing on the cinematic output of this important contemporary artist, with case studies of *The Confessional*, *Nô*, and *Possible Worlds*, this important new monograph explores these themes and concerns, and includes an exclusive and detailed interview with Robert Lepage.

"Robert Lepage is one of Québec's most important contributions to recent world cinema, making films that are crucial interventions in an emerging globalised industry. This book, which considers the director's entire cinematic oeuvre and puts it in the context of his innovative theatre, is most timely."
— Jerry White, University of Alberta

2003

£14.99 pbk   1-903364-33-7

£42.50 hbk   1-903364-34-5

208 pages

The Cinema of Kathryn Bigelow
Hollywood Transgressor

Edited by Deborah Jermyn & Sean Redmond

Kathryn Bigelow has undoubtedly been one of Hollywood's most significant female film-makers, well known in popular terms for films such as *Point Break* and *Blue Steel*, yet she remains relatively unexplored in academia. This collection explores how Bigelow can be seen to provide a point of intersection across a whole range of issues at the forefront of contemporary film studies and the transformation of Hollywood into a post-classical cinema machine, with a particular emphasis on her most ambitious and controversial picture to date, *Strange Days*. Her place within New Hollywood is as a film-maker that blurs genre conventions, reinscribes gender identites and produces a breathless cinema of attractions.

"Surely the only director to have successfully broken into the patriarchal stronghold of contemporary Hollywood ... At last, we have a collection which discusses her entire oeuvre."
– Pamela Church Gibson, The London Institute

2003

£13.99 pbk   1-903364-42-6
£42.50 hbk   1-903364-43-4
208 pages

The Cinema of Wim Wenders
The Celluloid Highway

Alexander Graf

The Cinema of Wim Wenders is a new study of the films of this most prominent of German directors, and penetrates the seductive sounds and images for which he is best known. The book analyses the individual films in the context of a pre-occupation central to all of Wenders' work and writings: why modern cinema - a recording art, solely composed of sounds and images - naturally developed into a primarily narrative medium, a domain traditionally associated with words and sentences? With its emphasis on analysing the films themselves, this book identifies and critically elucidates Wenders' chief artistic motivation: that the act of seeing can constitute a creative act in its own right.

"Offers a coherent introduction to the work of Wim Wenders. It isa a sheer joy to follow the logical flow of Graf's arguments; this is a solid analysis of the director's philosophy regarding the moral function of films and the tension betweem image and narrative."
– Franz A. Birgel, Muhlenberg College

2001

£13.99 pbk   1-903364-29-9
£42.50 hbk   1-903364-30-2
208 pages

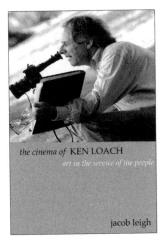

the cinema of KEN LOACH
art in the service of the people

jacob leigh

2001

£13.99 pbk   1-903364-31-0

£42.50 hbk   1-903364-32-9

208 pages

The Cinema of Ken Loach
Art in the Service of the People

Jacob Leigh

The Cinema of Ken Loach examines the linking of art and politics that distin-guishes the work of this leading British film director. His films manifest recurrent themes over a long period of working with various collaborators, yet his han-dling of those themes changes throughout his career. This book examines those changes as a way of reaching an understanding of his style and meaning. It evaluates how Loach incorporates his political beliefs and those of his writers into his work. The book augments the thematic interpretation with contextual information gleaned from original archive research and new interviews.

"A finely detailed, sympathetically critical examination of some major films and TV dramas. In addition to being a pleasure to read, the book contributes intelligently to debates about realism, and deserves to become a standard reference for anyone interested in Loach's work and the wider issues it raises."

– Matin Stollery, Southampton Institute

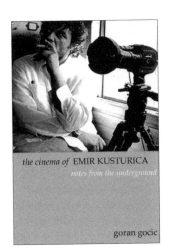

the cinema of EMIR KUSTURICA
notes from the underground

goran gocic

2001

£13.99 pbk   1-903364-14-0

£42.50 hbk   1-903364-16-7

208 pages

The Cinema of Emir Kusturica
Notes From the Underground

Goran Gocic

Notes from the Underground is the first book on Sarajevan film-maker Kusturica to be published in English. With six highly acclaimed films to his credit, Kusturica is already established as one of the most important of contemporary film-makers, with each of his films winning prizes at the major festivals around the world. His films include *Underground* (1995), *Arizona Dream* (1992) with Johnny Depp and, most recently, *Black Cat, White Cat* (1998). *Notes from the Underground* delves into diverse facets of Kusturica's work, all of which is passionately dedicated to the marginal and the outcast, and includes an exclusive interview with the director.

"This is a comprehensive and fascinating study of one of Europe's most important film directors. A sharp and percep-tive monograph and long overdue as far as English-lan-guage film criticism is concerned: this is a must read."

– John Orr, Edinburgh University